# VAT IN EUROPE

AUSTRALIA AND NEW ZEALAND
The Law Book Company Ltd.
Sydney : Melbourne : Perth

CANADA AND U.S.A.
The Carswell Company Ltd.
Agincourt, Ontario

INDIA
N.M. Tripathi Private Ltd.
Bombay
*and*
Eastern Law House Private Ltd.
Calcutta and Delhi
M.P.P. House
Bangalore

ISRAEL
Steimatzky's Agency Ltd.
Jerusalem : Tel Aviv : Haifa

PAKISTAN
Pakistan Law House
Karachi

# ERNST & YOUNG
# VAT IN EUROPE


Edited by
(in alphabetical order)

Andele Boomsma

Anne Ermel

Jim Somers

Jean-Marc Tirard



LONDON
SWEET & MAXWELL
1989

Published by
Sweet & Maxwell Limited of South Quay Plaza,
183 Marsh Wall, London E14 9FT
Computerset by P.B. Computer Typesetting, Pickering, N. Yorks.
Printed in Great Britain by
Butler & Tanner Ltd, Frome and London

**British Library Cataloguing in Publication Data**

Ernst & Young, VAT in Europe
1. European Community countries. Value-added tax
I. Ernst & Young
336. 2′714′094

ISBN 0–421–42110–X

This book has been prepared by the Ernst & Young European VAT Committee.

Contributors


Kjell Andersen
Ernst & Young, Drammen

Andele Boomsma
Ernst & Young, Amsterdam

Roger Couteau
Ernst & Young, Brussels

James Dixon
Ernst & Young, London

Brigitte Ebeling
Ernst & Young, Frankfurt

Anne Ermel
Ernst & Young, Paris

Nicola Fiorini
Ernst & Young, Verona

Albino Jacinto
Ernst & Young, Lisbon

Jos Junker
Ernst & Young, Luxembourg

Jan Kleerup
Ernst & Young, Stockholm

Morgens Krewald
Ernst & Young, Copenhagen

Themis Lianopoulos
Ernst & Young, Athens

Eduardo Sanfrutos
Ernst & Young, Madrid

Jim Somers
Ernst & Young, Dublin

# Contents

# Preface

This book has been prepared as a general guide to the Value Added Tax implications of commercial activities in the European Community, and Norway and Sweden which have both implemented a VAT system similar to the Sixth EC Directive model.

The same headings have been used in the same order for each country enabling the reader to find quickly the rules applicable to a particular situation.

It must also be stressed that tax legislation in general is changing continuously and Value Added Tax is no different. It is even more important in the EC environment where the harmonisation process leads the Member States to modify gradually their law in order to comply with EC common rules. Furthermore the removal of fiscal barriers by 1993 will mean that some of the basic rules presently applicable will be modified.

All EC Member States have implemented the Sixth Directive in their national law. Because the 12 Member States joined the Community at very different dates (over 30 years) they have achieved uneven progress in the compliance with the EC Directives. In two countries (Greece and Portugal) the introduction of VAT is very recent and there is uncertainty as to the interpretation of the law by the tax authorities or by the courts. In practice, there are important differences in the way in which the European VAT rules are applied in the 12 Member States of the European Community.

This book is by no means exhaustive and is not intended to cover in detail the VAT law and practice in each country. It does however give the basic principles and mentions difficult areas.

In particular circumstances professional advice is recommended to avail of planning opportunities and to avoid adverse tax consequences such as a charge to tax, disallowance of input credit, penalties, etc.

Jean-Marc Tirard, formerly Partner-in-charge of Tax Services, Ernst & Whinney, France, initiated this project and chaired the European VAT Committee prior to the merger of Ernst & Whinney with Arthur Young. The Committee is now chaired by Jim Somers, VAT Director of Ernst & Young, Dublin.

VAT law as explained in this book is that in force as of March 31, 1989.

# TABLE OF E.C. DIRECTIVES

*References are to paragraph numbers*

# TABLE OF STATUTES

*References are to paragraph numbers*

# TABLE OF TREATIES

*References are to paragraph numbers*

# 1. Introduction

## THE EUROPEAN ECONOMIC COMMUNITY

The project of a United Europe goes back to the year 1945 when **1–001**
Western European governments felt the need for closer cooperation after the devastation of the war.

In 1951 a treaty was signed by Belgium, the Netherlands, Luxembourg, Germany, Italy and France establishing the European Coal and Steel Community (ECSC). This was the start of a gradual process of European integration. While limited to one sector this cooperation soon evolved towards the idea of a European entity with common institutions and integrated national economies.

In 1955 a conference in Brussels started work on a proposal which was submitted to the ministers of Foreign Affairs in 1956 and which was used as the basis for negotiations on two treaties. Finally, in Rome in 1957 the two treaties establishing the European Economic Community (EEC) and the European Atomic Energy Community (EURATOM) were signed by Belgium, France, the Netherlands, Luxembourg, Italy and the Federal Republic of Germany. After ratification by the six Member States, they became effective on January 1, 1958.

The Community was enlarged to nine Members in January 1, 1973 with the United Kingdom, Ireland and Denmark joining.

On January 1, 1981, Greece acceded to the Treaty of Rome. Then on January 1, 1986 Spain and Portugal also became members of the Community.

The 12 countries of the present European Community have a total population of 323 million. The European Community will be the largest single market in the world. It already accounts for 30 per cent. of world trade.

## THE AIMS OF THE EUROPEAN COMMUNITY

### *The Treaty of Rome*

The Treaty of Rome, establishing the European Economic Commun- **1–002**
ity, is in nature the constitution of the Community. It contains the

principles and objectives which have been agreed by the Member States. The Community is, in essence, a union of European states mainly for economic purposes. The provisions of the Treaty aim at the progressive removal of economic barriers between the Member States and a correlative integration of the economies of the signatories into a single common market. As such, the Treaty was assigned specific objectives to sustain the realisation of a true common market.

The first of these is the free movement of goods. The Treaty's essential goal is the creation of a Customs union within which no duties, tariffs, restrictions or quotas will exist. This union has been partly achieved since July 1968 when customs duties were abolished on the movement of goods between member States and when a Common Customs Tariff was adopted for trading with the non-European Community countries. The reduction and eventual elimination of national trade quotas is still to be achieved as well as the removal of all systematic controls at frontiers.

Another objective is the establishment of a common agricultural policy with common rules concerning competition, coordination of the national market organisations and control of imports into the Community on occasions when foreign goods might affect the position of similar products in one of the Member States.

It is essential that not only goods be allowed to move freely within the European Community but also workers, businesses, services and capital. Directives have been issued and Regulations adopted gradually to provide for the freedom of establishment of nationals in any of the Member States, and the freedom to supply services within the Community. The Member States have also agreed to remove restrictions on the movement of capital by residents of the Community and to eliminate discrimination based on the nationality or on the place of investment of the capital.

Finally the Treaty contains provisions for the setting up of a common transport policy with agreed rules for international transport in, out and through the territory of the Community.

## *The White Paper*

**1–003** The very broad economic goal of the Treaty of Rome requires that many other areas be harmonised insofar as they have essential effects on a totally integrated free economy.

In 1985, in order to accelerate the completion of the internal market, the Commission proposed to the European Council a complete legislative programme. Presented in the form of about 300 Directives the "White Paper" outlines 279 measures to be presented to the Council of Ministers aiming at the complete elimination of barriers, whether physical, technical or fiscal. December 31, 1992 has been set as the target date to achieve these goals. Since 1985, nearly one-third of the Commission's proposals have been adopted and implemented. Proposals cover a great variety of matters such as rules governing competition, dumping, state subsidies, and taxes imposed by Member States, etc. In order to avoid the obstacle that divergent laws may present to the functioning of an internal market, the Community is also seeking an approximation of laws and in some instances is developing a European body of laws.

In December 1988, the Commission issued its fourth report on the Implementation of the White Paper on completing the Internal Market. This report updates the legislative time table contained in the White Paper.

## THE COMMUNITY'S INSTITUTIONS

The three treaties which created the European Coal and Steel Community, the European Economic Community and EURATOM provided for specific institutions for each of these communities. On July 1, 1967 following a treaty, the executive bodies of the community of the three organisations were merged and the institutions which exist at present were established. The main executive bodies include a Parliament, a Council of Ministers, a Commission and a Court of Justice. **1–004**

### *The European Parliament*

The Parliament of the European Community is composed of 519 delegates elected directly by the nationals of the 12 Member States. **1–005**

The Parliament has general advisory and supervisory powers. Its role is of a consultative nature.

Since 1979 when the Parliament was first directly elected its role within the Community has increased. In 1986 a new cooperation procedure was introduced whereby the Parliament would have to be consulted not only once but twice where certain provisions of the treaty, or where 1992 measures, were concerned.

It holds an annual session but special sessions may be called by a majority of the members or at the request of the Commission or the Council. The Parliament may put questions to the Commission.

### *The Council of Ministers*

The essential function of the Council of Ministers is the realisation of the Treaty of Rome's objectives. For this purpose, it has been given the power to take Decisions, to adopt Directives, to issue Regulations and to make Recommendations. As a general rule, it is the Commission which has the right of initiative in Community activities. However the Council of Ministers may request the Commission to make proposals or to undertake any specific studies it feels are necessary for the achievement of a single market. The Treaty has conferred on the Council the special task of setting the rules under which the committees (EEC, Steel and Coal and EURATOM) should function and of deciding on the salaries and allowances of the Commission and the Court of Justice members. **1–006**

The Council of Ministers is composed of ministers from the various Member States. They become president of the Council for six months in turn.

The work of the Council of Ministers is carried out at two types of Council meetings: the General Affairs Council, attended usually by Ministers of Foreign Affairs from the 12 Member States, which coordinates the activities of the Council and specialised Councils which deal with specific subjects such as education, finance, justice, and commercial policy with non-EC countries, etc.

The Commission proposals are submitted to the Council of Ministers, where they are discussed, reviewed and altered by the Council itself or by the Committee of Permanent Representatives of the Member States, assisted by various expert working groups.

The decisions of the Council such as the adoption of Regulations and Directives are taken usually by qualified majority vote. However, a unanimous vote is required in all tax matters or when the Council wishes to amend a proposal of the Commission.

## *The Commission*

**1–007** The Commission is the executive body of the Community institutions. It ensures that the Treaty and the decisions taken to implement it are carried out by the Member States. It also prepares Recommendations or gives Opinions on matters covered by the Treaty. Like the Council, the Commission issues Directives and Regulations, takes Decisions and makes Recommendations. It is important to stress that Regulations, both from the Council and the Commission, are binding in all their terms and directly applicable in all the Member States. Directives are binding as to the result to be achieved by the Member State to which they are addressed. National authorities must initiate the appropriate legislation to give legal effect to EC Directives.

Decisions of the Commission are binding on those to whom they are addressed. Recommendations or Opinions are not binding.

The Commission consists of 17 members: each Member State being represented by at least one national but there being no more than two persons of the same nationality. Members are appointed by mutual agreement between the government of the 12 EC countries.

## *The Court of Justice*

**1–008** The general function of the Court of Justice is to ensure the application of laws according to the interpretation and implementation of the Treaty of Rome.

It comprises 13 judges assisted by six advocates-general and a registrar. The Court of Justice has jurisdiction in suits brought by the Commission or by one Member State against another Member State which has failed to comply with the rules enacted by the Treaty.

It has the power to decide on the legality of the actions of the Council and the Commission. Member States, the Council and the Commission may ask the Court of Justice to condemn the actions of the Commission or the Council on the grounds of lack of jurisdiction or violation of the Treaty or misuse of powers. When the Court confirms that an action or a provision is not legal, that text becomes null and void.

In addition, the Court has the power to rule on questions referred from a court of a Member State. These rulings must deal only with the interpretation of the Treaty and the legality of the actions of the EC Institutions. Finally, the Court has jurisdiction in disputes arising out of claims for damages (except in the case of an existing contract) in disputes between the Community and its employees and in all matters relating to the European Investment bank.

## THE FINANCIAL MEANS OF THE COMMUNITY

The Community at its start, functioned on financial contributions of the **1–009** Member States. In 1970, a decision of the Council implemented a new system of self-financing in the Community. Under this new system the Community is now financed in part by a portion of the custom duties collected by the Member States on goods imported from non-EC countries, by agricultural levies and by financial contributions from the Member States. Since 1977, the financial contributions from Member States have been replaced by a percentage of the value added tax collected by each Member State, calculated on a uniform basis. In June 1984 an agreement was reached to increase the resources of the Community. From 1986, 1.4 per cent. of the value added tax collected by each of the 12 EC countries is allocated to the Community.

## THE VALUE ADDED TAX

Before the Treaty of Rome was adopted most European countries had **1–010** cumulative turnover tax systems whereby several taxes were imposed at the various stages of production. The unique feature of the valued added tax system as implemented by the European Community is its non-cumulative nature as opposed to the classic cascading taxes it has replaced. It is based on a tax credit system which allows every taxable person along the chain of production to recover the value added tax which was incurred upstream. It is in principle, the final consumer alone who, in the end, bears the weight of the tax.

The tax is actually paid by each taxable person up the line before final consumption but it is paid only on what is roughly the profit margin. The following example shows how the neutrality of this VAT system is achieved, which allows:

- exemption of all the intermediary consumptions,
- an equal amount of tax from a VAT cost, on all products or services whatever the commercial chain, whether direct from the producer to the consumer or through wholesalers and retailers.

### Importer

| | |
|---|---|
| Goods are imported for a net value of .................... | 1,000 |
| VAT is paid at importation (VAT at 15%) ............. | 150 |
| Total price paid ................................................ | 1,150 |
| The importer sells the goods to a wholesaler for a net price of .......................................... | 1,200 |
| VAT on the sale amounts to ................................ | 180 |

Upon sale the importer will pay to the VAT authorities 180 (VAT charged to his customer) less the 150 VAT paid at the time of importation, *i.e.* a net amount of 30.

### Wholesaler

| | |
|---|---|
| Wholesaler purchases the goods for ........................ | 1,200 |
| Plus VAT of ..................................................... | 180 |
| He sells the same goods to a retailer for a price of ............................................... | 1,500 |
| Plus VAT in an amount of .................................. | 225 |

Wholesaler will remit to the VAT authorities 225 less 180, *i.e.* a net VAT of 45.

### Retailer

| | |
|---|---|
| Price of the goods purchased ................................ | 1,500 |
| Plus VAT of ..................................................... | 255 |
| He sells the goods to a final consumer for ............... | 1,700 |
| Plus a VAT of .................................................. | 255 |

The retailer will remit to the VAT authorities 255 less 225, *i.e.* a net VAT of 30.
The total amount of VAT paid along the chain of production is:

| | |
|---|---|
| Importer (on importation) ................................... | 150 |
| Importer (on sale) ............................................ | 30 |
| Wholesaler ...................................................... | 45 |
| Retailer .......................................................... | 30 |
| | 255 |

Thus the final consumer, when he purchases the goods for a total price of 1,955 suffers a tax of 255.
If the goods had been sold directly to the final consumer for a net price of 1,700, the seller would have invoiced a VAT of 255, *i.e.* the same amount of tax is due whatever the commercial chain.

Neutrality is also achieved within the Community by means of exempting (or zero rating) exports and taxing imports. Thus the tax paid by the final consumer in any country is the same whether he obtains the goods or services from his own country or from abroad.

The neutrality of VAT which should be total along the successive transactions is, however, only partly achieved in certain circumstances. This is the case when the recovery of VAT incurred on certain specific items (cars, for instance) is prevented by legislation or when participants in the chain are only taxable on part of their transactions (partially exempt) and therefore limited in the amount of VAT incurred on their purchases which they may recover.

## HARMONISATION OF VAT LEGISLATION WITHIN THE EUROPEAN COMMUNITY

### *General*

The Treaty of Rome (1957) contains specific provisions dealing with harmonisation of legislation in certain areas. Article 99 of the Treaty deals with taxation in particular. It reads as follows: **1–011**

> "The Commission shall consider how the legislation of the various Member States concerning turnover taxes, excise duties and other forms of indirect taxation, including countervailing measures applicable to trade between Member States, can be harmonised in the interest of the common market.
>
> The Commission shall submit proposals to the Council, which shall act unanimously without prejudice to the provisions of Articles 100 and 101."

Article 100 of the Treaty authorises the Council of Ministers to issue Directives, based on proposals of the EC Commission, aimed at further harmonisation of domestic legal and administrative provisions which have a direct impact on the formation and functioning of the Common Market. It states:

> "The Council shall, acting unanimously on a proposal from the Commission, issue directives for the approximation of such provisions laid down by law, regulation or administrative action in Member States as directly affect the establishment or functioning of the common market.
>
> The Assembly and the Economic and Social Committee shall be consulted in the case of directives whose implementation would, in one or more Member States, involve the amendment of legislation."

In 1967, ten years after the signing of the Treaty of Rome, the EC Council of Ministers adopted two Directives which resulted in the implementation of Value Added Tax by all Member States (*i.e.*, First and Second Council Directives on Value Added Tax). Although these Directives laid the foundation for a standardised system, they still left the Member States considerable scope for derogations and special arrangements.

The First Directive provided that all Member States replace existing cumulative tax systems with a non-cumulative value-added tax system. The Second Directive introduced some basic concepts (*e.g.*, definition of taxable person, supply of goods and services, basis of taxation, etc.). However, many other important points were left to the Member States.

Further harmonisation was required to provide the EC with its own financial means, as well as to eliminate fiscal frontiers in the future and promote greater freedom of movement of people, goods, services and capital. This led to the Sixth Council Directive on VAT, effective as of May 17, 1977, which provided for a uniform basis of taxation.

The Sixth Council Directive, nevertheless, allowed Member States to continue certain incompatible arrangements for an agreed period of time. Moreover, the Sixth Directive did not require harmonisation of VAT rates nor did it eliminate fiscal frontiers.

Further Directives on the harmonisation of legislation of Member States relating to VAT have been adopted or proposed. A review of these Directives and whether or not they have been implemented is provided in Appendix B of this book.

## *Advisory Committee*

**1–012** Article 29 of the Sixth Directive provides for an Advisory Committee on VAT. This Committee consists of representatives of the EC Member States and the EC Commission, with a Commission representative as chairman. The Committee reviews measures proposed by the Member States for which the EC Directive stipulates consultation. The Committee also considers specific questions concerning application of the Directive upon request by either the chairman or a representative of the Member States.

## *EC Council Directives*

**1–013** Directives issued by the EC Council of Ministers are the primary vehicle for harmonisation of national legislation. Note that these Directives do not attempt to create uniform rules for the whole community but try to harmonise national legislation to achieve community goals

Contrary to Regulations (which are binding and have a direct effect in all Member States), Directives are binding only as to the result to be achieved (Article 189 of the Treaty). Thus, Directives leave the choice of form and method of implementation to national authorities. Directives therefore require national legislation to implement their policies.

The European Court of Justice in Luxembourg has ruled in various decisions that a Directive may have direct effect, provided that the period granted to Member States to implement such a Directive has lapsed. The Court has ruled that the concept of direct effect means that a provision of Community law can be relied upon by individuals before national courts, whether or not such provisions have been adopted as national law. This applies even where national law is in conflict with the EC provision. EC law does not prevent application of more favourable national law.

Under these circumstances, taxpayers may be entitled to rely on the provisions of a Directive as against opposing national law. It is assumed generally that the Sixth Council Directive on VAT has a direct effect in so far as its provisions do not give Member States the freedom to derogate or are explicit.

The right to invoke EC law has in practice only been granted to persons (individuals and legal entities). Until now, no EC cases have arisen regarding use of EC law by governmental administrations. Article 189 of the EC Treaty does not indicate whether a national tax administration may rely on an EC Directive when a provision of national law, pleaded by a taxpayer, is contrary to that Directive. However, if a national administration were allowed to use EC law against its subjects where the EC Directive (whether intentional or not) had not been implemented in national law, it would seem that the intent of EC law would be contradicted.

## *Appeal Procedures to Luxembourg EC Court of Justice*

Article 177 of the EC Treaty *allows* all national courts of the Member States to refer questions on interpretation of EC law to the EC Court in Luxembourg. However, the highest national courts (whose decisions are final and are normally followed by the lower courts), are *obliged* to refer questions on interpretation of EC law to the EC court for a preliminary ruling, whenever such a question arises in cases put before them. Thus, Article 177 guarantees uniform interpretation of EC law throughout the community. **1–014**

## *European integration and objectives for future harmonisation*

European Community activities in the VAT field have so far been limited to harmonisation of VAT systems in the Member States by means of Directives. Since the Directives allow Member States to determine their own legislation within the limits set down, there are substantial differences in practice between various countries. Also, the physical and administrative involvement of customs authorities with border traffic has been maintained. **1–015**

At the border, VAT is still levied on import of goods and VAT refunds are granted on the export of goods. This VAT barrier functions as a kind of lock through which the different VAT rate levels between the Member States are neutralised. Consequently, goods coming from abroad are no better or worse off than domestic goods. Moreover, through these fiscal barriers between Member States, a situation is reached in which fiscal sovereignty is maintained and VAT revenue is received by the country where the final use takes place ("country of destination" principle).

In order to realise a common market by the end of 1992, in August 1987 the European Commission issued proposals, as regards VAT, summarised as follows:

- — removal of the EC's internal fiscal barriers;
- — introduction of a VAT clearing house for transactions within the Common Market;
- — harmonisation of VAT rates and structures.

## The 1987 Proposals of the Commission

### *Removal of fiscal barriers*

**1–016** Upon the removal of the EC's internal barriers, as proposed by the EC Commission, it will no longer be a question of "import" and "export" between Member States of the EC. The concepts of "export" and "import" for VAT purposes will only apply to goods and services exported to, and imported from, non-EC countries. Intercommunity transactions will be dealt with in exactly the same way as normal domestic supplies. Domestic entrepreneurs will charge VAT to their foreign customers according to the normal domestic rate and then pay this to the customs authorities. The 0 per cent rate for "exports" will cease to exist. Conversely, foreign entrepreneurs will charge the VAT rates existing in their countries to their customers. Foreign VAT will be deductible in the purchaser's domestic VAT return.

When obtaining goods and services, an entrepreneur is thus confronted with the various VAT rates applicable in the other Member States. Despite the various VAT rates, generally, no distortion of competition will occur. The right to deduct input tax means that VAT will not be a cost item. Therefore the rate to be paid will not be an important factor when choosing a supplier.

Distortion of competition may, however, occur on purchases by final consumers *i.e.*:

- — private persons;
- — exempted entrepreneurs (*e.g.*, doctors, hospitals, universities, banks, insurance companies, etc.);
- — governmental bodies.

In order to discourage persons and institutions without entitlement to an input credit from buying goods in those Member States with the lowest VAT rate, special arrangements will be required, in addition to harmonisation of VAT rates.

The proposed modifications are of particular importance for the transactions within the Common Market. For transactions with non-EC countries, the present system is to be continued, including the physical and administrative involvement of customs authorities.

### *VAT clearing system*

**1–017** The second part of the Commission's proposal concerns the introduction of a VAT clearing-house, which aims to ensure that regardless of where VAT is collected, the revenue will accrue to the Member State of consumption ("country of destination" principle). This clearing system will allow a Member State to pay or collect VAT at regular intervals, depending on whether it is a net importer or exporter.

Each month, countries with a positive balance of intercommunity trade would deposit the amount of net export VAT into a central account. Countries with a negative balance of intercommunity trade would reclaim their net import VAT from this account. The balances between Member States could be derived by requesting two items of additional data in the entrepreneur's VAT return (*i.e.*, "import" and "export" within the Common Market).

### *Harmonisation of VAT rates and structures*

The harmonisation proposal of the EC Commission concerns, in particular, the rates of VAT, excise duties and the tax base. **1–018**

A European VAT system with only one rate would be most efficient. All goods and services would be subject to the same rate which would avoid administrative and classification problems created by a multi-rate system.

With the exception of Denmark and the United Kingdom, the EC Member States have one or more reduced and/or increased rates besides the normal rate. The Commission wishes to align the various VAT rates applied through the EC so that frontier controls can be removed without undue distortions of trade (for example, in case of cross-border shopping between neighbouring countries where tax rates are very different) and proposes the abolition of the increased rates and application of two rates of VAT only.

The Commission proposes a reduced rate for "social goods" (or basic necessities) in the range of 4 per cent. to 9 per cent. and a range of 14 per cent. to 20 per cent. for the standard rate applicable to other goods and services. "Social goods" are defined as food (excluding alcohol), energy for heating and lighting, water, pharmaceutical products, books, newspapers, magazines and passenger transport.

The rates are based on the VAT rates currently in force in Member States (note that the Commission has ignored the zero rate applicable in, *e.g.*, Ireland and the U.K.). The Commission hopes to prevent unacceptable price differences (particularly between neighbouring Member States), while at the same time leaving some freedom to the Member States to establish VAT rates for themselves.

Excise duties, often viewed as taxes on luxuries and other products, are also to be harmonised by the end of 1992. The application of bands (such as those proposed for VAT) to excise duties cannot be realised. This is because a turnover tax such as VAT is levied on the commodity price including excise duties. This could lead to considerably higher price differences than the proposed range of 5 per cent. to 6 per cent. This fact, in conjunction with the planned removal of custom barriers, will necessitate true uniformity in excise duties.

Generally, the Commission proposes to set the uniform excise duty rates at the average currently in force in the EC. This average rate deviates significantly from the present rates in various Member States in a number of cases.

It is proposed to complete and clarify the uniform basis on the Sixth EC Directive on VAT. There will be little or no room left for variations in the tax base between countries with respect to VAT rates, derogations and exemptions.

1–019 There are various concerns which make it unlikely that the proposals of the EC Commission will be adopted without amendments. For example, with respect to the dual rate system as proposed, it is generally felt that a rate difference of 5 per cent. to 6 per cent. between neighbouring countries is too much. A margin of 2 per cent. to 3 per cent. is the maximum considered acceptable. For Ireland and the United Kingdom, the main political problem is the abolition of the zero rate, whereas the proposals of the Commission would deprive Denmark of 11 per cent. of its total tax revenue. A solution to these problems will have to be found.

Furthermore, various Member States have expressed serious reservations about the clearing-house system and strongly recommend the introduction of alternatives for specific areas where possible, such as:

— introduction of an EC fiscal unity/group registration which would exclude the levy of VAT for intercompany supplies;
— creation of suspension of VAT for authorised trades;
— application of the postponed accounting system throughout the EC (14th EC Directive);
— introduction of a notification system allowing a zero rate for input and export transactions by entrepreneurs regularly importing and/or exporting, provided these transactions are reported to the tax authorities;
— amendment of the place of supply for intercommunity transactions together with introduction of a reverse charge mechanism for supply of goods, which would shift the liability of VAT to the recipient of the supply.

At this point, it is not possible to foresee how and to what extent the proposals of the EC Commission will be amended and what the final result will be.

## New "DRAFT" Proposals

1–020 The Members States have strongly opposed these 1987 proposals. The VAT clearing house as described was considered far too ambitious and too unreliable, whereas abolition of the zero rate was opposed particularly by Ireland and the United Kingdom. Moreover, for some countries the proposals of the Commission would deprive them of a substantial part of their tax revenue.

In response to the criticisms and the practical and political difficulties levelled at these proposals and in order to facilitate agreement among the Member States, the Commission decided to make certain amendments to its original proposals which were published in May 1989.

In order to limit distortions of competition, the Commission suggests the creation of a specific collection system for the most sensitive products. For instance, in the case of cars and mail-order sales, there would be derogations from the principle of taxation at the rate of the producer's country. In the case of cars, VAT would be collected at the time of registration at the rate applicable in the country of destination. For mail-order sales, the Commission is prepared to accept taxation of the sales in the country of destination of the goods.

As regards exempted entrepreneurs and governmental bodies, it has been proposed that their purchases in other Member States should give rise to a self-supply procedure in the country of establishment or that a differential tax equal to the difference between the VAT paid on the purchase and the national VAT on similar goods and services should be payable.

As the VAT clearing system (see para. 1–017) has been subject to serious criticism, the Commission proposed that it be replaced by a clearing system on a macro-economic scale, based on foreign trade statistics. Various measures would also be implemented to reduce the amount of transfers from exporting countries to importing countries. For instance, intra-community sales between affiliates of the same transnational group, which account for a very large portion of exchanges between Member States, could be performed without VAT being applied until resale.

As regards rates, the breadth of the band is commonly viewed as excessive and liable to cause distortions of competition, especially as regards the standard rate. The Commission therefore proposes replacement of the 14 per cent. to 20 per cent. band which it had suggested initially (see para. 1–018) by a minimum rate which it has not determined yet, but which could be in the order of 15 per cent. It has also acknowledged, on a transitional basis, maintenance of zero rating for a limited number of goods by Member States wishing to retain it.

As regards excise duties, the Commission is supposed to be willing to adopt a more flexible position by agreeing to the single rates set in its initial proposals in 1987 being regarded as long-term objectives. Until its objectives are achieved, the Commission will propose, according to products, either minimum rates, or bands of rates around such objectives.

At this point, it is not possible to foresee how and to what extent these new proposals of the EC Commission will be amended and what the final result will be.

# 2. Belgium

## 1. GENERAL BACKGROUND

VAT, which replaced the so-called "Taxe de transmission," was put into effect in Belgium on January 1, 1971. The Sixth EC Directive was introduced into the Belgian tax system by law in December 1977 and became effective on the first of January 1978. **2–001**

A body of the Ministry of Finance called "Administration de la T.V.A." supervises all operations of taxable persons in Belgium. VAT due on importation is dealt with by the Customs and Excise.

## 2. WHO IS TAXABLE?

### *General*

A taxable person is any person who independently and regularly supplies goods or services as defined by Belgian VAT law. The sale of goods or the rendering of services may occur as a principal or auxiliary purpose, with or without a profit motive. **2–002**

The definition of a taxable person in Belgian law is generally consistent with the definition used in the Sixth Directive.

Taxable persons who carry out general operations within the meaning of the law by non-equivocal deeds, (*i.e.*, by setting up an organisation for delivery of goods or services which will be made regularly) are subject to tax as soon as those deeds are performed. Consequently, all deliveries of goods and rendering of services carried out by this taxable person are subject to VAT. A company will be subject to VAT only if it carries on a taxable activity.

#### Transactions with branch/subsidiary

Subsidiaries of foreign firms supplying taxable goods and services in Belgium are treated in the same manner as other taxable persons. Supplies deemed to take place in Belgium between subsidiary and parent company are, therefore, in principle, subject to VAT. Supplies of goods and services between the head office and a branch are, however, not subject to VAT.

#### Government bodies

Government bodies are generally not considered to be taxable persons. However, when they are making supplies on a regular basis, they may qualify as entrepreneurs and become subject to VAT in order to prevent distortion of competition.

### *Fiscal unity/group registration*

**2–003** A "group or fiscal unity concept" does not exist in Belgium.

### *Foreign entrepreneurs*

**2–004** In Belgium, taxable person status applies to individuals and companies having no domicile or office within Belgium. The tax treatment of a taxable person operating from outside Belgium depends upon whether or not he has a permanent establishment in Belgium. When he has such a permanent establishment, he is treated as a normal Belgian taxable person and pays VAT when supplying goods and services or importing goods into Belgium.

#### Representative office

Representative offices of foreign entrepreneurs dealing with activities of a preparatory or auxiliary nature can register as a domestic entrepreneur and thus recover the input VAT. However, the tax authorities do not always allow this and may refuse recovery of the input VAT on the basis that there is no output.

#### VAT representative

If he has no permanent establishment, the foreign taxable person must, as a rule, appoint an approved responsible agent in Belgium before supplying goods or rendering services irrespective of whether such a transaction is subject to VAT or exempted under articles of the tax code.

Appointment of a responsible agent is compulsory when:

- the taxable person established abroad imports goods and enters them for home use on payment of tax in his name;
- the taxable person established abroad takes delivery in Belgium of goods which are intended either for sale in Belgium or for export;
- the taxable person established abroad carries out in Belgium construction work, assembly operations, maintenance or repair work;

— the taxable person established abroad hires out goods in Belgium.

Should the non-resident entrepreneur fail to appoint a responsible representative, he will not receive a credit for input VAT.

The foreign taxable person does not require an approved, responsible agent in respect of:

— services of an intellectual nature rendered in Belgium (research and inspection work, market research, advertising business, assignment or granting of intellectual rights, such as patents, registered trademarks, copyrights);
— services of a material character occasionally rendered in Belgium.
— transactions of an occasional character consisting of reselling, in his country, goods which have been bought in Belgium or imported therein;
— delivery of goods and the rendering of services in Belgium which are exempt from the tax pursuant to the Code (for example, international transport of goods);
— when the taxable person imports for home use, the payment of tax on behalf of a customer established in Belgium;
— when goods are imported for warehousing, transit or temporary importation.

**Reverse charge mechanism**

Sometimes the person receiving services for business use from abroad is obliged to account for VAT on the value of the services. The recipient of such services is regarded as supplying the services to himself.

### *Importers*

Persons who import goods into Belgium are subject to VAT at the **2–005** same rate as applies to the sale of similar goods within Belgium. VAT is to be paid by the importer when the goods cross the Belgian border. Where authorised, payment is generally deferred for entrepreneurs until the first tax return following importation (postponed accounting system, see para. 2–009, "Chargeable event/Time of payment").

## 3. WHAT IS TAXABLE?

As a rule, the supply of goods and services is taxable only if it takes **2–006** place in Belgium or when goods are introduced into Belgian territory (*i.e.*, importation).

The main types of transactions are:

## Supply of goods

Goods are supplied when they are put at the disposal of the purchaser or his agent, in compliance with a contract which passes title in return for payment or which permits use without transfer of ownership, for example:

— the transfer of ownership of goods by agreement;
— the handing over by a contractor of goods made up from materials supplied in whole or part by his customer.

The sale of certain items which are deemed luxury goods, (for example, yachts, airplanes, gliders) is subject to VAT even when the sale does not take place in the normal course of business.

The term "goods" includes all movable and tangible property. Supplies of fuel, refrigeration and energy, etc. are also considered goods.

## Supply of services

The services which are subject to VAT are specifically listed in the VAT law. Such services are only subject to VAT if there is a contract with remuneration, for example, provisions of management, staff hire, the leasing of goods, hire of workmen or intellectual work performed in an independent way, etc.

## Self-supply of goods/services

If a taxable person supplies himself or his employees with goods of his business for private needs, this operation is considered to be a supply of goods and the VAT previously deducted is to be refunded to the state.

Another case of self-supply is the situation where movable goods are used as capital goods by the entrepreneur which he produced or which he acquired or imported as non-capital goods.

## Importation of goods

Importation of goods is the introduction of goods into free circulation in Belgium. Importation is a taxable event. However, goods may cross the border without VAT, using the regime of transit. Goods may stay also in a bonded warehouse without VAT becoming due. Sometimes goods can be re-exported after processing.

# 4. PLACE OF SUPPLY

Supplies of goods and services are subject to VAT only if they take place in Belgium. **2–007**

## *Supply of goods*

A supply of goods takes place in Belgium when at the time of transfer the goods are in Belgium.

Exceptions:

— When the goods sold are installed by the supplier, the supply is deemed to take place where the goods are installed.

— When transport of the goods is necessary for delivery, the supply is deemed to take place where the transport begins.

## *Supply of services*

### General rule

As a general rule the place where a service is supplied is the place where the supplier has established his business, has a fixed establishment from which the service is supplied or has his domicile. **2–008**

### Exceptions

Services carried out for any work connected with real estate and certain other services, *i.e.*, teaching, sports, transport, are exceptions to the above and are taxable where the real estate is located or where the services are rendered materially.

The place where the recipient of the service is located is the place where the service is rendered for services such as:

— transfers and assignments of copyrights, patents, licences, trademarks and similar rights;

— transfers and assignments of goodwill and obligations to refrain from engaging in a particular business activity or from exploiting a right referred to above;

— advertising services. However, advertising services connected with the letting and exploitation of immovable property in Belgium which is held for business purposes and performed by a Belgian entrepreneur for an entrepreneur resident within the EC (but outside Belgium) are considered to be supplied in Belgium and, therefore, taxable transactions for purposes of Belgian VAT. This is because the service is deemed to be rendered at the immovable property, which is treated as a fixed establishment of a foreign entrepreneur (similar services performed by a Belgian entrepreneur for a non-entrepreneur who is a resident of a country outside the EC are, however, not considered taxable transactions in Belgium);

- intellectual services performed within the ordinary course of their professional activity by consultants, accountants, engineers and those engaged in the supply of similar services;
- professional transactions engaged in by banks and other financial institutions with the exception of the renting of safes;
- the supply of staff;
- the activities of agents in relation to the above-mentioned services;
- the leasing of movable tangible property other than means of transport.

### Reverse charge mechanism

Sometimes the VAT is collected from the Belgian customer of the foreign entrepreneur. This happens when the foreign entrepreneur has no permanent establishment or VAT representative in Belgium. Then the tax liability for both the supply of goods and services shifts from the foreign entrepreneur to the Belgian taxpayer. Generally, this situation would arise in the case of services of an "intellectual" nature.

## 5. BASIS OF TAXATION

### *Supplies within Belgium*

**2–009** VAT applies to the total amount of the purchase price and other consideration payable for the goods or services, including, for example, insurance and transport costs.

The following items are excluded from the taxable base:

- amounts deductible from the price as a discount for early payment and price reduction given by the supplier to which the purchaser is entitled at the time the tax becomes due;
- the VAT itself;
- interest charges for late payment;
- costs for ordinary and usual packaging materials for which the supplier agrees to reimburse the purchaser if the materials are returned;
- amounts advanced by the supplier for expenses he incurred in the name and for the account of the other contracting party.

When the consideration does not (wholly) consist of a sum of money, it is to be estimated at the normal value, which can be defined as the price which can be obtained in Belgium for the same goods on an arm's length basis.

### *Self-Supplies*

The taxable base for self-supplied goods is the purchase price of comparable goods. If, however, there is no comparable price, the taxable base is the cost of supplying such goods, *i.e.*, the cost price.

### *Imports*

VAT is payable on the value of the goods upon which customs duties are levied plus such duties. The VAT itself does not form part of the taxable basis.

### *Chargeable event/Time of payment*

An invoice relating to the goods or services supplied must be issued by the fifth day of the month following that in which the goods or services were supplied. The VAT is to be paid to the State at the time of the monthly or quarterly returns. The same rules apply with regard to the issuing of invoices and payment of tax in respect of self-supplies.

When goods are imported, the tax is paid to the customs authorities. However, provided he has obtained the required authorisation, a resident entrepreneur can defer payment until he files his periodic VAT return and he can then claim a credit for the tax.

VAT due is normally accounted for on the basis of the value of the invoices issued in an appropriate VAT period. Sometimes entrepreneurs can account for VAT on a cash basis when they do not issue invoices. These are generally very small retailers who can opt for a regime exempting them from most formalities, such as issuing invoices and filing returns.

### *Credit notes/bad debts*

Where a price reduction is agreed after an invoice has been issued, a partial recovery of the VAT paid can be effected by issuing a credit note.

When a taxable person believes a debt will not be paid, he can recover the VAT paid on the supply when the bad debt is entered as such in the books. The related VAT will be refunded.

## 6. TAX RATES

The present rates are as follows: **2–010**

1% — on gold transactions

6% — reduced rate applies to goods of basic necessity and to services of a social nature
17% — intermediate rate applies to goods of current consumption and to services which are particularly important from an economic, social or cultural view-point
19% — standard rate applies to all supplies of goods and services not covered by other rates
25% — plus eventually 8% — increased rate applies to goods which, according to the tax regulations, are deemed to be luxury goods.

## 7. EXEMPTIONS

### *Exemption with credit for input tax*

**2–011** Input tax relating to goods and services used for export operations is recoverable.

Certain imports, such as personal effects of travellers, personal goods imported on permanent transfer of private residence, goods imported by diplomats, packing containers and means of transport which will be reexported, are exempt from VAT.

### *Exemptions without credit for input tax*

Recovery of input tax incurred in respect of certain exempt activities which are listed in the tax code is not permitted. These activities include those carried on by banks, insurance companies, lawyers, notaries, doctors, etc., as well as certain duties, educational, cultural and sports activities.

### *Non-taxable transactions*

#### Transactions within the same legal entity

Supplies within the same VAT entity are not subject to VAT because they are considered to be outside the scope of VAT.

#### Transfer of business

The transfer of an entire business or an independent part thereof as a sale or a contribution of assets is not considered to be a delivery of goods when the recipient is subject to VAT.

#### Subsidies/Penalty payments/Compensation

Subsidies, *i.e.*, the intervention of a third party in a supply, are subject to VAT. Penalty payments are not subject to VAT when they are the consequence of damages to the supplier. Compensations do not normally fall within the scope of VAT.

### *Election to be subject to VAT*

In some cases, entrepreneurs may elect to be subject to VAT, for example, the sale of a new building or operations such as deposits and withdrawals.

## 8. CREDIT/REFUND FOR INPUT TAX

### *General rule*

In computing the amount of tax payable, a taxable person may deduct the tax relating to goods and services purchased or imported by him which are used for the purposes of his taxable business. **2–012**

A credit is not allowed for VAT paid on:

— goods and services used for non-business purposes;
— goods and services used for exempt transactions;
— tobacco, alcohol, hotels and meals, entertainment expenses and 50 per cent. of the expenses relating to cars.

If, at the end of a tax period, VAT paid to suppliers exceeds the VAT billed to customers, the balance will be refunded to taxable persons who make monthly VAT returns, if it is in excess of BF 60,000. For quarterly VAT returns, the balance is refunded if the excess is BF 25,000.

In any case, at the end of the calendar year, any excess of BF 800 or more is refunded.

### *Adjustment of entitlement to credit*

For a certain period (four book years for movable depreciable goods and nine book years for immovable goods following the year of purchase) the entitlement to a credit for input tax at the time of purchase may be adjusted on a *pro rata* time basis, depending on whether or not the goods continue to be considered as fixed assets.

### *Partial exemption*

Persons who make both taxable and exempt supplies as well as supplies outside the scope of VAT are entitled to recover VAT incurred in making the taxable supplies only. A preliminary ratio per calendar year is computed, but the exact ratio, taking into consideration the actual figures, is calculated (at the latest) on April 20 of the year following that in which a revision is due.

### *Time of recovery*

A credit for input tax may be claimed on the VAT returns for the tax period in which the supplier made his supply. Of course, this VAT is only refunded if the VAT liability is less than the VAT credit. Note that it is irrelevant, for the purposes of obtaining a VAT credit, whether or not the invoice has been paid.

### *Refund for foreign entrepreneurs*

**2–013** A refund is also available for a taxable person (who is not located in Belgium but is within the Common Market) in respect of VAT suffered on goods or services purchased in or imported into Belgium. Such a taxable person must fulfil the following conditions:

- file a special claim form with:
  Bureau Central de T.V.A. pour Assujettis Etrangers,
  Rue Van Orley 15
  1000 Bruxelles;
- indicate the nature of the activities for which he requests a VAT refund;
- attach a certificate issued by the taxpayer's own VAT authorities indicating that he is subject to VAT; and
- attach the original invoices or import documents.

The request must relate to a period of not less than three months and not more than one year. The request must be introduced no later than June 30 of the year following the one to which it relates. The refund should normally be made within six months.

With regard to a taxable person located outside the Common Market, the conditions are as follows:

- a form 803 F in three sets is to be filed with Bureau Central de T.V.A. pour Assujettis Etrangers, Rue Van Orley 15 – 1000 Bruxelles.

The applicant must provide proof that he has an economic activity by submitting:

- a certificate from his resident country. This certificate must be in French, Dutch or German;
- a copy of the applicant company's by-laws and balance sheet relating to the last fiscal year. This document must be certified as an exact copy and the signature must be legalised.

Only one request may be introduced per calendar quarter. Each refund request may include only invoices not more than five years old.

As a general rule, a refund is only granted in accordance with Belgian law. Consequently, VAT is not refundable for the items referred to above under "General rule," at para. 2–012.

## 9. ADMINISTRATIVE OBLIGATIONS

### *Registration*

Registration is required when an activity which is considered subject to VAT is effectively performed. However, the intention of performing such an activity is sufficient provided that this intention is sustained by an organisation created for the purposes of performing the activity. **2–014**

### *Books and records*

Those subject to the VAT laws and regulations are required to observe certain requirements regarding invoices, books, accounts, monthly or quarterly returns and other documents.

According to the Code of Commerce, a trader (including a company or branch) must keep the following books:

— a journal for the entry of the day-to-day transactions;
— a record ("livre des inventaires—inventarisboek") for the annual registration of the "inventory" of assets and liabilities (balance sheet and support details—income statement).

The VAT inspector must be informed of the commencement, change in location or nature and cessation of activities to which VAT law applies.

Incoming invoices and credit notes, documents supporting the import of goods and documents related to the transfer of fixed assets should be recorded daily in a register of incoming invoices.

The outgoing invoices and internal documents related to transfers out of inventory for private use and transfers out of inventory to fixed assets should be recorded in a register of outgoing invoices.

Collections related to transactions which are subject to VAT but for which no invoices are issued should be recorded day-by-day in a collection register. There should be separate columns (or registers) for collections by cash, postal check and banks.
This register is not required to be kept where appropriate financial ledgers are maintained.

Except in cases where a dispensation is granted, incoming and outgoing invoices and documents should be kept for a period of five years beginning on January 1 following the date of the document.

### *Invoices*

An invoice must be issued for each transaction. This requirement applies also to partial payments for goods or services. The minimum **2–015** information required on the invoice (a copy of which must be kept by the supplier) is as follows:

— date of invoice—this must not be later than the fifth working day following the month in which goods were delivered or services performed:
— sequential number in register of outgoing invoices;
— name and address of the supplier;
— VAT registration number of the supplier;
— name and address of the purchaser/recipient. In the event the purchaser/recipient is also subject to VAT law and regulations, it is recommended that his registration number also be shown;
— the date of delivery of the goods or completion of the services rendered;
— the usual description (including the quantity) of the goods supplied or the nature of the service rendered inclusive of all the data required to determine the applicable tax rate. If various goods are supplied free of charge to the customer, the total quantity actually delivered should still be mentioned;
— the selling price and other data required to determine the basis of VAT;
— the applicable VAT rate(s) and equalisation tax rate(s), if any;
— the amount of VAT;
— the amount of equalisation tax, if any;
— the reason for exemption in the case of transactions not subject to VAT.

Invoices do not need to be issued to individuals for goods supplied or services rendered to them unless those goods or services rendered are used by the individual for business or professional purposes. However, the rendering of an invoice to an individual is compulsory for the following transactions:

— sale of motor cars and other items, such as yachts, etc., which are considered to be luxury goods;
— new buildings;
— work carried out on real property;
— sales by instalment payments and rents.

### *VAT returns*

Monthly returns should be submitted to the appropriate VAT "Office de Contrôle" within 20 days following each calender month.

Quarterly returns apply to enterprises, the yearly turnover of which (exclusive of VAT) does not exceed BF 20,000,000.

### *Powers of Authorities*

Should a return be lodged with the tax authorities later than the required date, or non-authorised deductions be made by a taxpayer, the tax authorities can impose administrative penalties going from 10 per cent. to 200 per cent. of the non-authorised deductions and interest amounting to 0.8 per cent. per month.

The statutory time limit for additional assessments is five years from the day the VAT liability arose.

### *Objection/Appeal*

Where a person is dissatisfied with a formal determination of the amount to be paid to the tax authorities, he may lodge a claim with a court.

## 10. SPECIAL VAT REGIMES

### *Agricultural and forestry enterprises*

Farmers have a special regime. When they are supplying services or goods, they need not apply VAT formalities. However, a taxable person who supplies farmers must refund to the farmer the VAT amount included in the invoice price. **2–016**

### *Financial institutions*

Banking and financial activities are generally exempt.

### *Free port/Bonded warehouse*

Free port facilities are not available in Belgium. However, a bonded warehousing system exists where goods can be stored without being subject to import duties and VAT.

### *Small entrepreneurs*

Small entrepreneurs who are normally located in retail businesses are taxed on a fixed amount in order to simplify the formalities.

### *Travel agencies*

Travel agencies qualify for a special regime. Where a travel agent acts as an agent for someone else who organises the travel he is liable to VAT only on his margin (commission). Where travel agents directly organise the travel themselves they are subject to the normal VAT rules.

## *Transfer and leasing of real property*

Buildings (with the exclusion of the ground on which they are erected) are subject to VAT, provided they are transferred before December 31 of the year following that in which a fixed assessment of withholding tax on these buildings has been levied.

After this date, the buildings are subject to registration duties of around 12.5 per cent. Use of the VAT regime is optional.

Leasing of buildings is outside the scope of VAT. It is not possible to elect to be subject to VAT on the rents.

# 3. Denmark

## 1. GENERAL BACKGROUND

VAT (in Danish, MOMS) came into force on July 3, 1967. Most subsequent changes were introduced in 1978 under the harmonisation process of the EC, where, in particular, a number of new services became taxable under the VAT Act, 1967. **3–001**

The Act covers the Kingdom of Denmark except for the Faroe Islands, Greenland and the Free Port of Copenhagen.

VAT is administered by the Customs Authorities who are also responsible for the release of information about new VAT regulations. The day-to-day administration is handled by its 30 regional branch offices.

## 2. WHO IS TAXABLE?

### *General*

VAT must be paid by anyone who independently runs a business enterprise supplying goods or taxable services. **3–002**

The obligation to pay VAT also extends to co-operative and other societies.

A taxable enterprise has to register with the Customs Authorities when it has an annual taxable turnover of more than DKK 10,000. (1.274 ECU). This rule also applies to seasonal activities.

#### Transactions with branch/subsidiary

Transactions between a parent company and its subsidiary are treated as transactions between independent parties.

Transactions between a head office and its branch are exempt from VAT, unless the parties are registered separately or the branch or head office is located in a foreign country. In the latter case, the transaction is treated as either an export or an import.

### Government bodies

For the central government, counties, municipal institutions and public utility enterprises (*e.g.*, water supplies, electricity, etc.), the obligation to pay VAT is limited to cover the sale of goods or services made in competition with commercial enterprises. For example, there is no VAT on public certificates or the issuing of passports.

## *Fiscal unity/Group registration*

If an enterprise consists of more than one unit, division or branch, then taxation as one single enterprise is required. If separate accounts are kept for the individual units, divisions or branches, they may, upon request, be registered and taxed separately.

A company with one or more subsidiaries is not automatically regarded as one entity, but may, upon request, be registered as one single enterprise, provided all the companies involved are carrying out taxable business. Thus, it is not possible to register both taxable and non-taxable entities as one enterprise.

If enterprises have been registered as one enterprise, they are jointly and severally liable for the VAT in respect of the enterprises covered by the joint registration.

## *Foreign entrepreneurs*

**3–003** Foreign undertakings are liable to Danish VAT when making taxable supplies of goods and services within Denmark or when importing goods into Denmark.

Foreign undertakings with a fixed establishment in Denmark, including branches or agencies, carrying out taxable activities in Denmark are liable to Danish VAT.

A foreign enterprise having no registered office, residence or the like in Denmark may, on application, obtain reimbursement of VAT paid on goods and services purchased or imported for the commercial purpose of such enterprise in Denmark (see para. 3–015).

### Representative offices

A representative office of a foreign enterprise providing services of a supporting and auxiliary nature (for example, taking in orders) may, even if no suppplies are made in Denmark, apply for voluntary registration. This enables it to obtain a refund of VAT on local purchases of goods or services without having to go through the mutual recovery procedure referred to in paragraph 3–015 "Refund for foreign entrepreneurs." This facility, however, is not available for representative offices of enterprises carrying out activities which are exempt from VAT in Denmark (*e.g.*, banks).

### VAT representative

If the foreign entrepreneur carrying out taxable activities (*i.e.*, supplies or imports) in Denmark has no branch, office or the like in Denmark, he must be registered by a person (or a company) who has a permanent address in the country. The person or company will act as a local representative for the enterprise and he will be severally and jointly liable for the VAT attributable to the foreign entrepreneur.

### Reverse charge mechanism

For certain services "imported" into Denmark, the resident recipient of the services will be liable to VAT, rather than the non-resident supplier.

This special rule applies, for example, to services of consultants, lawyers and accountants, copyrights, patents, advertising and the hiring out of moveable property. For more details, see paragraph 3–009, "Reverse charge mechanism."

## *Importers*

Enterprises importing goods for business purposes must register separately in accordance with the provisions of the Tariff Act 1972. These rules similarly apply for VAT purposes. Likewise, a private individual is liable to pay VAT on importation of goods. However, no registration is required. **3–004**

Imported goods are taxed at the same rate as if the goods were supplied from within Denmark.

# 3. WHAT IS TAXABLE?

Danish VAT is levied on the supply of goods and services in Denmark and the import of goods. Occasional transactions are also taxable. **3–005**

## *Supply of goods*

On the basis of the 1972 Act and case law, VAT is levied on all goods, new as well as used, when the right to dispose of these goods is transferred by the owner. For example, a hire purchase qualifies as a supply of goods which takes place at the actual time of delivery, regardless of any agreements made in respect of instalment payments.

The assembly of, *e.g.*, a building or machine or an installation is also regarded as a supply of goods.

The term "goods" is not defined in the Act. Gas, water, electricity, heating and livestock are, however, to be regarded as goods. The following items are not regarded as goods and are not subject to VAT:

— bonds, shares and other securities.
— real estate. However, the owner of the real estate may register voluntarily in certain situations (see para. 3–016).

## *Supply of services*

As of October 1, 1978, VAT is levied on all services, apart from those specifically exempt (see para. 3–012). The term "services," however, is not defined in the Act. Services include, for example:

— leasing of movable and immovable tangible property;
— transfer of patents, copyrights, licences, etc.;
— supply of staff;
— advertising;
— services of consultants, engineers, lawyers, etc.

## *Self-supply of goods/services*

**3–006** Self-supply is the transfer of goods or services within the enterprise. In general, such transactions are not subject to VAT.

However, the Authorities may decide that an enterprise is liable to VAT on goods and services used by the enterprise itself. For example, the construction of buildings on the constructor's own land for the purpose of sale or letting has been deemed subject to VAT.

Where goods or services are purchased by the enterprise but partly used for private purposes, a special provision applies. At the time of the purchase, credit for input VAT is given, but the input VAT is adjusted for the part relating to the private use, normally an estimated value. For the private use of certain items, *e.g.*, the enterprise's telephone, standard rates apply.

Where goods or services are purchased by the enterprise but wholly used for private purposes, no input VAT is creditable.

In cases where goods are purchased for business purposes, but later on are removed from the enterprise for private purposes, such a removal will be treated as a taxable turnover of the goods. VAT will then be levied on the market value of the goods.

## *Importation of goods*

The taxability of imported goods is based on the act of importation itself. The liability to pay VAT is usually settled with Customs at the time of importation, regardless of whether or not the person importing the goods is a taxable person. Exemptions may apply for specific situations. For example, household equipment brought along by a person who is moving to Denmark to take up residence is exempt from VAT.

A registered enterprise can postpone payment of VAT by paying on a monthly basis in accordance with a statement received from the Customs Authorities.

# 4. PLACE OF SUPPLY

VAT only applies to supplies within Denmark. **3–007**

## *Supply of goods*

Goods located abroad and sold by a Danish enterprise, will be considered outside the scope of Danish VAT, even if the Danish or foreign enterprise is registered in Denmark for VAT purposes. However, if such goods are imported into Denmark, VAT will be levied on importation.

Goods being exported from Denmark are exempt from VAT. As a result, no VAT is actually levied, whereas at the same time the right to a credit is maintained.

## *Supply of services*

### General rule

The Act does not define what constitutes the rendering of services nor does it contain specific rules where the supply of a service is deemed to take place. The legislation is, however, based on guidelines contained in the Sixth EC Directive as to the place where the services are rendered. In general, services are (assumed to have been) rendered where the entrepreneur rendering the service is resident or has a fixed establishment from where the service is rendered.

### Exceptions

For certain services this general rule is not applied, despite the **3–008**
supplier's place of business or residence.

Services connected with real property are deemed to take place where the real property is situated. For example, services performed by a real estate agent, project planning, etc.

Transport of goods and persons is deemed to take place where it actually occurs. Note, however, that transport of goods directly to and from a foreign country is exempt with credit; transport of passengers is usually exempt without credit, see para. 3–012, "Exemptions".

Services of a scientific, cultural or entertainment nature are deemed to be supplied where the arrangements are actually and physically performed.

Valuation of or work in respect of movable tangible property is deemed to take place where the property is situated.

For certain other services (listed below), the general rule is also changed so that the place of supply is deemed to be the place where the recipient is established or has his residence, provided that:

— the supplier is an entrepreneur outside the EC and the recipient is a non-entrepreneur in Denmark; and

— the supplier is an entrepreneur within the EC and the recipient is a partially exempt entrepreneur or even a non-entrepreneur in Denmark.

The services in question are:

— transfers and assignments of copyrights, patents, licences, trademarks, designs and similar rights;
— advertising services;
— "intellectual" services, such as consultants and engineers, project planning, services of lawyers, accountants and similar services, data processing and information services;
— supply of staff;
— the hiring out of movable tangible property, except for all forms of transportation;
— services consisting of a commitment to refrain from any professional activity or right referred to above;
— the services of agents who act in the name and for the account of another, when they procure for their principal the services referred to above.

### Reverse charge mechanism

**3–009** For certain services "imported" into Denmark, the resident recipient of the services will be liable to VAT, rather than the non-resident supplier. This special rule applies to the following services:

*Group A*

— transfers and assignments of copyrights, patents, licences, trademarks, designs and similar rights;
— advertising services;
— "intellectual" services, such as consultants and engineers, project planning, services of lawyers, accountants and similar services, data processing and information services;
— the supply of staff;
— the hiring out of movable tangible property, except for all forms of transport;
— services consisting of a commitment to refrain from any professional activity or right referred to above;
— the services of agents who act in the name and for the account of another, when they procure for their principal the services of this group;

*provided* these services are rendered by a supplier resident outside the EC territory to a Danish recipient.
If the services listed above are rendered by a supplier resident within the EC territory, the reverse charge mechanism will not apply. In this case, the foreign supplier will remain liable for the VAT due.

*Group B*

— services related to real estate in Denmark, *e.g.*, services from a real estate agent and project planning;

— valuations of or work in respect of movable tangible property;
— cultural, artistic or entertainment activities taking place in Denmark.

Note that no liability to pay Danish VAT arises for the Danish recipient of the services listed under A or B if he is:

— registered as an entrepreneur; and
— entitled to a *full* credit for input tax.

If the Danish recipient is a registered entrepreneur, but entitled to a *partial* credit only, (*i.e.*, partially exempt enterprises), he will, however, become liable to pay VAT. Exempt enterprises and private persons not registered as entrepreneurs will be liable to VAT.

## 5. BASIS OF TAXATION

### *Supplies within Denmark*

VAT is charged on the total amount of consideration paid by the buyer. This can, for example, include: **3–010**

— other duties or taxes which have been levied on the goods at previous stages of distribution or by import;
— packing, transport or distribution expenses;
— agent's commission;
— cash discounts and other discounts which are subject to conditions that have not been met at the time of delivery.

If there is a community of interests between supplier and buyer of goods and taxable services (*e.g.*, one party holding a financial interest in the other enterprise), the Customs Authorities may determine a taxable base other than the one agreed between the parties and levy VAT accordingly.

### *Self-supplies*

The taxable base for self-supplied goods and services is the value of the transaction to a third party, *i.e.* arm's-length value. If goods or services are used for private purposes by the owner, shareholders or employees, etc., the taxable value is determined at the purchase or production price.

### *Imports*

The taxable value for imported goods will be the same as the taxable value for Customs duty purposes, as defined in the Tariff Act. The taxable value must include freight charges, insurance premiums, etc., incurred until the goods reach their first destination in Denmark, plus Customs duties and other taxes levied.

### *Chargeable event/Time of payment*

The general rule is that a taxable transaction occurs when the goods are actually supplied. However, where invoices are made out with respect to supplies, the time of invoicing is to be regarded as the time of supply, provided the invoice is made out before or directly after completion of the supply.

A taxable entrepreneur must submit periodical accounts to the authorities, usually based on a calendar quarter. Settlement must be made no later than one month and 20 days after the end of each period.

With every supply of goods or services, it is normal to issue an invoice connected to the taxable transaction. The invoice must normally be made directly after the supply.

However, no invoice is required for sales to private customers. These entrepreneurs (normally retailers) may account for VAT on a cash basis. Retailers and other entrepreneurs who mainly sell to private customers may also omit to issue an invoice to registered enterprises unless the recipient requests an invoice.

### *Credit notes/Bad debts*

An enterprise may deduct from the taxable turnover credit notes for returned goods, cash discounts and other discounts, which are subject to conditions which have not been met at the time of delivery, provided:

- the discounts were given to a registered enterprise which is entitled to a full credit for input tax; and
- a credit note is made indicating the VAT with respect to the discount allowed.

A refund of VAT on bad debt is normally available when the loss has been realised. A loss is realised under the following circumstances:

- bankruptcy;
- compulsory set-off of debts;
- set-off of debt with creditors;
- failed enforcement proceedings;
- compulsory sale;
- a proper valuation of facts and the amount involved.

## 6. TAX RATES

The present rates are as follows:

0% — not applicable, see para. 3–012, "Exemptions with credit for input tax"; **3–011**
22% — all goods and services, which are not exempted.

## 7. EXEMPTIONS

### *Exemptions with credit for input tax*

The following exemptions are with credit for input tax:

- goods exported by an enterprise and services performed in a foreign country; **3–012**
- transport of goods in Denmark directly to or from a foreign country, as well as related services such as customs clearance loading, unloading, etc., provided these are rendered by the transport enterprise itself and charged on the same invoice;
- work performed on goods for a foreign account provided that the enterprise exports the goods after the treatment and technical design and styling of goods for foreign account provided that the goods are to be manufactured abroad;
- project planning, design and other taxable services concerning buildings and other real estate located outside Denmark;
- necessary equipment delivered for use in aircraft and ships in international traffic (other than sports aircraft and pleasure craft) and services performed on such aircraft and ships;
- sale and hire of ships of not less than five gross register tons, and of aircraft other than sports aircraft and pleasure craft,
- repairs, maintenance and installation work performed on aircraft and ships referred to above, and on their permanent equipment, and materials supplied by the enterprise concerned for these purposes;
- sale of newspapers which are normally published in not less than one monthly issue;
- subscriptions for foreign periodicals from a foreign publisher on behalf of a subscriber.

The Minister of Taxation or the Customs authorities may decide whether and to what extent supplies delivered to ships or aircraft for use on board or for sales to passengers, etc., may be excluded from taxable sales.

### *Exemptions without credit for input tax*

The following exemptions are without credit for input tax:

- hospital treatment, medical practice, dentistry and other dental services. This means that nearly the whole health care sector is exempted, unless not approved by the authorities, *e.g.*, homeopathy;
- social services and aid;

— school and university education, language training. However, some educational programmes are not exempted, *e.g*, driving lessons;
— cultural activities, including libraries, museum, zoological gardens and the like. However, radio and television transmissions, theatre and cinema performances, concerts, etc., are taxable;
— sporting activities and arrangements, including arrangements to which betting or the like is attached. However, motor racing and arrangements in which professional sportsmen and athletes participate are taxable. Football matches are included only when professionals participate in both teams;
— passenger transport. However, commercial passenger bus transport, other than regular service, shall be taxable;
— postal services. However, telecommunication and parcel post services are taxable;
— letting, leasing and administration of real estate. However, letting of rooms in hotels, inns, motels, etc., letting out for periods shorter than one month, and letting out of camping, parking and advertising space are taxable;
— insurance activities;
— bank, savings bank, and financing activities. However, hiring out of bank boxes is taxable;
— lotteries, etc.;
— literary and musical, as well as other artistic, activities;
— travel agencies and information activities, etc. and tourist offices;
— services performed by undertakers, etc., in direct connection with funerals.

## *Non-taxable transactions*

### Transactions within the same legal entity

**3–013** Transactions between a head office and its branch are not subject to VAT, unless the branch or the head office is situated in a foreign country. If so, the transaction is treated as either an export or an import.

However, VAT liability may arise according to the rules concerning place of services and the reverse charge mechanism (see para. 3–009).

Transactions between a parent company and its subsidiary are subject to VAT, unless jointly registered, see para. 3–002, "Fiscal unity/Group registration".

### Transfer of business

Taxable sales do not include sale of stocks, machinery and other assets, provided they are sold in connection with the sale of all or part of an enterprise and the new owner operates a registered enterprise. Within eight days of the sale, the seller must notify the Customs Authorities of the new owner's name and address, and the sales price for the stocks, machinery and other assets sold. With regard to a potential adjustment, see paragraph 3–014 below.

However, this rule does not apply when an arrangement of sale and lease back is established. In such cases, VAT is charged at the normal rate.

### Subsidies/penalty payments/compensation

Subsidies given to an enterprise are only exempt from VAT if given as a gift and without consideration.

There is no VAT on penalty payments (for example, for premature termination of a lease), unless it is also payment for a supply.

Usually, there is no VAT on damage claims neither on payments from an insurance company nor on payments for unfulfilled contracts.

## *Election to be subject to VAT*

A voluntary registration applies only for a very limited number of normally exempted enterprises. The more important areas are letting or leasing of real estate.

# 8. CREDIT/REFUND FOR INPUT VAT

## *General rule*

VAT owed to the Treasury by registered enterprises is calculated as the difference between the output VAT and the input VAT, import included. **3–014**

In principle, all input VAT on purchases including VAT on investments made during a VAT period is recoverable.

However, there is no recovery for input VAT related to a non-taxable turnover.

Moreover, input VAT is not recoverable for:

- meals for the enterprise's owner and employees;
- acquisition and use of housing accommodation for the enterprise's owner and employees;
- remuneration in kind of the enterprise's employees;
- acquisition and operation of creches, kingergartens, recreation centres, holiday homes, summer cottages, etc., for the enterprise's employees;
- entertainment expenses and gifts;
- hotel accommodation;
- acquisition and operation of passenger motor vehicles adapted for transport of not more than ten persons.

### Adjustment of entitlement to credit

Special provisions apply in relation to input VAT on certain investment goods:

- machinery, inventory and working plant, provided that the cost is more than DKK 50.000, (ECU 6.280); and
- immovable property.

On the sale of an enterprise, no adjustment is to be made by the seller if the purchaser is a registered entrepreneur who is willing to undertake the obligation of recomputing the allowable credit.

Adjustments need only be made during a five-year period (10 years for immovable property) and will be calculated on the basis of one-fifth, (one-tenth for immovable property) including the year of delivery, of the VAT paid at the time of acquisition for the year when a change occurs.

### Partial exemption

**3–015** Input VAT on purchases in connection with exempt transactions may not be reclaimed. However, where VAT is incurred on purchases which are attributable to both taxable (exemption with credit included) and non-taxable supplies, the input VAT incurred must be apportioned *pro rata* between taxable and non-taxable supplies for the period of turnover.

It is not possible to divide one enterprise into profit centres to obtain a better position for a VAT refund, instead of the *pro rata* refund, for example, by using floor space, number of employees, etc., However, the enterprise may reorganise and form two entities, *e.g.*, a parent company and a subsidiary.

If an estimated ratio is used, an adjustment to actual must be made by the end of the accounting year.

There are no special provisions available to allow a partly exempt enterprise to be treated as fully taxable.

### Refund for foreign entrepreneurs

A foreign entrepreneur making taxable supplies in Denmark may register for VAT if he has an office or other business establishment in Denmark. He is then treated in the same way as a Danish enterprise. If no such establishment exists in Denmark, a VAT representative should be appointed. A credit or refund is then claimed when filing the normal periodic VAT return.

A special refund procedure applies for VAT paid on goods and taxable services purchased or imported in Denmark for commercial purposes for a non-registered entrepreneur, *e.g.*, advertisement expenses and exhibition costs. A refund of this Danish input VAT can be obtain upon application, under the following conditions:

— the business must *not* have an office or registered address in Denmark;
— the business must be subject to VAT according to the rules applied in Denmark, if the activity was carried out there; this means that for banking activities, insurance business and travel agencies, it is not possible to obtain VAT refunds;
— the foreign business must *not* supply goods or services in Denmark;
— the foreign business can only obtain a refund under the same conditions as a Danish business subject to VAT.

This means that there is no refund of VAT on purchases relating to the specific items for which a credit for input tax is disallowed, referred to in para. 3–014 above.

To obtain the refund, it is necessary to fill in a standard form in Danish and send it in to the Customs authorities at:

Address: Distriktstoldkammer 6
Skodsborgvej 303
Postbox 200
2850 Naerum

The application must be filed together with the original VAT invoices and a statement indicating the purpose of the expenses. A statement from the relevant competent authority to prove that the enterprise is subject to VAT in its country of domicile must also be enclosed. Such statement is only valid for a period of one year from the date of issue. The enterprise must also provide a statement that it has not exercised any activity subject to VAT in Denmark in the course of the reimbursement period.

The application must refer to purchases of goods or taxable services over a period of at least three months and not exceeding one calendar year. It must concern a VAT amount of less than DKK 1,500. Where the application covers a calendar year or the rest of a calendar year, the amount may, however, not be less than DKK 200.

## 9. ADMINISTRATIVE OBLIGATIONS

### *Registration*

Any entrepreneur who is taxable (see para. 3–002) must apply to the Customs authorities for registration. He will then be entered into the Register of Urban Trade or the register covering agricultural occupations. After registration has been completed, a certificate of registration will be issued to the enterprise. Enterprises, whose taxable sales of goods and services do not exceed DKK 10,000.— per annum, are not taxable. **3–016**

For enterprises selling non-taxable services, a voluntary registration is possible. This may be beneficial to, for example, an entrepreneur who is renting out real estate in order to obtain a refund of the input VAT. A voluntary registration covers a minimum period of two years during which de-registration cannot take place.

It is possible for registered enterprises carrying out export business to apply for and obtain a VAT refund after one month instead of the usual three months.

## *Books and records*

Registered enterprises' purchases and sales of taxable goods and taxable services must be recorded in accounts which can serve as a basis for the calculation and control of the VAT amounts for each taxation period.

Such records must contain separate accounts for VAT receivable and VAT payable. VAT accounts may be kept by periodical entries, provided that VAT can be directly calculated on the basis of the enterprise's records of purchases and taxable sales of goods and services.

With respect to purchases and sales of taxable goods and services, registered enterprises and enterprises exempted from VAT must retain books and records, including invoices, invoice copies, cash register tapes, etc., for five years after the end of the accounting year.

Registered enterprises must perform inventories at least once a year. Account records must be filed for five years after the end of the accounting year.

## *Invoices*

Invoices must be issued to consignees for all taxable goods or services supplied by registered enterprises. If payment is required for partial deliveries before the entire delivery has been completed, separate invoices must be made out for any such partial deliveries. The following details must be specified: consigner, consignee, description, quantity and price of the goods delivered or services performed.

The supplier must indicate the amount of the VAT on the invoice and specify the price without VAT for each item on the invoice.

A credit note must be issued for goods returned to offset an issued invoice. This rule also applies in cases where the supplier allows a price reduction after the issue of the invoice, provided that the reduction is not a discount.

The supplier must file copies of invoices, credit notes and cash vouchers.

In cases where an invoice or a cash voucher covers both taxable and non-taxable supplies, the invoice must specify the taxable supplies. Such supplies must be listed and added up separately.

## *VAT returns*

**3–017** Within one month and 20 days after the end of each taxation period, registered enterprises must submit to the Customs authorities a return of the amounts of VAT payable and VAT receivable for the period and the amount of sales which are non-taxable. Amounts shall be shown in Danish kroner, fractions thereof being disregarded. Such returns, which must be signed by the enterprise's responsible manager(s), must be submitted on special forms which should also be used for settlement of the net-VAT balance.

Taxation periods must be calendar quarters. Filing on a monthly basis is not possible. For an enterprise registered as farming, fishing or related activities, the period is six months.

If the VAT return for any tax period is late, then the tax liability for that period is increased by 1 per cent. (min. DKK 300—max. DKK 1,000), and if the VAT is not paid on time, interest is to be paid at the rate of 1.3 per cent. per month.

The authorities are entitled to estimate VAT to be paid if no return is received.

## *Powers of authorities*

The Customs authorities are authorised to inspect premises used in connection with the operations of enterprises which are required to register, and to inspect the stocks held by such enterprises, their books of account, other records, correspondence, etc.

The books and records shall, at the request of the Customs authorities, be surrendered or sent to the Customs authorities.

Suppliers to enterprises, which are required to register, shall, upon request, give the Customs authorities information about goods and services delivered to such enterprises.

## *Objection/Appeal*

Any disputes with the Customs authorities may be submitted to a board of appeal of six members, which should possess a general knowledge of administrative and business matters. The board has the final power to make administrative decisions on:

- questions concerning the scope of VAT liability;
- questions concerning taxable value;
- questions concerning the scope of the exemptions;
- questions relating to VAT deductibility items;
- questions as to how public utility deliveries shall be defined;
- appeals against estimated assessments made by the Customs authorities.

The final decisions are made by the Court of Justice.

# 4. France

## 1. GENERAL BACKGROUND

A tax on consumption was first introduced in France in 1920. This tax was gradually modified and finally called "value added tax," in French "taxe sur la valeur ajoutée (T.V.A.)" in 1968. Important modifications were made to harmonise the French legislation with the Sixth EC Directive on VAT with effect from January 1, 1979. **4–001**

The term French territory means France including Corsica and Monaco. VAT is applicable in the overseas departments (Martinique, Guadeloupe, Réunion) but special rules are applicable. In particular, transactions between France and these departments are treated as exports or imports, see para. 4–013, "Refund for foreign entrepreneurs".

VAT in France is administered by the income tax authorities, with the exception of VAT levied on imports which is administered by Customs (Administration des Douanes).

## 2. WHO IS TAXABLE?

### *General*

Any person supplying taxable goods or services in the course of business, whether on a regular or occasional basis is taxable (assujetti). The term "business" applies to all the activities of producers, traders and suppliers of services which are carried out independently. The activities of employees are outside the scope of VAT. **4–002**

The legal status of the person is irrelevant and VAT will thus apply indifferently to corporate bodies, individuals, liberal professions, residents or non-resident.

There is no monetary limit below which VAT is not due.

#### Transactions with branch/subsidiary

VAT is not due on transactions within the same legal entity. Supplies of services between a branch and its foreign head office are therefore not subject to VAT. On the contrary, services supplied by a foreign company to its French subsidiary, or vice versa, will be a taxable supply.

### Government bodies

Government bodies are not subject to VAT in respect of their activities of an administrative, social, or cultural nature. However, they are liable to VAT in respect of their commercial activities or their activities which are deemed to be in competition with other commercial concerns.

## *Fiscal unity/Group taxation*

The concept of fiscal unity does not exist in French VAT law. Each taxable person (individual or legal body) must account for the tax independently of any other taxable person. It is not possible for a group of taxable persons to file joint returns.

## *Foreign entrepreneurs*

**4–003** Entrepreneurs without an establishment in France but delivering goods in France or supplying services which are taxable in France are subject to VAT. A foreign entrepreneur is taxable in France when he acts as the importer of the goods.

Generally, a non-resident entrepreneur is considered as having an establishment for VAT purposes if he keeps in France a regular place of activity such as an office, shop, factory or only a fixed domicile from which the activity is exercised. A non-resident entrepreneur with an establishment in France is treated as a local company and should comply with all the rules applicable to French entrepreneurs. In particular it will have to file regular returns and will be able to offset directly input VAT against output VAT.

### Representative office

Representative offices of foreign entrepreneurs are not regarded as taxable persons when they only carry out activities of a preparatory or auxilliary nature. The foreign entrepreneur is entitled to ask the French VAT authorities to refund the input VAT incurred in France through its representative office, see para. 4–013, "Refund for foreign entrepreneurs".

### VAT representative

Foreign entrepreneurs without establishment in France but making taxable supplies in France are required to appoint a VAT representative who will be responsible for fulfilling the administrative obligations and for payment of the tax due by the foreign entrepreneur.

**Reverse charge mechanism**

Foreign entrepreneurs who supply in the state, services such as copyrights, patents, hiring out of movable goods, advertising services, consultancy, provision of staff and financial services, etc., do not have to account for VAT in France since the tax on such services is due by the recipient, see para. 4–007, "Reverse charge mechanism".

However the reverse charge does not apply when the same services are supplied to and used by a non-entrepreneur in France (*e.g.* an individual). If the foreign entrepreneur is established outside the EC he will be liable to VAT in France and the appointment of a VAT representative is compulsory.

### *Importers*

Goods brought into France are liable to VAT at customs clearance. The tax is due by the importer. If the goods are sent directly by the foreign firm to the final customer in France who appears as the actual importer, VAT due on imports will be payable by the French customer.

## 3. WHAT IS TAXABLE?

VAT is due on the supply in France of goods and services, as well as on **4–004**
the importation of goods.

To be taxable a supply must be made for consideration. The consideration is usually the price paid for the goods or the services. It may also be the goods or services received in exchange for the supply. Supplies made at cost are taxable.

### *Supply of goods*

The term supply (delivery) usually refers to the actual transfer of ownership of the goods from one person to another against payment. It can be effected by a sales deed but in the absence of any legal documents the handing over of the goods is also treated as a supply. This is the case in:

— hire purchase contracts;
— seizure of goods by legal officers;
— sales with retention of ownership until full payment;
— exchange of goods;
— contribution in kind to a corporate body.

The term goods applies to all tangible movable properties. Utilities such as electricity, gas, heat or refrigeration qualify as "goods." This also applies in the case of land and buildings, see para. 4–019, "Real estate".

## *Supply of services*

The term services applies to all transactions which are not treated as supplies of goods.

The transfer of intangible property such as rights on trademarks, patents, know-how, software, etc., is regarded as supply of services. The following transactions also qualify as services:

— leasing, renting;
— transport of persons or goods;
— commissions;
— building construction work;
— research and expertise;
— agreement to refrain from an activity.

## *Self-supplies of goods/services*

**4–005** In certain cases which are specified by law, an entrepreneur is deemed to supply goods to himself and therefore is liable for VAT on the goods.

A self-supply is deemed to occur:

— when goods acquired in the course of a business and giving rise to an input tax credit are finally used, appropriated or devoted to non-business purposes. This is the case, for example, where goods are appropriated by the directors or employees of a company for their personal use;
— when goods are extracted, manufactured, built or transformed by the entrepreneur himself for the need of his business. There is a self-supply even if the manufacturing, building or transformation is carried out by a third person at the request of the entrepreneur.

This rule is intended to avoid distortion of competition by preventing an entrepreneur from obtaining goods free of VAT when he would not have any or only a limited right of recovery either because he is not making any taxable supplies or because recovery of the input VAT is disallowed. A self-supply is always taxable when it concerns capital assets. It is taxable only in limited cases when it concerns other goods.

Self-supplies of services are not taxable.

## *Importation of goods*

The introduction of goods to the territory of France triggers liability for import VAT. Under certain circumstances payment of VAT can be delayed until the goods are finally put onto the French market (see para. 4–018 "Bonded warehouses"). In limited cases, the importation of goods into France is exempt from VAT, see para. 4–011, "Exempt imports".

# 4. PLACE OF SUPPLY

VAT is chargeable in France only if the supply of goods or services takes place in France. The rules for determining the place of supply are different for goods and services. **4–006**

## *Supply of goods*

Where the goods are to be transported:

— the goods to be delivered are in France before transportation: the supply is taxable in France with the important exception of export sales.
— the goods to be delivered are abroad before transportation: the supply is subject to VAT in France at the point of importation and either payable by the foreign supplier or by the final customer in France.

Where the goods are not transported:

— the supply is taxable in France if the goods are in France at the time of delivery or transfer of ownership.

Goods which have been assembled or installed in France before they are delivered are also taxable in France.

## *Supply of services*

### General rule

The general rule is that the place where services are deemed to be supplied is the place where the entrepreneur supplying the services has his place of business, his fixed establishment or his usual place of residence from which the services are supplied.

### Exceptions

For a number of specified services, the general rule is not applicable. These are:

— Services connected with real estate, such as the services of estate agents, architects, etc., are deemed to be supplied where the real property is located.
— Transport of goods and persons and closely related services (such as loading, unloading), are deemed to be supplied where transport takes place. Only transport which takes place in France is taxable. Exemptions apply to international transport and to exported goods, see para. 4–011, "Exemptions".
— Renting means of transport is deemed to be supplied in France:

(1) if the lessor is established in France and the services are used in France or in another EC country;
(2) if the lessor is established outside the EC and the services are used in France by the lessee.

— Cultural, artistic, sporting, scientific, educational and entertainment services are supplied where they are physically performed.

**4–007** The following services are deemed to be supplied where the recipient of the service usually resides or has a fixed establishment:

- transfers and assignments of trade marks, licences, copyright, patents;
- advertising services;
- services of consultants, engineers, chartered accountants, consultancy offices;
- data processing and supply of information;
- financial, banking and insurance services;
- supply of staff;
- acceptance to refrain from carrying out an activity or exercising any rights;
- renting of movable properties (apart from the renting of means of transport).

According to this rule no VAT will be due in France when the recipient of these services is established outside France. However, the tax will be due in France if the services are provided to a non-entrepreneur located in another EC country.

### Reverse charge mechanism

A foreign supplier without a fixed establishment in France who provides the following services to a French taxable entrepreneur will not have to charge French VAT since the liability for the tax is shifted to the French recipient. These services are:

- transfers and assignments of trade marks, licences, copyright, patents;
- advertising services;
- services of consultants, engineers, chartered accountants, consultancy offices;
- data processing and supply of information;
- financial, banking and insurance services;
- supply of staff;
- acceptance to refrain from carrying out an activity or exercising any rights;
- renting of movable properties (apart from the renting of means of transport).

In the case of a foreign supplier established outside the EC who provides these services to a non-entrepreneur in the state, French VAT will be due by the foreign supplier if the services are used in France. The appointment of a VAT representative will then be necessary.

# 5. BASIS OF TAXATION

## *Supplies within France*

VAT is assessed on the total price received, or to be received, as consideration for the supply of the goods or services. On that basis, ancilliary expenses, additional payments, commissions, wrapping expenses, interest relating to the supply (as opposed to financial interest) insurance charged by the seller, customs duties are part of the taxable basis. If no monies are received, VAT must be assessed on the total value of the goods or services received in exchange for the supply. **4–008**

If cash discounts are granted on the invoice, it is the net amount which is subject to VAT.

## *Self-supplies*

VAT due on self-supplies is calculated on the basis of the purchase price of the goods or otherwise on the cost to the supplier. In the case of goods manufactured by an entrepreneur for his own business, the cost will include the value of the raw materials, of the services used in the manufacture and/or the salary expenses if the work was carried out by the entrepreneur's own employees.

The purchase price or the cost is determined at the time the goods are first put into use.

## *Imports*

VAT due on the importations of goods is assessed on the value determined for customs purposes, to which should be added freight and insurance costs to the first place of destination in the country, as well as the taxes or duties paid on the importation, except for VAT.

VAT is also due on late payment interest relating to imported goods. A special procedure has to be set up with the Customs authorities to settle the tax when the amount of such interest is unknown at the time of importation.

## *Chargeable event/Time of payment*

Different rules apply to goods and to services. VAT on goods becomes due as soon as the goods have been delivered. This is the case even if the corresponding invoices have not been issued. The full VAT will be due even if the price has not been paid for the goods or if it is paid by instalments. **4–009**

VAT on services is normally due on receipt of the payment from the customer. This rule allows the supplier to delay the payment of the tax until he has been fully paid by his customer. However entrepreneurs supplying goods as well as services may find it simpler to declare their taxable transactions using the same rule. They can therefore opt to pay VAT on services at the same time as VAT on goods ("option pour les débits") which normally coincides with the invoicing. A letter should be addressed to the tax authorities to inform them that this option is being exercised. VAT due on imported goods is payable at the time of customs clearance.

VAT due is paid every month on the goods delivered and the monies received for services during the previous month, see para. 4–016, "VAT returns".

### *Credit notes/Bad debts*

A refund of VAT can be obtained by an entrepreneur who issues a credit note to his customer.

VAT on uncollected debts can be recovered by the supplier provided a special procedure is followed.

## 6. TAX RATES

**4–010** The following main rates presently apply in France:

| | |
|---|---|
| 0% | see para. 4–011, "Exemptions with credit for input tax". |
| 5.5% | (reduced rate) applies mainly to food, water, medicine, products from agriculture and fishing as well as to transport of persons, books, lodgings, hotel accommodation, services of travel agents. |
| 18.6% | (standard rate) is applicable to all supplies of goods or services not subject to another specified rate. |
| 28% | the 1988 Finance Act introduced this new rate for cars and motorcycles above 240 $cm^3$. Following the 1989 Finance Act, it also applies to luxury goods (precious stones, pearls, gold, furs, caviar) as well as to cameras, videos, video tapes and tobacco. |

Specific rates apply to newspapers (2.1%), and to land for construction (13%).

## 7. EXEMPTIONS

**4–011** A transaction is considered as exempt when, while being within the scope of VAT, it is excluded from being subject to the tax by a special provision of the law. As a rule, exempt supplies prevent an entrepreneur from recovering the tax incurred on purchases made in connection with these exempt supplies. However, the law provides that a number of exempt supplies are entitled to input credit.

## *Exemptions with credit for input tax*

The following exemptions are with credit for input tax:

- goods transported out of France by a resident or non-resident entrepreneur;
- delivery of goods to be placed under customs duty suspensions;
- services connected with goods under customs duty suspensions, such as transportation, handling, warehousing, wrapping;
- insurance expertise on exported goods;
- work, repairs performed for the account of a foreign client, on goods to be exported;
- services connected with the importation of goods, the cost of which was already included in the amount on which tax at importation was based;
- sale and renting of ships and aircraft engaged in international trade or professional fishing;
- repair, transformation, maintenance performed on ships and aircraft mentioned above;
- international transport of persons or goods;
- equipment subsidies granted by the Government or municipalities;
- financial and banking services when supplied to non-EC recipients.

Exporters may purchase in France, free of VAT, all the goods (and related services) which they intend to export within the limit of an annual quota equal to their export transactions of the preceding year.

### Exempt imports

Limited exemptions apply to goods introduced in France by travellers. Personal and household belongings are not taxed when someone is setting up his main residence in France. VAT relief is also available under certain conditions for goods which are temporarily imported or which are re-imported after repair abroad.

## *Exemption without credit for input tax*

The following exemptions are without credit for input tax:

- medical care or services provided by hospitals, doctors, dentists, laboratories;
- transactions on human blood, milk or organs;
- social or cultural services of associations or foundations;
- educational services provided by schools and universities as well as by private teachers;

- state postal services;
- insurance, reinsurance transactions (input VAT may be creditable in certain cases);
- financial and banking services (input VAT may be recovered in limited cases);
- lawyers, artists, translators, sportsmen;
- leasing of unfurnished residential or commercial buildings;
- subsidies obtained for non-taxable transactions.

## *Non-taxable transactions*

### Transactions within the same legal entity

4–012 Supplies within the same legal entity are not taxable. Supply of services made between a foreign head office and its branch in France (or vice versa) are treated as internal non-taxable transactions.

### Transfer of business

The transfer of a business or of a complete and independent branch of activity is not subject to VAT. This exemption does not prevent the recovery of the input VAT paid in relation to the transfer.

### Subsidies/Penalty payments/Compensation

Subsidies granted by government bodies are generally liable to VAT when they are directly linked to the cost of a taxable supply, or when they purport to offset operating losses.

Subsidies granted by one company to another (often referred to as a waiver of debt) are liable to VAT when the two companies have commercial links. The tax is due by the beneficiary of the subsidy if he is established in France. When the links are only financial no VAT is due on the amount of the subsidy.

Generally the VAT status of subsidies is a difficult area and professional advice should be obtained to ensure that it is correctly treated.

Penalty payments made for premature termination of contracts are normally liable to VAT.

Sums of money repairing a damage are not subject to VAT. Careful analysis is nevertheless required to establish that the compensation cannot be considered as being part of a taxable operation.

## *Election to be subject to VAT*

Taxable persons making certain exempt supplies may elect to be subject to VAT. Election will enable them to charge VAT and correlatively to recover the input tax relating to these supplies. Election may be made for the following activities:

- supply of goods and services by authors, artists, interpreters, translators, sportsmen, lawyers;
- leasing of unfurnished real property for business purposes;
- supply of certain services by municipalities (*e.g.* supply of water);
- banking and financial services. Election is possible only for a limited number of specified transactions;
- farming.

## 8. CREDIT/REFUND FOR INPUT TAX

### *General rule*

The principle is that all the VAT paid on goods and services by a French entrepreneur is recoverable. However this principle applies only if the input tax was incurred with a view to achieving taxable transactions. This important restriction prevents entrepreneurs from recovering input VAT on: **4–013**

- goods and services obtained for exempt supplies. Exports and international trade transactions are allowed a full deduction although they are exempt from VAT;
- goods and services used for private consumption. This also applies to hotel accommodation, travel and restaurant expenses paid by companies for their employees or third parties;
- goods or services used to provide goods or services free of charge or very much below market price.

No credit is available for input tax on:

- private cars even when used in the course of a business. The same restriction applies to services obtained in connection with private cars such as repairs, transport, renting;
- transport of persons (by road, air, railway, etc.) and ancilliary services such as reservation.

### *Adjustment of entitlement to credit*

A credit for input VAT obtained in respect of capital assets may have to be adjusted if one of the following events occurs before the beginning of the fourth year (for movable goods) or the ninth year (for immovable goods) following purchase:

- transfer of the capital assets (for consideration or free of charge), if the transaction is not subject to VAT;
- transfer of the capital assets from a taxable to an exempt sector of activity;

— termination of business;
— termination of all taxable activities.

Part of the input tax will have to be repaid on a *pro rata* time basis.

In a similar way, if credit for input VAT was not available or only partially available at the time of the acquisition of the asset, an additional credit may be obtained if the asset goods are sold within the same period (four or nine years) and if the sale is subject to VAT on the total price and not only on the margin.

## *Partial exemption*

**4–014** Entrepreneurs making both taxable and exempt supplies are allowed to recover only the input VAT relating to taxable supplies.

If the goods or services purchased can be attributed to being used for taxable supplies the credit for input VAT will be fully allowed. On the contrary, if attribution is made to exempt supplies it will be totally disallowed.

If the goods or services purchased are used both for taxable and exempt supplies the creditable input tax is calculated in the ratio of the turnover of supplies which are entitled to credit to the total turnover.

The applicable ratio is calculated for each calendar year. During the year a provisional ratio is used either based on that of the previous year or on expected sales in the case of a new business. The final ratio must be determined at the latest by April 25 of the following year and the credit obtained for the previous year must be adjusted accordingly.

## *Time of recovery*

Input VAT cannot be recovered before it has actually been accounted for by the supplier. Consequently it becomes creditable normally as soon as the goods are supplied and when the services are actually provided.

However, France allows immediate recovery only if the goods purchased qualify as capital assets. For all the other goods and services recovery is possible the month following that of the delivery or payment.

When recoverable input VAT is in excess of output VAT an application can be made to the tax authorities to obtain a refund of the excess.

## *Refund for foreign entrepreneurs*

Foreign entrepreneurs not established in France and who do not supply goods or services in France may obtain a refund of the VAT paid on goods or services purchased in France, as well as of the VAT incurred at the time of importation.

Claims for refund must be requested on a special form addressed to:

Centre des Non Résidents
9 Rue d'Uzès
75084 PARIS CEDEX 02

The claim must be completed in French and filed at the latest before June 30 following the end of the calendar year during which VAT was paid in France. The original invoices and a certificate (provided by the foreign tax authorities) establishing that the foreign entrepreneur is a taxable person in his country must accompany the claim.

Entrepreneurs from outside the European Community must prove that the VAT for which they claim a refund was paid in order to market their products in France. Non-EC entrepreneurs must appoint a VAT agent in France to file the claim in their names.

For the purpose of refund, the French overseas departments (Martinique, Guadeloupe, Reunion, and Guyana), Sweden, the Canary Islands as well as Ceuta and Melilla are considered as EC members.

No recovery is available for a number of items, see para. 4–013, "Credit for input tax".

## 9. ADMINISTRATIVE OBLIGATIONS

### *Registration*

An entrepreneur engaged in an industrial, commercial or professional activity is subject to VAT whatever his annual turnover may be. **4–015**

Within the first two weeks of starting operations, entrepreneurs must register with their local income tax office.

### *Books and records*

Entrepreneurs who are subject to VAT must keep adequate accounting books to justify all their transactions. When they are charging different VAT rates, their corresponding sales must be accounted for separately.

### *Invoices*

Invoices must contain the following information:

- name and address of the client;
- price of the goods or services excluding tax;
- rate of the tax and corresponding VAT due.

Apart from these specific VAT requirements the invoices issued must show all the compulsory information required by commercial law: supplier's name or corporate name, form of the company (SA, SARL, etc.), address, registration number, share capital, date of invoice, description of the supply.

Failure to comply with these requirements prevents the recovery of input VAT.

## VAT Returns

**4–016** Every month, the entrepreneur must file a VAT return to declare his taxable transactions of the preceding month. Date of filing may differ from one entrepreneur to another but is due at the earliest on the 15th and at the latest on the 24th of the month following the transactions declared.

Quarterly returns are allowed only if the monthly VAT due is below FF 1 000. Output VAT, after deduction of input VAT, is payable at the time of filing.

When the return shows a VAT credit, *i.e.* on excess of input over output VAT, it can be carried forward and used until completely offset against output VAT. A refund can also be obtained.

## Powers of the authorities

The tax authorities may estimate the tax to be paid if an entrepreneur has failed to file VAT returns within 30 days of a formal request to do so.

The tax authorities have a period of three years to correct a VAT transaction. The period ends on December 31 of the third year following the transaction when the fiscal year coincides with the calendar year.

An input credit which has been omitted from a VAT return can still be claimed until the end of the second calendar year following the omission.

Failure to submit returns in time entails the payment of interest at the rate of 0.75 per cent. per month plus a penalty of 10 per cent. to 80 per cent. of the VAT due.

Late payment of tax entails the payment of interest at the rate of 0.75 per cent. per month plus a penalty of 5 per cent.

## Objections/Appeals

An entrepreneur may request a reduction or a repayment of his tax if it was wrongly assessed. Claims must be filed with the local tax authorities before the end of the second calendar year following assessment or payment of VAT.

Appeals are heard by the trial court (Tribunal administratif) within two months of the tax authorities' refusal. Further appeal is possible before the Administrative Appeal Court and the Supreme Court (Conseil d'Etat).

# 10. SPECIAL VAT REGIMES

Special VAT rules apply to a number of activities. The general outlines of the main special regimes are summarised below: **4–017**

## *Small businesses*

Small entrepreneurs whose turnover is below FF 500 000 (suppliers of goods) or FF 150 000) (suppliers of service) may account for VAT according to a simplified procedure ("forfait"). The amount of VAT due for the year is assessed on the value of the taxable transactions after deduction of input VAT. The taxable basis is negotiated with the tax authorities.

Small entrepreneurs whose turnover is below FF 3 000 000 (suppliers of goods) or FF 900 000 (suppliers of services) may file their return according to a simplified method.

In all cases, small entrepreneurs may opt to account for VAT according to the normal rules.

Small entrepreneurs such as individual traders or associations may get total VAT relief if they owe an annual amount of VAT below FF 1 350. They can obtain a special reduction if the total VAT due for a year is below FF 5 401.

Craftsmen may obtain a special reduction of their tax, under certain conditions, if VAT due for a year does not exceed FF 20 000.

## *Farmers*

The term "farmers" should be understood to include all the activities relating to agricultural as well as livestock productions.

They may be classified into three categories:

- farmers compulsorily subject to VAT. This applies when their average income over two years exceeds FF 300 000;
- farmers who have elected to be subject to VAT. Election may be limited to part of their activity or apply to all their activities. It is valid for three years;
- farmers who are not taxable to VAT. They all benefit from a lump sum refund intended to compensate for the non-creditable input VAT incurred on the acquisition of goods and services. The refund is made on an annual basis.

## *Banking and financial institutions*

Most of the transactions of these institutions are exempt from VAT (see para. 4–011 "Exemptions without credit"). Their few transactions which are taxed usually give them a very low recovery *pro rata*. They may elect to be subject to VAT for a number of specified transactions to improve their recovery rights. **4–018**

### Second-hand goods

Second hand asset goods which are sold by an entrepreneur to another for the purposes of his business are not subject to VAT. Input credit may have to be adjusted if the sale take place within a certain period of time, see para. 4–013, "Credit for input VAT".

Second hand goods sold by traders are subject to VAT either on the total price or on the margin. If VAT is paid only on the margin, the trader is limited in the recovery of the input tax.

### Arts and Antiques

Art pieces such as paintings, water colours, sculptures, tapestries etc., are exempt from VAT when sold directly by the artists.

When they are sold by traders, the taxable basis may either be the margin or the sale price (excluding VAT) reduced by 30 per cent.

Imports of art pieces are often exempt from VAT or subject to the tax on 30 per cent. of the sale price.

### Travel agencies

A special regime applies to travel agents who hold a professional licence and who act in their own capacity and not for the account of their customers.

The services they provide are exempt from VAT in respect of the part which is used outside the EC. Travel agents are taxed at the rate of 5.5 per cent. on the difference between the payments received and the related expenses incurred during a giving period of time (month or half year). They cannot recover the input VAT relating to their expenses.

### Bonded warehouses

**4–019** Goods imported into bonded warehouses do not have to pay VAT and customs duty until they are removed for sale in the community. Importation of goods into a bonded warehouse is subject to the prior approval of the customs authorities. The agreement applies for a limited period of time and specifies the conditions in which the goods are to be kept. Only minor processes are allowed (packing, handling, etc).

### Free zone

The free zone of Gex, Savoie and Haute-Savoie (an area in France near the Swiss border) allows entrance of goods in suspension of VAT and customs duty. All transactions or modifications of the goods in that area are subject to customs control.

## *Real estate*

### VAT regime applicable during the construction of the building

The acquisition of land used for construction is normally subject to VAT at a rate of 13 per cent.; buildings are subject to VAT at a rate of 18.60 per cent. Builders can normally deduct VAT paid on land and construction works. They can obtain a refund of tax credits under certain conditions. **4–020**

### VAT regime applicable at the time of the transfer of the building

VAT or transfer duties are due depending on whether or not the building involved is new.

If the building is sold before its completion, sales are always subject to VAT at a rate of 18.60 per cent.

If the building is sold during a period of five years following its completion, the first sale (or the second one if the seller was an estate broker [marchand de biens]) which takes place during this period is subject to VAT at a rate of 18.60 per cent. Other sales are normally subject to transfer duties at a rate of approximately 18 per cent. or 8 per cent., depending on the nature of the building (office building or residential).

If the building is sold more than five years after its completion, it is always subject to transfer duties at a rate of 18 per cent. or 8 per cent.

### VAT regime applicable while the building is rented

For unfurnished residential building: rental income is never subject to VAT;

For furnished residential building or furnished office building: rental income is always subject to VAT, respectively at a rate of 5.5 per cent. and 18.60 per cent.

For unfurnished office building: no VAT is normally due on rental income, but the owner of the building may opt to pay VAT at a rate of 18.60 per cent. as long as the lessee carries out an industrial or commercial activity.

### Recovery of input VAT paid on the purchase of the building

If the owner of the building uses it to carry out a taxable activity, he can deduct the VAT paid on the building.

If the owner leases the building he can deduct VAT if rental income is subject to VAT.

# 5. Germany (Federal Republic of)

## 1. GENERAL BACKGROUND

The Value Added Tax Law (Umsatzsteuergesetz) came into effect on January 1, 1968. Before this date Germany had a cumulative all-stage turnover tax which had been in effect for nearly fifty years. From January 1, 1980 the Value Added Tax Law was amended so as to bring the German legislation into line with the requirements of the Sixth and the Eighth EC Directives. **5–001**

Value Added Tax (VAT) is levied when an entrepreneur executes a supply of goods or services in the territory of imposition and on the importation of goods. Territory of imposition means those territories which fall within the scope of the law, with the exception of those territories which are excluded for customs purposes and duty free zones (Zollanschlusse, Zollfreigebiete). External territories are those territories which do not belong to the territory of imposition nor to the German Democratic Republic or East Berlin. The German Democratic Republic and East Berlin are not part of the territory of imposition nor of the external territory.

The VAT is administered by the tax office responsible for the tax affairs of the enterprise, *i.e.* normally the place where the enterprise is located. VAT matters of foreign enterprises without a branch or fixed establishment in Germany are handled by the Bundesamt fur Finanzen in Bonn or by specially determined tax offices responsible for non-resident entrepreneurs.

VAT on imports is dealt with by the Customs duty office.

## 2. WHO IS TAXABLE?

### *General*

An entrepreneur (taxable person) is any person who independently carries on a commercial or professional activity. The enterprise comprises the entire commercial or professional activity of the entrepreneur. Any activity for the purpose of obtaining income on a continuing basis is commercial or professional even in the absence of an **5–002**

intention to make profits or in the case of an association acting only vis-à-vis its members. VAT is levied on taxable transactions carried out in Germany and West Berlin by an entrepreneur, regardless of whether the entrepreneur is a citizen or resident of Germany or has a place of management in Germany.
The taxable person or entrepreneur may be one of the following:

- a legal person
- an individual
- an association of individuals
- a combination of legal persons or,
- any other economic entity.

Private persons who engage in an occasional transaction are not deemed to be entrepreneurs within the meaning of the VAT law.

Registration is required as soon as the definition of entrepreneur is satisfied. VAT is not levied where the previous year's total (worldwide) turnover did not exceed DM 20,000 and the current turnover will not exceed DM 100,000 and VAT has not been shown on the invoice. Consequently input tax would not be deductible. This treatment is optional.

### Government bodies

Juridical persons under public law (state, municipalities) are not liable to VAT as long as they fulfil Governmental functions only; however, if they are engaged in commercial or professional activities, within the scope of their operations, of a commercial kind or in agricultural or forestry operations, these juridical persons under public law will qualify as entrepreneurs.

### Transactions with branch/subsidiary

Transactions between the head office and a branch of the same company are internal transactions and are therefore not taxable even where the head office and branch are in different countries. On the contrary, transactions between a foreign company and its German subsidiaries, or vice versa, will be a taxable supply.

## *Fiscal unity/Group registration*

**5–003** Under certain conditions, a parent company and its controlled subsidiary company, which is financially, economically and organisationally integrated, can be regarded as a fiscal unity (Organschaft) for VAT purposes and group taxation may apply. This leads to the result that sales and services of the controlled company are reported on the return of the parent company. This applies also to exempt and partially exempt entrepreneurs. Transactions between the parent company and the controlled subsidiary company are considered to be internal transactions and therefore not taxable.

The application of the fiscal unity (Organschaft) concept for VAT purposes is determined on the circumstances; no special application to the tax authorities is necessary.

Until December 31, 1986 this fiscal unity concept was applicable even in cases where the parent and its controlled subsidiary were resident in different countries. However, in order to comply with the Sixth EC Directive, Germany has amended the Value Added Tax Law with effect from January 1, 1987 and has limited the application of the fiscal unity concept to intra-group transactions carried out between those parts of the group which are located in Germany. This is a very important change and it is recommended that tax implications of all cross-border transactions between integrated companies be reviewed.

All members of the group are registered in the name of the parent; if the parent is resident outside Germany, the registration is made in the name of the most important part of the enterprise in Germany.

The parent is liable to account for the total VAT but each member of the group can be made liable for its part of the VAT.

## *Foreign entrepreneurs*

Non-resident entrepreneurs who do not have their registered office or **5–004** branch office in Germany become liable to VAT if they supply goods or services in Germany. Generally, the non-resident entrepreneur performing taxable supplies in Germany has to register with the German tax authorities and has to pay his VAT liability.

Non-residents who maintain a fixed establishment in Germany have to register with the tax authorities like a domestic entrepreneur.

### Representative offices

Representative and information offices of foreign entrepreneurs, which only perform activities of a preparatory or similar nature, do not qualify as a fixed establishment for VAT purposes. For refund of VAT, see paragraph 5–016 below.

### VAT representative

The appointment of a fiscal representative is not necessary in Germany

### Reverse charge mechanism

A special provision exists where taxable work supplies (Werklieferungen) or the supply of services by non-residents is concerned. The German recipient of the work supply or the service is obliged to withhold the VAT from the consideration and to pay it to his tax office, provided the recipient is an entrepreneur or a juridical person under public law. Depending on the personal circumstances the recipient may claim this VAT as an input tax (reverse charge mechanism).

As a second alternative the recipient need not withhold the VAT if he is entitled to a full input tax claim and if the performing entrepreneur does not show any VAT on his invoice; so-called zero arrangements (Null-Regelung). Non-resident entrepreneurs falling under this special provision need not register with the tax authorities.

### *Importers*

The VAT on imports becomes due when goods are imported to Germany and cleared by the customs. The importer (transporter, entrepreneur, individual) is liable for payment of the tax.

## 3. WHAT IS TAXABLE?

**5–005** The supply of goods or services effected for consideration within the territory of Germany by a taxable person, as well as the importation of goods, is subject to VAT.

### *Supply of goods*

Supplies of an entrepreneur are performances by which he or a third party acting on his behalf, enables the customer or a third party acting on his behalf, to dispose of an object in its own name (procuration of the right of disposal).

Supply of goods includes the transactions between the principal and the commission agent in the case of a commission agency, and a work supply, if the entrepreneur has undertaken the treatment of processing of an item thereby using material which he procures himself, unless such materials are merely of an accessory or ancilliary character.

#### Chain transactions

If several entrepreneurs enter into transactions concerning the same goods but the actual right of disposal is transferred directly from the first entrepreneur to the last recipient in the chain, then each entrepreneur within the chain is deemed to have conducted a taxable transaction in the form of a simultaneous supply of goods (chain transactions).

### *Supply of services*

Services are performances which do not qualify as a supply of goods. They may also comprise omission or toleration of an act or of a situation.

Services also include transfer of patents, trademarks, licences, granting of loans, renting of property, staff hire, legal and technical assistance, transport services, advertising, data processing, granting of licences etc.

### *Self-supplies of goods/services*

The application by a taxable person of goods forming part of his business assets for his private use or that of his staff or more generally, the application for purposes other than those of his business, is treated as supplies for consideration. The same applies where goods forming part of the business assets are applied to the private use of the taxable person or his staff or to the supply of services carried out free of charge by the taxable person for his private use or that of his staff. Additionally, certain expenses which are not deductible according to the income tax law may be treated as taxable turnover (*e.g.* gifts to customers with a value of more than DM 50 per annum and per customer, expenses for entertainment with customers if the relating accounting requirements are not fulfilled, etc.) **5–006**

### *Imports of goods*

The importation of goods into Germany is generally a taxable event. Some exemptions apply, *e.g.* for personal luggage of travellers, household goods of persons moving to Germany, goods to be re-exported after a certain period of time.

The time for payment of VAT on imports may be deferred if the goods are brought into a bonded warehouse. In this case VAT will become due if and when the goods are dispatched for free circulation in Germany.

## 4. PLACE OF SUPPLY

German VAT is applicable if transactions are carried out in Germany; therefore it is important to determine the place of supply. **5–007**

### *Supply of goods*

A supply is executed at the place where the goods are located at the time of the procuration of the right of disposal. That means, if goods are physically present in Germany at the time of supply, the transaction becomes liable to VAT. This applies even if the goods are exported later on.

In the case where goods are located outside Germany at the time of supply, German VAT will not apply. Subsequent import into Germany, however, will qualify for VAT on import.

If the goods are dispatched or transported either by the supplier or by the person to whom they are supplied or by a third person then the place of supply is the place where the goods are located at the time when dispatch or transport to the person to whom they are supplied begins.

Where goods are installed or assembled by or on behalf of the supplier, the place of supply is the place where the goods are installed or assembled.

Special provisions may apply if the goods to be supplied enter, with transport or shipment to the customer or on his behalf to a third party, from the outside territory into Germany or from Germany into an EC Member State. In this case the supply is deemed to be executed in the importing country provided that the supplier or his agent is the debtor for the VAT to be paid upon the importation.

### Chain transactions

The general rules also apply in case of chain transactions. Each entrepreneur within the chain is deemed to have carried out a taxable transaction in the form of a simultaneous supply of goods at the moment of transfer of the power of disposal by the first entrepreneur to the last recipient. The location of all transactions depends on the place where the goods are located at that moment or at the place where the transport begins.

## *Supply of services*

### General rule

**5–008** As a general rule, the place where a service is supplied is the place where the supplier has established his business or has a fixed establishment from which the service is supplied.

### Exceptions

There are various exceptions to this general rule to determine the place of the supply of services:

1. The place of the supply of services closely connected with immovable property including the services of estate agents and experts, architects, etc. is the place where the property is situated.
2. The place where transport services are supplied is the place where the transport takes place.
3. The place of supply of services relating to cultural, artistic, scientific, educational, entertainment or similar activities, including the activities of the organisers of such activities, is the place where those services are physically carried out. The same applies to handling, storage or further services connected with transport services as well as to work on movable tangible property and valuations of movable tangible property.
4. The place of supply of the services listed below to entrepreneurs is deemed to be where the customer has established his business or has a fixed establishment to which the service is supplied. If the customer is a non-entrepreneur resident outside the EC, then the place of supply of services is the place where he has his

permanent address or usually resides. Where the customer is a non-entrepreneur resident within the EC, the general rule applies.

This applies to the following services:

- transfers and assignments of patents, copyrights, trade-marks and similar rights; 5–009
- services such as advertising or public relations, including the services of advertising contractors and advertising agencies;
- the services of lawyers, patent lawyers, tax advisors, accountants, experts, engineers, members of the board of directors as well as the legal, economic and technical advice given by other entrepreneurs;
- data processing;
- the grant of information including industrial processes and experiences;
- certain financial transactions and services connected with the trade of gold, silver and platinum (does not apply to coins and metals made from these precious metals);
- the supply of staff;
- the relinquishment of the exercise of the right mentioned in the first item above;
- the complete or partial relinquishment of the exercise of professional or commercial activities;
- the procurement of the other services denominated under the points above;
- the hiring out of movable tangible property, with the exception of transportation equipment.

In order to avoid double taxation, non-taxation or the distortion of competition, a special regulation applies to the supply of services by entrepreneurs not resident within the EC. If an entrepreneur who operates his business from a place outside the territory of the EC, supplies a service which is denominated under 4 above:

- to a juridical person under public law not qualifying as an entrepreneur; or
- a service which is otherwise taxed where the entrepreneur operates his business to an entrepreneur residing in Germany; or
- to a fixed establishment of a foreign entrepreneur in Germany; or
- to a juridical person under public law in Germany;

then such service is deemed to be rendered in Germany if it is utilised or exploited here.

### Reverse charge mechanism

Under certain conditions the liability to VAT for taxable work supplies or the supply of services is transferred from the foreign entrepreneur to the recipient of the supplies. For details, reference is made to paragraph 5–004, "Reverse charge mechanism."

## 5. BASIS OF TAXATION

### *Supplies within Germany*

**5–010** The basis of taxation in respect of supplies of goods and services is the consideration which has been or is to be obtained for such supplies. The provisions with respect to the basis of taxation are governed by the exchange principle. The consideration must be connected directly with the performance rendered. VAT does not form part of the consideration. The taxable amount does not include amounts received by a taxable person from his purchaser or customer for expenses paid in the name and for the account of the purchaser or the customer and which are entered in his books on a suspense account (transitory items). The taxable person must furnish proof of the actual amount of this expenditure and may not deduct any tax which may have been charged on these transactions.

### *Self-supplies*

Some supplies are taxable even without payment of a consideration. The application of goods or use of goods for purposes other than those of business, are assessed on the going-concern value which could be the purchase price, the cost price, the full cost or the open market value.

### *Imports*

The basis of taxation of imports is the value of the imported goods according to the provisions of the customs law. Different treatment is applied to imports of equipment used for electronic data and containing data or computer programmes.

If imported goods are not liable to customs duty, the basis of taxation is the consideration paid. Where no consideration is payable the value for customs purposes is the basis of taxation.

The basis of taxation includes transport cost, duties and other levies but not German VAT on importation.

### *Chargeable event/Time of payment*

**5–011** As a general rule, VAT becomes due at the end of the month in which the goods are supplied, the services are completed or when the goods are imported into Germany. The due date for payment is 10 days after the month concerned, disregarding the time of receipt of the consideration. A one month extension for payment may be achieved upon application if one eleventh of the prior year's tax liability was paid in advance to the tax authorities.

Where the goods are not supplied and the services are not completed but a partial consideration is received, liability to VAT arises at the end of the month in which the partial consideration was received. This does not apply if the amount received is less than DM 10,000 (without VAT) and an invoice showing the VAT separately was not issued by the performing enterprise.

VAT on imports becomes due at the time the imported goods enter into Germany. Upon application a one month extension for payment may be allowed if the importing enterprise is entitled to full input tax claim.

Furthermore, deferral of payment can be obtained while the goods are stored in a bonded warehouse.

### *Cash/Invoice Basis*

Small enterprises with a worldwide turnover exceeding in the prior year not more than DM 250,000 may account for VAT on a cash basis.

### *Credit notes/Bad debts*

If the entrepreneur gives a credit and issues a credit note he is allowed to reduce his VAT liability accordingly. The customer, on the other hand, has to reduce his input tax deduction.

Furthermore VAT can be adjusted if the entrepreneur does not or only partially receives payment and proper evidence to prove this can be submitted.

## 6. TAX RATES

The present rates are as follows:

0% (zero rate) is not available in Germany. For certain turnover transactions, however, an exemption with credit for input tax does exist, see para. 5–013 below, "Exemptions". **5–012**

7% The reduced rate applies to supplies of certain raw materials, foodstuffs, books, services of dental technicians, theatres, orchestras, circus presentations, etc.

14% This general tax rate applies to all other supplies of goods and services.

## 7. EXEMPTIONS

### *Exemptions with credit for input VAT (zero rate)*

**5–013** Where an entrepreneur makes exempt supplies he is not allowed to charge VAT (exception, see para. 5–020, "Election for taxable supplies") nor is he entitled to reclaim input tax suffered. However, a credit for input VAT incurred in connection with certain exempt activities can be obtained for the following:

- the export of goods;
- turnover transactions for navigation and air traffic;
- certain cross border transport services;
- supplies of gold to Central Banks;
- the procurement of exports, cross border transport services, etc.;
- certain supplies of the Federal Railway Company.

Under certain conditions supplies to NATO are tax-exempt as well.

### *Exemptions without credit for input VAT*

The following supplies are exempt from output tax and do not qualify for credit of related input VAT incurred:

- financial transactions such as the granting and the negotiation of credits as well as the administration of credit securities, transactions as to monetary claims, transactions in the deposit business, sale of shares, etc. (exceptions, see para. 5–015, "Credit/refund for input tax");
- transactions falling under the Real Estate Acquisition Tax Law;
- insurance transactions including related services performed by insurance brokers and insurance agents;
- the leasing or letting of immovable property. Not exempt is the leasing in the hotel sector, the letting of premises and sites for parking vehicles, short term lease of camping sites or letting of permanently installed equipment and machinery;
- transactions resulting from activities as a physician, dentist, etc.

### *Non-taxable transactions*

#### Transactions within the same legal entity

**5–014** Transactions within the German part of a fiscal unity for VAT purposes, as well as transactions between head office and branch (disregarding the location) are treated as internal transactions and therefore not liable to VAT.

### Transfer of business

Various countries consider the sale of a business to be outside the scope of VAT. Germany, however, applies the regular VAT provisions to such a sale; *i.e.* each asset is considered separately for VAT purposes.

### Subsidies/Penalty payments/Compensation

Certain transactions are deemed to be outside the scope of VAT because the payments received are not treated as a consideration for a supply. This applies to the receipt of investment grants, the payment of damage claims according to Civil Law, the receipt of subsidies, etc.

## *Election to be subject to VAT*

In the case of exemptions without credit any related input VAT paid with respect to the output transaction becomes a cost factor. There is a limited number of circumstances in which the entrepreneur has the right to waive the tax exemption and opt for VAT in order to qualify for input VAT credit

The following exemptions benefit from this option provided the supply was made to other entrepreneurs:

— certain financial transactions;
— supplies falling under the Real Estate Acquisition Law;
— supplies of immovable property provided the property is not used for habitation or non-entrepreneurial purposes;
— certain supplies relating to the use of common property by apartment owners;
— activities of blind persons who do not employ more than two people.

# 8. CREDIT/REFUND FOR INPUT TAX

## *General rule*

The entrepreneur can deduct the following input tax: 5–015

— tax suffered on supplies of goods or services which were carried out for his enterprise (not for private purposes), provided the input tax is shown separately in the invoice;
— VAT paid in respect of goods imported for his enterprise (VAT on import).

Excluded from input tax deductions is the VAT paid on supplies of goods and services and imports which the entrepreneur uses for the execution of the following supplies:

- — tax exempt transactions;
- — transactions carried out abroad which would be tax exempt if executed within Germany;
- — supplies of goods and other services carried out without consideration which would be tax exempt if supplied for consideration.

This exclusion from input tax deduction does not apply if the related transaction is or would be:

- — a tax exempt export of goods; or
- — a tax exempt supply of certain financial services and related directly to goods exported into a territory outside the EC; or
- — a tax exempt supply of certain financial services where the recipient of the services is resident outside the EC, or the recipient is resident in an EC country, but the service is directly related to an export of goods in a non-EC country.

### *Adjustment of entitlement to credit*

An adjustment of entitlement to input tax credit will be made on a *pro rata* basis if the circumstances governing the tax deduction in the first calendar year of use should change within the first five years (immovable property, ten years). This will lead to additional credits or additional tax liabilities depending on whether the use of the goods changes from exempt to taxable transactions or vice versa.

### *Partial exemption*

As regards goods and services which are used by a taxable person both for supplies in respect of which VAT is deductible and supplies in respect of which VAT is not deductible, such proportion of the VAT suffered shall be non-deductible as it is economically attributable to supplies which lead to exclusion from input tax deduction. The entrepreneur may estimate this proportion in an appropriate way. Instead of the above allocation the entrepreneur may determine the non-deductible VAT according to the ratio of the total transaction volume leading to the exclusion from input tax deduction to other transaction volume but imports are not treated as supplies in this connection. The *pro rata* allocation is excluded if it leads to unjustified tax advantages.

### *Time of recovery*

**5–016** Input credit can be claimed for the month in which the supply was made if the entrepreneur is in possession of the appropriate invoice. If the input tax exceeds the output VAT the balance will be refunded upon application.

### *Refund for foreign entrepreneurs*

Non-resident entrepreneurs who have neither their registered office nor branch office in Germany and who do not make taxable supplies (with certain exceptions) in Germany are entitled to recover VAT billed to them by applying a special refund procedure. The non-resident entrepreneur has to register with:

Bundesamt fur Finanzen,
Postfach,
5300 Bonn 3

or with a responsible district tax office.

The refund must be claimed by using special forms (the same forms are used in all EC Member States) which indicates the aggregate amount of input tax to be refunded. The request must be sent, together with a certificate indicating that the applicant is registered as an entrepreneur in his country of residence and with the original invoices showing the amount of VAT, not later than six months after the end of the calendar year concerned. Repayment of VAT will take about two or three months. An extension to the last date for filing may be applied for prior to the end of the six months period. The tax authorities will issue a tax assessment notice indicating the amount of refund.

The refund may be claimed by entrepreneurs resident within and outside the EC.

It is not necessary to appoint a fiscal representative for VAT purposes, however, for practical reasons it is recommended to authorise a tax advisor to handle the formalities.

Where the non-resident entrepreneur performs taxable supplies of goods in Germany he has to register with the competent tax office and has to file monthly/quarterly/yearly VAT returns. A surplus of input tax will be refunded.

## 9. ADMINISTRATIVE OBLIGATIONS

### *Registration*

Every entrepreneur who carries out taxable transactions in Germany **5–017**
must register with the local tax office where the enterprise is located irrespective of the amount of turnover. After registration the entrepreneur will get a tax number (Steuernummer) under which the necessary VAT returns must be filed.

## Books and records

The entrepreneur must keep accounts in sufficient detail to permit the proper application of the Value Added Tax law and inspection by the tax authorities. The accounts must show amongst other things:

— the consideration for the supplies and services separated into taxable and tax exempt transactions;
— taxable transactions must be recorded separately where different tax rates are applied;
— consideration received for supplies not yet executed (payment in advance);
— if the entrepreneur is entitled to only partial input tax deduction, the allocation method has to be verified;
— the basis for the assessment of VAT on imports as well as the amount of import tax.

These records must be kept for a period of 10 years. The tax authorities may carry out a tax audit and inspect the above accounts as well as the outgoing and incoming invoices. This can be done as long as the statutes of limitation have not expired, which is generally four years after the end of the year in which the VAT return was filed.

## Invoices

**5–018** Every entrepreneur must issue an invoice in respect of all goods and services supplied by him to another entrepreneur and must keep a copy thereof. The invoice has to state the following information:

— the name and the address for the supplying entrepreneur;
— the name and the address of the recipient of the supply;
— the quantity and the description of the supplied goods or the type and volume of services;
— the date of the supply of goods or services;
— the consideration for the supply of goods or services;
— the tax amount relating to the consideration.

It is not necessary to indicate the tax number.

## VAT returns

Preliminary returns have to be filed monthly if the tax liability in the preceding calendar year was more than DM 6,000, quarterly if the last year's tax did not exceed DM 6,000 or annually if the last year's tax did not exceed DM 600. The preliminary returns as well as the tax liability are due on the 10th day after the end of the respective month, quarter or year. A one month filing extension may be allowed if a down payment of one-eleventh of the tax liability of the prior year is made. In addition the entrepreneur has to submit an annual tax return which is due on May 31 of the following year. Permission for extension of filing of the annual tax return may be obtained upon application. Any tax liability resulting from the annual tax return is due one month after filing it.

## *Powers of the Authorities*

### Estimate of tax paid (estimated assessment)

If the VAT returns are not filed until the due date, the tax authorities **5–019**
will issue tax assessment notices and will assess an estimated tax liability.

### Statutes of limitation

The period of limitation for assessment of taxes is four years from the end of the year during which the tax return was filed.

### Correction of returns

As long as the VAT returns are preliminary ones, an application for correction can be filed. The monthly returns are preliminary, as long as a tax assessment notice was not issued by the tax authorities. Additionally the tax authorities may declare a tax assessment notice to be preliminary.

### Penalties for late filing

A penalty of up to 10 per cent. of the tax liability can be assessed if the tax returns are not filed by the due date, including extensions granted.

### Penalties for late payment

The penalty for late payment amounts to 1 per cent. per month of the balance payable.

## *Objections/Appeals*

The taxpayer has the right to file an appeal with the tax authorities against a VAT assessment notice within one month after receiving it. Further appeals are possible to the District Tax Court or to the Supreme Tax Court if the tax authorities do not amend the tax assessment notice as applied for.

## 10. SPECIAL VAT REGIMES

### *Agricultural and forestry enterprises*

5–020 A special tax treatment with reduced tax rates applies to certain determined transactions in the agricultural and forestry section. Additionally there are special provisions relating to the percentage of input tax credit to be allowed as well as provisions on other tax reductions.

As a result these supplies are often taxed at a 0 per cent. rate.

Upon application the entrepreneur can apply the general tax rules.

#### **Antiques**

The supply of antiques is subject to the normal tax provisions.

### *Banking/Financial activities*

Under the general conditions, banking and financial activities are VAT exempt and input taxes connected with these transactions are not deductible.

An exception, however, applies to input taxes in connection with financial transactions supplied to customers resident outside the EC. Therefore, it is recommendable to review the transactions of banks or bank representative offices very carefully in order to determine the percentage of deductible input tax.

### *Election for taxable supplies as a tax planning idea*

As described in paragraph 5–013 above there are a number of cases in which the entrepreneur has the option to waive an exemption if the supply is made to other entrepreneurs. Such a waiver would allow the supplier to deduct the connected input tax; there is no disadvantage for the recipient of the goods or services if he is entitled to a full input tax credit.

The review of this provision is very important where supplies such as the sale or lease of real estate are concerned. The waiver of tax exemptions can enable the supplier to deduct input taxes connected with the construction of a building which would otherwise be lost.

However, this entitlement to input tax credit will be reviewed over a period of 10 years, see para. 5–015, "Credit/Refund for input tax". Therefore, one should avoid making a lease liable to VAT and then selling the real estate on a tax exempt basis within 10 years.

### *Fishing*

5–021 The import of fish which are caught by fishermen resident in Germany and imported on German vessels is exempt from VAT on importation.

## *Freeport areas*

Generally the freeport areas are not part of the territory of imposition of VAT. However, German VAT law has determined a number of activities which are treated as supplies executed within the territory of levy and consequently subject to VAT.

These are, *inter alia*:

— supplies of goods designated for use or consumption within such duty free zones;
— supplies of goods used for the maintenance of private means of transport, provided they are not supplies for the enterprise of the customer;
— private use in these areas;
— supplies of goods which are from an import tax point of view, in free movement, etc..

## *Oil industry*

The general rules apply.

## *Retailers*

There are no special provisions for retailers.

## *Second-hand goods*

There are no special regulations concerning the supply of second-hand goods.

## *Small entrepreneurs*

Entrepreneurs whose worldwide turnover did not exceed DM 20,000 (beginning 1990 DM 25,000) during the previous year and will not exceed DM 100,000 during the current year, will not be subject to VAT if they do not charge VAT on their invoices. An input tax credit is then not allowed. The treatment can be waived upon application; **5–022**

Small entrepreneurs applying the general VAT rules whose turnover does not exceed DM 60,000 per annum can claim a special tax reduction (which will be abolished at the beginning of 1990);

Small entrepreneurs with an annual turnover not exceeding DM 250,000 may report VAT on a cash basis.

### *Supplies to the German Democratic Republic*

A special VAT regime can apply for certain supplies to the German Democratic Republic. Under specific determined prerequisites, the reduced VAT rates of 6 per cent. or 3 per cent. may apply.

### *Travel agencies*

Special rules exist for the taxation of services rendered by travel agencies to a non-entrepreneur.

Travel services to entrepreneurs are taxed according to the general rules.

# 6. Greece

## 1. GENERAL BACKGROUND

Value Added Tax was introduced in Greece with effect from January 1, 1987 and replaced a number of indirect taxes the most important of which were the turnover tax and stamp tax. For VAT purposes, the territory of Greece excludes only the area of Mount Athos. **6–001**

VAT in Greece is administered by the Income tax authorities. However VAT on import is paid to the Customs department of the Ministry of Finance.

## 2. WHO IS TAXABLE?

### *General*

There is no monetary limit below which VAT is not chargeable. Any person supplying goods or services in the course of business, whether on a regular or occasional basis is taxable. Employees are outside the scope of VAT. **6–002**

#### Transactions with branch/subsidiary

VAT is not due on transactions within the same legal entity. Services supplied to a branch by its foreign head office (or vice versa) are therefore not subject to VAT. If goods are involved the rules concerning imports will apply. Crossborder supplies between a foreign parent company and its subsidiary in Greece or vice versa are taxable supplies.

#### Government bodies

The Greek State, municipalities, communities and other organisations governed by public law are not considered taxable persons in respect of activities in which they engage in pursuance of their objectives, even where they collect dues, fees or contributions. These bodies, however, are considered as taxable persons when they engage in such activities as telecommunications, supply of gas, electricity and thermic energy, transport of goods, port and airport services, passenger transport, running of trade fairs and exhibitions, etc.

## *Fiscal unity/group registration*

This concept does not exist in Greece.

## *Foreign entrepreneurs*

**6–003** Entrepreneurs with no establishment in Greece but delivering goods in Greece or supplying services which are taxable in Greece are subject to VAT.

A foreign entrepreneur is regarded as delivering goods in Greece when he acts as the importer of the goods.

Generally, a non-resident entrepreneur is considered as having an establishment for VAT purposes if he keeps in Greece a regular place of activity such as an office, shop, factory or only a fixed domicile from which the activity is exercised.

A non-resident entrepreneur with an establishment in Greece is treated as a local company and should comply with all the rules applicable to a Greek entrepreneur.

### Representative office

Representative offices of foreign entrepreneurs are not within the scope of VAT when they carry out preparatory or auxiliary activities.

### VAT representative

Foreign entrepreneurs making transactions in Greece are required to appoint a VAT representative who will be responsible for fulfilling the administrative obligations and for payment of the tax due.

### Reverse charge mechanism

Where certain services are imported into Greece by way of business, the importer shall account for Greek VAT as if he had made the supply himself, to himself. The services concerned are the following:

- transfers and assignments of copyright, patents, licences, trademarks and similar rights;
- advertising services;
- services of consultants, engineers, consultancy bureaux, lawyers, accountants and other similar services, data processing and provision of information (but excluding any services relating to land);
- acceptance of any obligation to refrain from pursuing or exercising, in whole or part, any business activity or any such rights as are referred to in paragraph 6–002 above;

— banking, financial and insurance services (including reinsurance, but not including the provision of safe deposit facilities);
— the supply of staff;
— the letting or hire of goods other than means of transport;
— the services rendered by one person to another in procuring for the other any of the services mentioned in the preceding paragraphs;

In all the above cases, the liability for the tax is shifted to the recipient of the services;

### *Importers*

Goods brought into Greece are liable to VAT at customs clearance. The tax is due by the importer.

## 3. WHAT IS TAXABLE?

VAT is due on: **6–004**

— the supply of goods or services effected for consideration within the Greek territory by a taxable person in the course of a business;
— the importation of goods irrespective of whether such importation is effected by a taxable or non-taxable person.

### *Supply of goods*

The term supply of goods includes the transfer of the right to dispose of tangible movable goods as well as of immovable properties.

The term "movable goods," includes energy which may be the subject of transaction, *e.g.* electricity, gas, refrigeration and heat.

### *Supply of services*

Supply of services is defined as any transaction which does not **6–005** constitute a supply of goods. This wide definition allows a large number of transactions to be classified as "services". Accordingly these transactions may include, *inter alia*:

— assignments of intangible property whether or not they are the subject of a document establishing title. Examples include the transfer of rights for the use of know-how and trademarks;
— obligations to refrain from an act or to tolerate an act or situation;

— the exploitation of hotels, furnished rooms and houses, camping grounds and similar installations, parking places, means of transport and caravans, the leasing of manufacturing locations and safes;
— the sale of food and drinks by restaurants, places of entertainment and other similar enterprises;
— the use of goods forming part of the assets of a business for the private use of the taxable person or his staff or more generally for purposes other than those of the business where the value added tax on such goods is deductible;
— supply of services carried out free of charge by the taxable person for his own private use or that of his staff or more generally for purposes other than those of his business;
— application by a taxable person of his own services for the purpose of his business where the tax on such services, had they been acquired from another taxable person, would not have been deductible.

### *Self-supplies of goods/services*

A taxable supply of goods or services is deemed to occur in the following situations:

— goods are extracted, manufactured, built or transformed by the entrepreneur himself for the use of his own business or for the private use of directors, employees or third parties;
— services are provided free of charge to directors, employees or third parties;
— when assets of an entrepreneur are used for private purposes by himself or his staff or more generally when used for purposes other than those of the business.

In such cases, the entrepreneur has to issue a specific document to report these self supplies to the tax authorities. The VAT is due by the entrepreneur on the cost of the goods or services provided. The tax can be recovered as an input VAT.

### *Imports of goods*

Importation of goods means the entry of goods in to the Greek territory.

## 4. PLACE OF SUPPLY

### *Supply of goods*

6–006 The place of supply of goods is deemed to be in Greece if at the time the tax becomes chargeable the goods are within the Greek territory.

In cases where a transfer of the right to import goods is effected, the place of supply is considered to be within the Greek territory although the goods may be outside the country.

## *Supply of services*

### General rule

The place of supply of services is considered to be Greece if, at the time the tax becomes chargeable, Greece is the country where the supplier has established his business, or has a fixed establishment from which the service is supplied or, in the absence of such a place of business or fixed establishment, he has a permanent address or habitual residence.

### Exceptions

Greece is considered to be the place of supply of services in the case of:

— services connected with immovable property situated in Greece including the services of estate agents and experts, engineers, architects and firms providing on-site supervision;

— transport services, if the transport takes place within Greece. In the case of international transport, according to the distance covered within the country;

— services connected with the establishment or assembly of imported goods if the related work is performed in Greece by the supplier of such goods who is established outside Greece.

— services connected with the hiring of all forms of transport if the lessor is established in Greece and the lessee uses the asset in Greece or in another Member State of the European Community or, if the lessor is established in a country outside the European Community and the lessee uses the asset within Greece;

— services supplied in Greece relating to:

  — cultural, artistic, sporting, scientific, educational, entertainment or similar activities, including the activities of the organisers of such activities and the supply of ancillary services; **6–007**

  — ancillary transport activities such as loading, unloading and similar activities;

  — valuations of movable tangible property.

### Reverse charge mechanism

When a foreign entrepreneur provides the following services to a Greek entrepreneur he will not have to account for Greek VAT since the tax will be due by the Greek recipient. This special rule referred to as the "reverse charge mechanism" applies to the importation of:

- transfers and assignments of copyrights, patents, licences, trademarks;
- advertising services;
- services of consultants, engineers, consultancy bureaux, lawyers, accountants, data processing and supply of information;
- acceptance to refrain from pursuing or exercising a business activity or a right relating to copyrights, patents, trademarks, etc.;
- the supply of staff;
- banking, financial and insurance services;
- letting or hiring of goods other than means of transport;
- the services of an agent when procuring any of the above mentioned services.

## 5. BASIS OF TAXATION

### *Supplies within Greece*

**6–008** The taxable amount in respect of supplies of goods and services is the consideration which has been or is to be obtained by the supplier of goods or services.

On that basis, incidental expenses, such as commissions, packing, insurance, transport and custom duties are part of the taxable basis.

### *Self-supplies*

The taxable basis of self-supplies of goods or services is the cost. Cost may easily be determined when goods are concerned. It is the cost of raw materials plus labour costs. It is more difficult to establish it in the case of services.

### *Imports*

VAT due on the importation of goods is assessed on the value paid by the importer to the supplier. The taxable amounts include as well all taxes, dues, levies and contributions paid to the state by other third parties, and also commission, transport and insurance costs, with the exception of VAT.

### *Chargeable event/Time of payment*

›VAT becomes due when the goods have been supplied and the services performed. The actual payment of the tax will have to be made at the time the VAT return is filed. For filing dates see para. 6–013, "VAT returns," below.

### Credit notes/Bad debts

The recovery of VAT can be obtained by a Greek entrepreneur who issues a credit note to his client.

An in-court settlement is necessary to establish that a debt cannot be recovered. In practice, in-court as well as out-of-court settlements allow an entrepreneur to issue a credit note and therefore to recover the VAT on his bad debts.

## 6. TAX RATES

The Greek VAT rates are: **6–009**

- 0% (see para. 6–010, "Exemption with credit")
- 3% applicable to books and magazines
- 6% applicable to products regarded as basic necessities
- 16% applicable when the goods or services are not subject to any other specific rate
- 36% due on products regarded as luxuries, such as televisions, videos, etc..

## 7. EXEMPTIONS

### Exemptions with credit for input tax

The following are examples of exemptions with credit: **6–010**

- — export of goods from Greece provided that the tax authorities are satisfied that the goods have in fact been exported;
- — insurance and reinsurance services rendered to non-EC residents including related services performed by insurance brokers and insurance agents;

### Exemptions without credit for input tax

A number of exemptions are granted from VAT, including:

- — services supplied by lawyers, doctors, dentists, veterinarians, nurses and physiotherapists;
- — the supply of educational services by public or private educational institutions;
- — tuition given privately by teachers covering all levels of education;
- — the income (rent) from buildings, excluding the exploitation of hotels, furnished rooms, parking places, etc.;

- hospital and medical care and the supply of goods incidental thereof provided by bodies governed by public law or by other institutions which operate under conditions comparable to those applicable to bodies governed by the public law.

There is no right to recover VAT on the purchases of the above exempted transactions.

- air, sea and rail transport of passengers from within the country to a destination outside Greece and vice versa, and services closely connected with such transport;
- delivery of gold to the Bank of Greece.

## *Non-taxable transactions*

### Transactions within the same legal entity

**6–011** Transactions within the same legal entity are considered as internal transactions and therefore are not taxable. Services supplied by a foreign head office to its Greek branch are not taxable to VAT.

### Transfer of business

The transfer of a complete business as a going concern is not subject to VAT.

### Subsidies/Penalty payments

Subsidies received from the Greek Government (essentially by exporters or investors) are never subject to VAT. Subsidies granted by an entrepreneur to another entrepreneur may be subject to VAT depending on the nature of the subsidies. It is not subject to VAT when the subsidy takes the form of a reimbursement of expenses.

Penalties payments are not subject to VAT.

## *Election to be subject to VAT*

Transactions are either subject to VAT or exempt. It is not possible to opt to pay VAT when an exemption normally applies.

# 8. CREDIT FOR INPUT TAX

## *General rule*

**6–012** An entrepreneur is, in principle, entitled to recover VAT paid on goods and services and on importation of goods acquired in furtherance of business. However, no credit is granted for input tax on:

— purchase or import of tobacco products;
— purchase or import of alcoholic beverages to the extent that these have been utilised in non-taxable transactions;
— banquets, entertainment and hospitality expenses;
— accommodation, food, beverage, transport and entertainment expenses of personnel or company representative;
— purchase or import of passenger cars for private use (up to nine seats) motor-bicycles and mopeds, vessels and aeroplanes for private use or sports, as well as the related fuel, repair, maintenance, rental and circulation expenses generally.

### *Adjustment of entitlement to credit*

The input VAT recovered on capital assets has to be adjusted if the assets are sold within five years. Repayment of the input VAT will be one-fifth for each year the assets where not used by the entrepreneur.

### *Partial exemption*

Entrepreneurs making both taxable and exempt supplies are entitled to recover input tax related only to their taxable supplies. When goods and services are attributable to the taxable activity, VAT can be recovered in full.

When goods and services are used for both taxable and non-taxable activities, the creditable input tax is calculated based on the ratio between taxable supplies and total supplies.

The applicable ratio is determined at the time each VAT return is filed.

### *Time of recovery*

Input VAT incurred in a VAT period (one month, two months or a quarter—see para. 6–013 below, "VAT returns") can be offset against output VAT of the same period.

When input VAT is in excess of output VAT, a refund can be obtained on application.

### *Refund for foreign entrepreneurs*

Foreign entrepreneurs with no fixed establishment in Greece may apply for a refund of the VAT they incurred in Greece.

## 9. ADMINISTRATIVE OBLIGATIONS

### *Registration*

**6–013** Registration with the tax office in the district in which the business is located is required of any person who makes or intends to make taxable supplies. There is no monetary limit below which registration is not required.

### *Books and records*

Proper books and records provided by the Tax Records Code should be kept by any entrepreneur who makes taxable supplies. Purchases and sales should be accounted for, based on the VAT rate.

### *Invoices*

The invoices must contain the following information:

— name and address of the client;
— its tax number;
— description of the supply
— price of goods or services excluding VAT;
— rate of VAT and corresponding amount of VAT.

### *VAT returns*

During the year temporary VAT returns are filed. The date of filing is determined by the category of books of account the entrepreneur must keep. Entrepreneurs whose turnover is below Drs 6,000,000 (category A) are required to keep only purchase books and have to file VAT returns on a quarterly basis on the 15th of the month following the end of the quarter.

Entities whose turnover is between Drs 6–80,000,000 (category B) are required to keep income and expenditure books and have to file their VAT returns on the 20th of the month following the end of a two-month period.

Corporations, limited liability companies, foreign companies and any other entity with a turnover above Drs 80,000,000 (category C) have to keep full sets of books (journal, general ledger, etc.) and their VAT returns have to be filed monthly on the 25th of the following month. A final VAT return for the entire year is filed within two months from the end of the accounting year. Payment of VAT is made to the tax authorities directly or to the post office upon filing of the VAT returns.

### Powers of the authorities

The following are some of the fines provided by the Greek tax laws: **6–014**

| | *Offence* | *Fine* |
|---|---|---|
| a/ | Late filing of VAT returns | 10% of tax per month up to 100% |
| b/ | Assessment of income taxes where an income tax return was not filed | 150% of the non declared tax |

The tax authorities may correct any VAT transactions during a ten year period.

Tax payers have a period of three years to correct their VAT tax returns or to apply for a reduction or a repayment of VAT when it was wrongly assessed.

### Objections/Appeals

When an entrepreneur is reassessed by the tax authorities he has to settle 20 per cent. of the VAT assessment even if he wants to dispute it. Within 20 days of the tax authorities report, the entrepreneur may appeal before a first instance court or agree to a compromise with the tax authorities. If the court's decision is in favour of the tax authorities the full amount of the reassessment has to be paid immediately, although further appeal is possible before a higher court and possibly before the Supreme Court.

## 10. SPECIAL VAT REGIMES

### Small enterprises

Small enterprises are defined as those whose annual income does not exceed Drs 6,000,000 and which, under the provisions of the Tax Records Code, do not keep books or keep books of the first category. Excluded from the definition are farmers for whom other special arrangements apply and enterprises which derive at least 60 per cent. of their income from wholesale or export sales. **6–015**

Small enterprises whose annual income does not exceed Drs 1,000,000 are exempted from the obligation of filing returns or the payment of tax. This exemption, however, does not apply to enterprises which commence business for the first time. Exempted enterprises cannot claim deduction of tax on their purchases (see para. 6–012) and invoices issued by them must not include value added tax.

The income of small enterprises other than those which are exempted, is determined on a deemed basis by the application of gross profit coefficients to the cost of their purchases excluding value added tax. The coefficients will be determined by the Ministry of Finance. These enterprises must file returns in the same way as all other enterprises.

Small enterprises may elect to be included under the normal value added tax arrangements and exempted enterprises may elect to be included under the status of small enterprises or under normal arrangements.

### *Farmers*

The special arrangements for farmers provide for the return of tax charged on their purchases of goods and services. This return is effected by the Greek State by applying flat rate percentages to the price, exclusive of tax, of the agricultural products and services delivered by the farmers.

Farmers under these arrangements do not file returns and cannot claim deductions of tax on any of their purchases. The special arrangements do not apply to farmers who carry on their agricultural operations through a company of any form.

As in the case of small enterprises, farmers may elect to be included under the normal value added tax arrangements.

### *Travel agents*

**6–016** Special arrangements apply to travel agents who, for the purpose of providing travel facilities to their customers, use the supply of goods and services of other taxable persons. All transactions performed by a travel agent in respect of a journey are treated as a single service by the travel agent to the traveller. This service is taxable in Greece if the place of establishment of the travel agent from which the service is provided is in Greece.

The taxable amount in these cases is the difference between the amount paid by the travel agent's customer, exclusive of value added tax, and the actual cost to the travel agent of supplies and services, including tax, provided by others where these supplies are for the direct benefit of the customer.

The tax charged to the travel agent by other taxable persons on the above transactions is not recoverable.

The above provisions do not apply to agents who are acting only as intermediaries paid by a commission.

# 7. Republic of Ireland

## 1. GENERAL BACKGROUND

VAT was introduced in Ireland on November 1, 1972 replacing a combined retail and wholesale tax system which had been in operation for the preceding nine years. 7–001

Ireland acceded to membership of the European Community on January 1, 1973.

Control of Value Added Tax is vested in the Revenue Commissioners. Internally, control of VAT is exercised by Inspectors of Taxes in conjunction with the administration of income tax, corporation tax and capital gains tax. At point of import it is controlled by Customs and Excise.

The VAT Act of 1972 is the principle legislation governing VAT. It has been amended by subsequent finance acts and is supported by regulations and statutory instruments. It was harmonised with the Sixth EC Directive by the 1978 VAT Amendment Act.

## 2. WHO IS TAXABLE?

### *General*

There is no equivalent in Irish tax law of the continental term "entrepreneur" although the term "taxable person" used in Ireland serves a similar purpose. Any person other than somebody acting as an employee, who supplies taxable goods or services within the State in the course of business and whose annual turnover exceeds, or is likely to exceed £15,000 from services or £32,000 from goods must account for VAT. A profit motive is not required; thus, certain non-profit making organisations are subject to VAT in accordance with the general principles. 7–002

A person who disposes of certain taxable interests in property must also register and account for VAT—see para. 7–025, "Special regimes—property".

Any person who disposes of a taxable person's goods in satisfaction of a debt must register and account for VAT. This applies to receivers and liquidators. The legislation also requires the registration of banks which dispose of goods when enforcing their security under mortgages or debentures, although this is not enforced in practice.

### Transactions with branch/subsidiary

Subsidiaries of foreign firms which supply taxable goods and services in Ireland are treated in the same manner as other taxable persons, even where the goods and services are supplied to the parent company situated outside the state. Transactions between branches of the same legal entity are not subject to VAT. Thus supplies between a branch and its head office or another branch are not taxable even if one of the parties is situated outside of Ireland.

### Government bodies

Except in regard to certain imported services, *e.g.* leasing within the EC (excluding means of transport) the State and local authorities are not taxable persons in respect of any of their other activities unless the Minister of Finance makes an order to this effect. To date, no order has been made. State and local authorities are of course liable to VAT at the point of import in respect of all goods imported by them.

## *Fiscal unity/Group taxation*

**7–003** The term "fiscal unity" is not used in the Irish legislation but there is provision whereby several taxable persons, including individuals, may be regarded as one for the purposes of VAT. Where the Revenue Commissioners are satisfied that it would be in the interests of efficient administration and that no loss of tax would be involved, they may treat a group of taxable persons, as a single taxable person. This facility does not extend to taxable persons who are not supplying taxable goods or services within Ireland, or to exempt or partially exempt companies. This position is, however, currently under review with the likelihood that exempt persons may be admitted to VAT groups in the future.

Under this system intra-group transactions with the exception of dealings in property may be ignored for VAT purposes. One member of the group, the "remitter," will submit a single "group" VAT return. The remitter's return will show output tax and input tax of the external transactions of the group. All members of the group will be jointly and severally liable to comply with the VAT obligations of each member.

The Inspector must be advised of any proposed change to a VAT group structure, *e.g.* a subsidiary being sold off and leaving the group or another taxable person wishing to join the group. When a company which has been a member of a VAT group is sold off the other members will still be liable for its VAT debts until the VAT group is formally changed by the Inspector.

## *Foreign firms*

Foreign firms which supply goods or services in Ireland are obliged to register and account for VAT if their annual turnover is in excess of the appropriate limit. **7–004**

Foreign firms which do not supply taxable goods or services in Ireland are not permitted to elect to register for VAT.

### Representative office

A representative office of an overseas business such as the sales and booking office of an international airline, which does not operate out of Ireland, is not required to register for VAT in Ireland when it makes no taxable supplies in Ireland.

Where a foreign firm sends goods to an agent or representative in Ireland for distribution, the foreign firm must register and account for VAT. The agent or representative (but not an employee) of the foreign firm should also register and account for VAT on the services he provides to the foreign firm.

### VAT representative

A foreign firm is not obliged to appoint a representative or responsible person to act on its behalf if it is making taxable supplies in Ireland. However, the Revenue has power, by notice in writing, to substitute for the foreign firm any agent, manager or factor residing in the state and who has acted on behalf of the foreign firm, and to hold that person accountable in respect of the foreign firm's liabilities. This power is rarely used.

### Reverse charge mechanism

Persons who receive from abroad, for business use, certain services (such as copyrights, patents, hiring of movable goods, advertising, consultancy and certain financial services) are obliged to account for VAT on the value of the services. The recipient of such services is regarded as supplying the services to himself. See para. 7–009, "Place of supply of services".

## *Importers*

Persons who import goods into Ireland are subject to VAT at the same rate as applies to the sale of similar goods within Ireland. **7–005**

With regard to services, the place of supply of services may be deemed by VAT law to be outside the State—see para. 7–009, "Place of supply of services."

Non-resident entrepreneurs who import goods into Ireland through an agent or representative are generally obliged to register for VAT and are liable for VAT on the importation of such goods. They are deemed to import the goods themselves, the agent merely acting on their behalf.

It is worth noting that non-resident entrepreneurs delivering goods directly to Irish customers are not liable for VAT on this transaction. In this instance it is the customer who is the importer and who is therefore liable to pay the tax. A true agency relationship must, of course, actually exist: many traders who act as principals, *e.g.* sole concessionaires or distributors but who are commonly referred to as agents, incur liability for VAT in their own right.

## 3. WHAT IS TAXABLE?

**7–006** VAT liability arises on the taxable supply of goods or services in Ireland for consideration by a taxable person in the course or furtherance of any business carried on by him and on the importation of goods into Ireland.

### *Supply of goods*

A taxable supply of goods means a voluntary or involuntary transfer of ownership whether by delivery of the goods or otherwise. The term "goods" includes not only new and second hand goods but also buildings and land which have been developed or are being developed.

Gifts of taxable goods made by a taxable person in the course or furtherance of business are liable to VAT unless their cost to the donor is £15 or less. This *de minimus* limit does not apply to a series of gifts to one person irrespective of their individual or total value.

Advertising goods given free for business use to trade customers such as advertising mirrors, beer mats and industrial samples, etc., are not taxable. The normal rules for input credits will apply but as this area can give rise to disagreement with the Inspector on interpretation expert advice should be sought.

Disposals of taxable goods used in a business in respect of which a VAT input credit has been obtained are taxable supplies and VAT must be accounted for. There is no relief in respect of the time during which the goods were used in the taxable business.

A taxable supply of goods also includes:

- the transfer of ownership of goods by agreement;
- the handing over of goods under a hire purchase contract;
- the handing over by a contractor of goods made up from materials supplied in whole or part by his customer;
- the application or appropriation of materials or goods by a taxable person to some private or exempt use, *i.e.* self-supply;
- the seizure of goods by a sheriff or other person acting under legal authority;
- the provision of electricity, gas, and any form of power, heat, refrigeration or ventilation.

### Mixed transactions

Special rules apply to mixed transactions consisting of supplies of goods and services. Basically the supply is regarded as a supply of goods where they represent two thirds or more of the total price. This rule however applies only where the contract is essentially an agreement for the supply of services. Where the supply consists totally of goods or totally of services but where the goods or services are liable at different rates, special rates apply—see para. 7–015, "Rates-package rule"—below.

### *Supply of services*

A supply of service can be defined as any supply in the course of business, which is not a supply of goods. It includes an agreement to refrain from engaging in a particular activity or the toleration of a commercial activity carried on by others. Food and drink provided in the course of operating such businesses as hotels, restaurants, cafes, public houses, catering businesses or businesses providing facilities for the consumption of food and drink and vending machines are treated as supplies of services rather than supplies of goods.

### *Self-supplies of goods/services*

There is a self-supply of goods, when a person diverts to private or **7–007** exempt use, goods which he has imported, purchased, manufactured or otherwise acquired and in respect of which he is entitled to a VAT deduction.

The provision of catering services for employees by an employer is regarded as a self-supply of services and VAT must be paid on the cost to the supplier. This is the only self-supply of services provided for in the Irish legislation.

### *Imports of goods*

The mere importation of goods is a taxable event irrespective of the status of the importer or the nature of the importation—with certain exemptions, see para. 7–016, "Exemptions". Goods imported into a bonded warehouse are liable to VAT. The tax is assessed on the value for customs purposes excluding any duties which are not being paid at the time of entry for warehousing.

## 4. PLACE OF SUPPLY

### *Supply of goods*

The place where goods are supplied is deemed for the purposes of **7–008** VAT to be:

1. Where the supply of goods requires their transportation, the place where transport begins;
2. In any other case the place where the goods are located at the time of the supply.

Assembly, installation and incorporation of goods into other goods in Ireland is taxable in Ireland irrespective of their transportation from abroad.

### Chain transactions

Where there is a series of agreements for the sale of the same goods from vendor to purchaser to sub-purchaser, etc. and all parties to the agreements agree that the goods should be delivered directly by the vendor to the last sub-purchaser, each seller in this chain is deemed to have made a supply of goods to the next sub-purchaser and is accordingly liable for VAT. The net effect, of course, will be that if all sub-purchasers sell in the course of business, all will be entitled to an input tax credit exactly equal to the amount of their liability on the sale. If one of them, however, is not selling in the course of his business and is not, therefore, registered for VAT, his sub-purchaser will not be liable to pay VAT on such purchase. If this sub-purchaser sells in the course of his business he will nevertheless have to charge his purchaser VAT and account for same to the Revenue.

## *Supply of Services*

### General rule

7–009 The general rule is that the place where services are deemed to be supplied for VAT purposes is the place where the person *supplying* the service has his establishment or (if more than one) the establishment of his which is most concerned with the supply or (if he has no establishment) his usual place of residence.

### Exceptions

The exceptions are:

— the place of supply of services connected with immovable goods is deemed to be the place where the goods are situated;
— transport services are deemed to be supplied where the transport takes place;
— the following services are deemed to be supplied where they are physically performed:
cultural, artistic, sporting, scientific, educational, entertainment or similar services. Thus an entertainer is deemed to supply his services in the country where he performs and not in the country which transmits or receives an associated television or radio programme;

ancillary transport activities such as loading, unloading and handling;
valuation of and work on movable goods.

### Reverse charge mechanism

The place of supply of services such as copyrights, patents, hiring of movable goods, advertising, consultancy and financial services, provision of staff and some others is generally where the recipient of the services has his business. This gives rise to the "Reverse Charge" concept in that the recipient is held to be liable to VAT on the value of the services he has received and will be entitled to the normal input VAT deduction if he is a taxable person. Thus, a fully taxable person will ultimately not have to pay VAT but an exempt person is obliged to register and is not entitled to input credit in respect of such service.

## 5. BASIS OF TAXATION

### *Supplies within Ireland*

Where the consideration takes the form of money the amount on **7–010**
which tax is chargeable is normally the total sum paid or payable to the person supplying the goods or services including all taxes, commissions, costs, and charges whatsoever but not including the VAT chargeable in respect of a transaction. VAT must therefore be returned on the VAT exclusive price. Where goods or services are supplied and the consideration does not consist of or does not consist wholly of an amount of money the amount on which tax is chargeable is the open market or arm's length value of the goods or services supplied.

Interest charged on late payment, etc. is taxable.

Special rules apply with regard to the amount to be charged where goods are made up from materials or components supplied by customers and expert advice should be sought.

### *Self-supplies*

Self-supplies of goods, *i.e.* the use of goods for which refund of VAT has been obtained by a taxable person in respect of an exempt or non-business activity, are liable to VAT, on the basis of their cost to the supplier. The provision of catering services for employees, by an employer, is regarded as a self-supply of services. Tax in respect of self-supplies becomes due when the goods are appropriated or when the services are supplied.

VAT must be paid on the cost of the goods or service to the taxable person. In practice the credit taken is recovered or disallowed—however, there are exceptions with regard to property and expert advice should be sought.

## *Imports*

7–011 The value of imported goods for the purposes of VAT is the value for customs purposes, plus any taxes, duties, and other charges levied either outside or by reason of importation, inside the State (excluding VAT) on the goods and not already included. Where the value is expressed in a foreign currency the amount must be converted to the national currency in accordance with EC rules.

However, goods imported into warehouses are taxed on the "short price," *i.e.* the value exclusive of any duty payable. When removed from a bonded warehouse by a taxable person, VAT will not be payable on any duty paid.

## *Chargeable event/Time of payment*

Liability to tax arises at the time when taxable goods or taxable services are supplied.

In dealings between taxable persons tax becomes due on the date of issue of the invoice (which must be issued within 10 days of the end of the month during which the taxable supply took place) or on the receipt of a payment in advance of the issue of an invoice. However, if the advance payment is received from a taxable person an invoice must be issued within 10 days of the end of the month.

The time when tax is due can be summarised as follows:

- in dealings with taxable persons, tax is due on the earlier of the following three dates:
  - the date on which the invoice was issued, or
  - the date on which payment is received in advance of the date on which the tax would normally be due; or
  - the date on which the invoice should have been issued;
- in dealings with unregistered persons tax is due when the taxable goods or services have been supplied.

Tax is normally payable on importation. However a deferred payment scheme may be authorised which will defer payment of the tax to the 15th day of the month following that in which the goods are imported.

## *Cash/Invoice basis*

7–012 VAT due must normally be accounted for on the basis of the value of invoices issued in the appropriate VAT period. However, where a taxable person supplies goods to the value of 90 per cent. or more of his annual turnover to non-registered customers (for example a retail shop) or supplies services to anybody, he may elect, in writing, to account for VAT on the basis of monies received. The cash basis provides automatic bad debts relief and ensures that VAT is only payable at the rate applicable at the time of receipt. This can prove to be a disadvantage if the rate increases between the taxable supply and receipt of the cash.

### *Credit notes/Bad debts*

A registered person may adjust his liability for tax in respect of goods returned to him, discounts or other price adjustments allowed or bad debts written off by him subsequent to his having paid the appropriate tax. A registered person must prove to the Inspector's satisfaction that the debt was pursued through the usual commercial channels and was then written off. A credit note should not be issued and the debtor is entitled to retain the VAT input credit on foot of the original invoice.

Where a price reduction has been allowed by one registered person to another after the issue of an invoice showing VAT and a corresponding tax adjustment is actually made, the person who has issued the invoice is required to issue a credit note showing the amount of tax by which his liability has been reduced.

However, where both the issuer and recipient are taxable persons and they both agree not to make any change in the amount of tax shown on the original invoice, a VAT credit note need not be issued.

## 6. TAX RATES

The present rates are as follows:

0%— The zero rate applies to services related to the export of goods such as docking, landing, loading or unloading facilities, including the provision of customs clearance, directly in connection with the disembarkation or embarkation of passengers or the import or export of goods. **7–013**
Exported goods, certain animal feedstuffs and fertilisers, books, food and drink with certain exceptions, oral medicines, children's clothing and footwear, medical equipment for the handicapped.

2%— Live cattle, sheep, goats, pigs, deer.

5%— Electricity.

10%— Fuel gas excluding motor fuel, developed property, building services, adult clothing and footwear, newspapers, hotel accommodation, restaurants, cinema, cabaret, museum and art gallery admission, tour guide services, certain car and boat hire, repair and maintenance or alteration of movable goods, health studios, the disposal of waste material, certain agricultural services, certain services of auctioneers, solicitors, estate agents in connection with the sale of agricultural land and the repair and service of cars and works of art.

25%— Goods or services not subject to one of the other rates or exempt from tax (including rent where the exemption has been waived).

### Package rule (Cocktail rule)

If an article comprising goods taxable at different rates is sold as a unit—for example, a book and cassette, a tie and tiepin—tax is payable on the entire amount at the rate applicable to the higher or highest VAT-rated item included. The same provision applies to services liable at different rates or to a mixture of goods and services.

See also para. 7–006, "Mixed transactions".

## 7. EXEMPTIONS

### *Exemption with credit for input tax (zero rate)*

**7–014** In many cases the zero rate referred to above works as an exemption with credit because the suppliers of zero-rated goods and services are entitled to input credit under the normal rules.

However, the following activities which are deemed to be exempt from VAT carry an entitlement to recovery of VAT:

— international passenger transport, and
— financial or insurance services supplied outside the EC.

### *Exemption without credit for input tax*

The supply of certain goods and services is exempt from VAT. The suppliers of such goods or services are not permitted to charge VAT, nor will an input credit be allowed where it is attributable to the purchase or importation of any of these goods or services.

These include:

— financial services—lending money or providing credit, any dealings in stocks, shares, debentures, the operation of current, deposit or savings accounts, management of certain unit trusts;
— education;
— medical and dental services and hospital care together with welfare and social security services provided by non-profit making organisations.
— Short term letting of property
— Services for the protection of children
— Admissions to plays, concerts, ballet and circuses
— Travel Agencies and tour operators
— Insurance services and insurance agents
— Veterinary surgeons
— National broadcasting and television services
— Betting and lotteries
— Promotion of and admission to sporting events and provision of sporting facilities

- — Collection, storage and supply of human organs, human blood and human milk
- — Funeral undertaking
- — Supply of live horses and greyhounds
- — Certain services of non-profit making organisations
- — Provision of sporting facilities
- — Catering services to patients of a hospital or to students of a school where they are supplied in the hospital or in the school.

Certain importations are exempt from VAT such as the personal effects of travellers, personal goods imported on permanent transfer of private residence, goods used in a business on the permanent transfer of that business to Ireland, temporary imports, goods reimported after being repaired abroad, goods in transit and raw materials for the manufacture of goods which will be exported. Certain restrictions and qualifications apply to some of these items.

## *Non-taxable transactions*

### Transactions within the same legal entity

Transactions including cross border transactions between branches of **7–015** the same legal entity and between members of a VAT group are not taxable. VAT credits will be allowed subject to the normal rules.

### Transfer of business

The transfer of a business or part thereof and the transfer of goodwill or other intangible assets of a business in connection with the transfer of a business or part thereof between two taxable persons is not regarded as a taxable activity. Credit for input tax will be allowed where appropriate in respect of such transactions. It is important to note that the business transferred does not have to amount to a going concern to qualify.

### Subsidies/Penalty payments/Compensation/Waiver of debt

Subsidies, penalties, grants and compensation payments will be regarded as outside the scope of VAT and thus not taxable if it is clear that they are not received in respect of a supply of taxable goods or services. Premature lease termination payments are however regarded as taxable. A price subsidy is generally taxable and a waiver of debt is regarded as a price reduction. Expert advice should be sought when dealing with any payments of this nature.

### Inter-group lending and bank deposit interest

Interest from inter-group lending, *e.g.* between holding and subsidiary **7–016** companies is not regarded as exempt, or outside the scope of VAT, unless the holding company is a bank or lending institution. Credit for input tax will be allowed where appropriate. Similarly, bank or building society interest earned by a taxable person will not normally be regarded as exempt income and recovery of input VAT will not be affected.

### *Election to be subject to VAT*

The following persons are not obliged to register for VAT but may do so if they wish:

— Veterinary surgeons
— Farmers
— Fishermen
— Persons in receipt of rents from lettings under a lease for a period of less than 10 years
— Persons whose turnover from activities which are otherwise taxable does not exceed £32,000 per annum in the case of a supply of goods or £15,000 per annum in the case of a supply of service.

If a person in any of the above categories also has other taxable activities, he may of course, be obliged to register for VAT in respect of all of his activities.

## 8. CREDIT/REFUND FOR INPUT VAT

### *General rule*

**7–017** In computing the amount of tax payable by him a taxable person may deduct the tax relating to most goods and services purchased or imported by him which are used for the purposes of his taxable business. No deduction may be made for the tax paid on goods and services used for any other purposes. To be entitled to the deduction the registered person must have a proper VAT invoice or a stamped copy of the customs entry.

As an exception to the general rule, input tax suffered in relation to certain activities which are exempt or outside the scope of VAT is deductible, such as:

— transport outside the State of passengers and their accompanying baggage;
— certain financial and insurance services supplied to a person who has his establishment outside the EC or directly in connection with the export of goods to a place outside the EC;
— supplies of goods and services outside the State which would be taxable supplies if made in the State;
— transfer of a business—see para. 7–015 above;
— inter group lending—see para. 7–016 above.

A deduction is not permitted in respect of tax suffered on any of the following:

food and drink;
accommodation;
personal services for the benefit of an employee even if the expense is incurred for business purposes;
entertainment expenses;
purchase and hire of passenger cars (except in the case of a garage, driving-school or car hire trader);
petrol (otherwise than as stock in trade).

Dealers in second hand motor vehicles may take an imputed credit in respect of the purchase of a motor vehicle from a private individual or a registered person who did not qualify for an input credit. The amount of the imputed credit is 20 per cent. of the purchase price. This scheme does not apply to any other business.

## *Adjustment of entitlement to credit*

There are no special rules with regard to the review of apportioned input credits in respect of capital goods as provided for in Article 20(2) of the Sixth Directive.

## *Partial exemption*

Persons who make taxable and other supplies such as exempt supplies **7–018**
and supplies which are outside the scope of VAT are entitled to recover VAT incurred in making the taxable supplies only.

Where the purchases or imports are used in making both taxable and exempt/outside the scope supplies, an apportionment of the input VAT is allowed. The allowable input tax credit is usually calculated in the ratio of the turnover of taxable supplies to the total turnover of all supplies. Alternatively the ratio may be determined on any basis which may be agreed between the taxable person and the local Inspector of Taxes. Thus, for example, some registered persons may claim that areas, assets, number of employees, employees' time, employees' remuneration etc. which are attributable to taxable supplies, represents a more equitable basis for calculating the allowable input credit. This apportionment is normally calculated on an annual basis.

## *Time of recovery*

A taxable person is entitled to recovery of input tax, subject to the rules to entitlement outlined above, when he has a valid VAT invoice or stamped customs entry. It is *not* necessary that he has paid for the goods or that the supplier has paid the output tax to the authorities.

The claim to input tax credit should be made in the VAT return for the period in which the invoice or import documents are issued.

### *Refund for foreign businesses*

7–019 Any person who is engaged in business outside Ireland and who does not supply taxable goods or services within the State may reclaim tax suffered in Ireland on certain goods and services acquired in Ireland or tax suffered on certain goods imported. These may arise in connection with attendance at exhibitions, training courses, the costs of a representative office or agency services.

Refunds will not be made in respect of tax which is not recoverable by registered persons in Ireland—see para. 7–017, "Credit—General Rule"—or in respect of goods or services where the foreign firm's business would be regarded as exempt if carried on in Ireland.

Claims should be submitted within six months of the end of the relevant calendar year but claims will normally be entertained for up to 10 years. The claim form must be supported by the appropriate original Irish VAT invoices and stamped customs entry documents. EC claimants must also produce a certificate that the claimant is an entrepreneur in his own country. The scheme also applies to persons engaged in business outside the EC. It is not necessary for the foreign business to appoint an agent or fiscal representative in Ireland. Claims for refund should be addressed to:

VAT Branch
Revenue Commissioners
South Georges Street
Dublin 2
Tel. 01–792777.

## 9. ADMINISTRATIVE OBLIGATIONS

### *Registration*

7–020 Any person who supplies taxable goods or services within Ireland in the course of his business or who elects to become taxable—see para. 7–002, "Who is Taxable" and para. 7–016, "Election for Taxable Supplies"—must register at the VAT office in the district in which the registered office (of a Company) or the main place of business (in all other cases) is situated. This includes persons who supply zero-rated goods and services but does *not* include persons who make exempt supplies only.

Provisional registration of an intending trader is permitted. When the registration application has been approved, a VAT number will be allocated by the Inspector. This will normally be the same number as that allocated to the taxable person for Corporation or Income Tax.

The registration will be cancelled if it transpires that the person is not or has ceased to be a taxable person. The Inspector must be informed of any relevant changes to the business in this regard.

Branches of the same legal entity may, in certain circumstances, be permitted to register separately. This will not, however, interfere with the overall liability of the legal entity. Application in writing must be made to the local inspector.

A person who is obliged to register and does not do so, does not avoid a liability to VAT even where VAT has not been charged to his customers.

## *Books and records*

Registered persons, including foreign firms registered for VAT must keep full records, for a period of six years, of all business transactions which may affect their liability to VAT. The records must be kept up to date and must be sufficiently detailed to enable a trader accurately to calculate his liability and the Inspector of Taxes to check the calculation, if necessary. Failure to keep proper records could result in a penalty of IR£800. A foreign firm may keep its books and records outside Ireland but must produce them for inspection in Ireland whenever requested to do so.

## *Invoices*

An inadequate invoice will deprive the recipient of his right to deduct **7–021**
VAT. Invoices and credit notes must contain:

- a VAT registration number;
- the date of supply;
- the name and address of the taxable person supplying the goods or services;
- the name and address of the person to whom the goods or services are supplied;
- a full description of the goods or services supplied;
- the quantity or volume of goods supplied;
- the consideration (exclusive of VAT);
- the rate or rates of tax and amount of tax at each rate chargeable.

Care should be taken when issuing invoices in respect of exempt activities or activities which are outside the scope of VAT that no tax is shown on the invoice. VAT incorrectly stated on an invoice is payable to the Revenue.

Where the zero rate applies it should be shown on the invoice as follows: "VAT @ 0%—nil." An invoice or credit note issued for VAT purposes in amounts expressed in a foreign currency must contain the corresponding figures in Irish punts—the net and total consideration and the VAT charged must be shown separately in Irish punts.

## *VAT returns*

Each taxable person must by the 19th day of the month following the end of each two month taxable period (January/February, March/April, etc.) file a return with the Revenue Commissioners showing the amount of tax deductible and due by him for the period and must pay the tax due by the same date. The return must be in Irish punts.

The Inspector of Taxes may allow some variation in the legal requirement to make returns on a strict January/February, March/April, etc., basis where, because of problems in a particular trade, the registered person may have difficulty in assembling, for the second month in a period, all the data necessary for the submission of their VAT return by the due date. Any such variation does not permit a postponement of tax due.

A registered person who is in a continuous repayment position *i.e.* an exporter or a supplier of zero-rated goods may also apply to the appropriate Inspector of Taxes for permission to make VAT returns on a monthly basis which will improve cash flow. Annual accounting will be available in 1989.

Where there is a repayment due to the registered person this will be made by way of cheque or setoff against tax outstanding to the Revenue Commissioners.

## *Correction of returns*

**7–022** Where a return needs to be amended this must be done without unreasonable delay. A supplementary return should be filed for the period during which the error or omission occurred, and any additional tax paid. Interest will arise from the original due date. Where the supplementary return involves a repayment of tax it will be repaid without the addition of interest.

## *Powers of the Authorities*

Authorised Revenue officers have extensive powers in regard to the inspection and seizure of records and there are penalties if an authorised officer is impeded in his duty by the registered person or his employees. The officers will normally review the VAT position for a period of 2/3 years preceding the audit date. However, the statutory limit is 10 years, except in the case of fraud or neglect where there is no limit.

The Revenue Commissioners may defer repayment of all or part of any tax refundable to any taxable person where they consider that the business activities of that person and of others are so interlinked that it would have been expedient to have applied a group registration to all the persons concerned and any of the persons so interlinked has not filed all VAT returns or paid all VAT due.

The Inspector may refuse to allow a group registration or may cancel a group registration without explanation. Group registration is totally at the discretion of the Inspector. His decision may be queried but cannot be appealed—see para. 7–023, "Appeals" below.

Where a taxable person fails to make a VAT return the authorities may issue an estimated assessment of the tax due. This can be displaced only by making a proper return or by proving that one is not a taxable person.

Where the Inspector is of the opinion that a taxable person has underpaid the VAT properly due he may issue an assessment based on the correct figures or on estimate. This assessment may be appealed. Assessments can be made at any time up to 10 years after the end of the appropriate tax period.

VAT is a preferential debt in bankruptcy or liquidation. Tax payable in respect of a twelve month period prior to the commencement of proceedings in bankruptcy or liquidation ranks equally with most other taxes and certain other preferential debts in priority to all other debts.

The Revenue Commissioners may formally determine whether or not a particular activity is an exempt activity and the rate at which tax is chargeable in relation to the supply of goods or services. **7–023**

### Penalties

The penalty for late filing or for failure to produce records is IR£800 in respect of an individual and IR£500 in respect of a body of persons. These penalties are rarely imposed.

The penalty for late payment is an interest charge of 1.25 per cent. for each calendar month or part of a month for which the payment is late. This applies also to VAT due on foot of an assessment. The due date for the payment of tax charged by assessment is the 19th day of the month following the latest month included in the assessment.

### *Appeals*

Where a person is dissatisfied with any formal determination of the Revenue Commissioners, with any assessment of the payable amount made on him or with any refusal or restriction of a repayment claim made by an Inspector of Taxes he may appeal to the Appeal Commissioners, in writing, within 21 days of the notification of determination, assessment or refusal.

The Appeal Commissioners, who are independent from the Revenue Commissioners, are the first Court of Appeal. They hear arguments from the appellant or his representative and from the Inspector of Taxes. If either person is dissatisfied with the Appeal Commissioner's decision he may appeal to the ordinary Courts.

## 10. SPECIAL VAT REGIMES

### Annual accounting

At present, annual accounting is not available in Ireland but it is **7–024** proposed to introduce this sometime in 1989. Under the current proposals the facility will not be restricted to entrepreneurs of a particular size or type. The authorities will select those who may avail of the facility and may impose payment on account and other obligations.

### Art

With effect from July 1, 1989 works of art including paintings, drawings, etchings, sculptures, etc., irrespective of age, which have been executed by hand will be liable at 10 per cent. All mass produced copies will be liable at 25 per cent.. Exported originals or copies are and will remain zero-rated.

### Farmers and veterinary surgeons

Farmers and veterinary surgeons are not obliged to register for VAT, but may do so if they wish. Farmers who do not register for VAT are compensated for the tax they are charged on their purchases by means of a 2.0 per cent. flat rate addition to the prices at which they sell their produce and services, etc., to VAT-registered persons. The VAT-registered person who buys produce or services from non-registered farmers may claim input credit of the 2.0 per cent. addition to the price paid. The flat rate addition does not apply to veterinary surgeons.

### Horses

Because of the special position of the thoroughbred industry in Ireland's economy, the sale of live horses is exempt.

Racehorse training services are chargeable at 25 per cent.. The amount on which tax is chargeable is the amount of fees which relates to training only and not those amounts which relate to associated services such as keeping, feeding, minding and generally looking after an animal's well-being. In the practical administration of the tax the Revenue Commissioners are prepared to accept as a general, but not invariable, rule that approximately 10 per cent. of the total charge made by trainers relates exclusively to training.

### Real property

7–025 A VAT liability arises on the disposal of a taxable interest in property in the course or furtherance of business. A taxable interest consists of either a freehold interest or a leasehold interest for a period of at least 10 years. The property must have been developed after October 31, 1972 and the person disposing of the property must have been entitled to input tax credit on the development or acquisition costs. The term "development" is widely defined and includes construction, demolition, extension, alteration or reconstruction of buildings as well as operations on land which materially alter the use. There is no registration limit for property dealings.

The outright sale of a taxable property is liable to VAT at 10 per cent. on the sale price.

A person who creates and disposes of a lease in a taxable property for a period of at least 10 years is liable to account for VAT at 10 per cent. on the value of the lease. The regulations provide for specific methods of valuation of leasehold interest of at least 10 years which are based on the expected rent yield. He must also account for VAT on the value of the reversionary interest, as a self supply. The reversionary interest has no value where the lease is for a period in excess of 20 years.

Where a taxable property is developed and leased for a period of less than 10 years then there is a deemed self supply of the property and the lessor must account for VAT on the cost of the property. However, where the tenants are taxable persons, the lessor should consider waiving his exemption on rents, in which case he should charge VAT on the rent and will be entitled to claim input credits in respect of the original development and ongoing maintenance costs. This right to waiver does not require the approval of the lessee.

Rents are liable to VAT at 25 per cent..

### Retailers

Retailers whose supplies consist of goods chargeable to VAT at more than one rate may avail of one of four schemes for the calculation of their output VAT which are approved for different businesses by the Revenue authorities. These schemes are based on the level of purchases at each rate but a taxable person may propose any other scheme which must be approved before use.

### Retail sales exports scheme

Foreign visitors are entitled to relief from tax on certain retail pur- **7–026**
chases of goods which are taken abroad by them.

### Second-hand goods and antiques

There is no special scheme for second hand goods traders and antique dealers. Car dealers who purchase motor vehicles from non-registered persons are entitled to an imputed VAT credit—see para. 7–017, "Credit General Rule" above.

### Shannon Customs-Free Airport and Ringaskiddy Free Port

VAT is not payable on importation of goods from outside the State into the Shannon Customs Free Airport and Ringaskiddy Free Port. Goods supplied to a registered person at Shannon Airport by a registered person from outside the airport qualify for zero rating. Goods supplied to a registered person at Ringaskiddy do *not* qualify for zero rating.

Goods supplied by a registered person at Shannon Airport to another registered person who is trading within the Shannon customs-free area or Ringaskiddy free port also qualify for zero rating but goods going in the opposite direction do not qualify for zero rating.

The supply of taxable services to persons within the customs-free area, whether or not they are registered, does not qualify for zero rating.

### Small enterprises

Small traders whose turnover does not exceed the statutory limit and who are supplying taxable goods or services may elect to become taxable persons, in which case all the rights and obligations of taxable persons come into operation.

### Travel agencies and tour operators

Travel agents and tour operators are exempt from VAT and cannot recover any VAT suffered.

# 8. Italy

## 1. GENERAL BACKGROUND

VAT was introduced in Italy on January 1, 1973 replacing another general tax on consumption called I.G.E. (general tax on revenues). The Italian name of VAT is I.V.A. (imposta sul valore aggiunto). The harmonisation of Italian legislation with the Sixth EC Directive was achieved on April 1, 1979. **8–001**

VAT is levied on the supply of goods and services in Italy made by entrepreneurs and professionals and on all imports of goods. For VAT purposes, Italy means the whole territory subject to the sovereignty of the Italian Republic with the exception of the municipalities of Campione d'Italia and Livigno.

VAT is administered by the Ministry of Finance which also administers direct taxes. Within the Ministry of Finance, VAT due on importation is administered by the Customs Department, otherwise VAT is administered by a specific department through a network of local VAT offices.

## 2. WHO IS TAXABLE?

### *General*

Entrepreneurs and professionals are taxable persons, *i.e.* liable to tax. **8–002**
The definition of an entrepreneur is very broad and includes anyone conducting an industrial, commercial or agricultural activity on a regular and independent basis, including the exploitation of intangible assets. The same can be said with respect to professionals in relation to professional and artistic activities. These definitions imply that:

— occasional supplies of goods and services are not subject to tax;
— employees are not taxable persons;
— the legal status of the entity qualifying as entrepreneur or professional is completely irrelevant in principle. In other words, entrepreneurs can be either resident or non-resident in Italy, can

be an individual or an association of individuals (*e.g.* partnership), a legal entity with profit aim (*e.g.* limited responsibility companies) or a legal entity pursuing public purposes (*e.g.* the State, municipalities and so on).

There is no income limit below which a taxable person can avoid registration for VAT purposes.

### Transactions with branch/subsidiary

Transactions between a branch and its head office are not regulated explicitly. They are usually subjected to tax. According to the draft of a new VAT law currently being discussed, these transactions are considered to be non-taxable transactions.

A subsidiary is considered to be an autonomous Italian resident entity and VAT is therefore applicable according to general rules.

### Government bodies

Special rules apply to non-profit organisations including government bodies such as the State or municipalities. These rules are intended to distinguish between entrepreneurial activities and non-entrepreneurial activities which are usually conducted by these entities. Certain supplies are, in any case, treated as taxable even if *not* made in the conduct of an entrepreneurial activity in order to avoid distortion of competition.

## *Fiscal unity/Group taxation*

To a limited extent, a group taxation may be permitted for VAT purposes. The group can only comprise a holding company and all limited responsibility companies (spa and srl) in which the former has owned, directly or indirectly, the majority of voting share capital from the beginning of the taxable year prior to the one in which the consolidation takes place. No consolidation is possible for individuals and partnerships and no foreign entity can be part of a group. The election for this special regime must be made each year before March 5. Group taxation enables the holding company to offset VAT credit and debit positions. Each member of the group remains independent in all respects except for the payment or reimbursement, either periodical or annual. Transactions within the group remain taxable and VAT is computed by each company according to general rules.

There is, therefore, no particular advantage in including an exempt entity in the group (which is nonetheless possible). The holding company is jointly and severally liable for the VAT due by any member of the VAT group.

## *Foreign entrepreneurs*

In principle, foreign entrepreneurs become liable to tax when supplying goods or services in Italy according to special rules, see para. 8.006, "Place of supply". **8–003**

A permanent establishment of a foreign entrepreneur in Italy is subject to tax in Italy as if it were an independent entity. Supplies made by and to the permanent establishment, are considered to be made by or to an Italian taxable person.

VAT law does not provide for the definition of permanent establishment, nor does income tax law. The OECD definition is usually used.

### Representative office—VAT representative

A representative office in Italy (as opposed to a permanent establishment) is not subject to VAT. The manager of the representative office may be appointed VAT representative. The VAT representative is jointly and severally responsible with the foreign enterprise for the fulfilment of all the duties imposed by VAT law.

### Reverse charge mechanism

In certain cases, liability to VAT is shifted from the supplier to the recipient. This applies in the case of a number of services which are considered to be rendered in Italy when the beneficiary of them is an Italian resident entity. In this case, the foreign entrepreneur may elect to have a VAT representative in Italy who will issue the relevant invoice. If no election is made, the Italian entity will pay VAT by issuing a so-called "auto-invoice" replacing the one which could have been issued by the VAT representative.

## *Importers*

VAT liability arises on clearance of the goods by the competent customs authority. Importers are those who qualify as such according to customs law. It can well be a private person, *i.e.* neither an entrepreneur nor a professional. VAT is levied according to the rules applicable to customs duties.

## 3. WHAT IS TAXABLE?

VAT is levied on the supply of goods or services effected for consideration within the country and on the import of goods. **8–004**

## *Supply of goods*

Supply of goods means the actual transfer of ownership of tangible assets, which include movables, immovables and utilities such as electricity. The following are also considered as supplies of goods even if they do not comply with the general definition in all respects:

— hire purchases which are taxable on delivery of the goods, though ownership is transferred when the last instalment is paid;
— the transfer of goods made by buying or selling agents acting in their own name but for the account of third parties;
— supplies of goods usually manufactured or traded by the entrepreneur made without consideration;
— exchange of goods.

A number of supplies are considered non-taxable transactions even if they comply with the general definition in most respects, see para. 8–013, "Non-taxable transactions".

Assembly and installation are considered to be supplies of services.

## *Supply of services*

Services are broadly defined as obligations to perform, refrain from or tolerate an act or situation for a consideration.

The following are also considered to be supplies of services if made for consideration:

— leasing and hiring of movables and immovables;
— lending of money and securities;
— transfers and licenses of copyrights, patents and know-how;
— the assignment of contracts, see para. 8–013, "Non-taxable transactions".

## *Self-supplies of goods/services*

**8–005** A self-supply of goods is the application by an entrepreneur (not a professional) of goods forming part of his business assets for his private use or for purposes other than those of his business, including liquidation and allotment to shareholders or partners. These transactions are subject to VAT in any case, irrespective of whether a VAT credit was granted or not for the relevant self-supplied goods at the moment of purchase or manufacture.

In principle, self-supplies of services are not taxed.

However, the exceptions are services constituted by transfers or licences of intangible assets (such as copyrights, know-how, etc.), leasing and hiring of movables and immovables, assignment of contract. They are treated as self-supplies of services when rendered without consideration to shareholders or partners.

### Imports of goods

Importation of goods means the introduction of goods into free circulation in Italy. This situation is referred to as a final importation. Importations are taxed as such, irrespective of the legal status of the importer. Temporary importations are not subject to VAT. VAT is levied when the customs clearance is obtained. Bonded warehouses are available to defer the payment of VAT while keeping the goods in stock in Italy. Goods in bonded warehouses are not considered as imported, *i.e.* they do not qualify as national goods.

## 4. PLACE OF SUPPLY

As already mentioned, VAT applies to supplies of goods and services taking place in Italy. It is therefore necessary to have a clear understanding of the territoriality rules. **8–006**

### Supply of goods

Transactions concerning immovables are deemed to take place in Italy when the immovables at issue are situated in Italy.

As to movables, transactions concerning them are subject to VAT when such movables are physically present in Italy at the moment the relevant transaction takes place. According to wording used by customs legislation, this means that the goods must be national, nationalised (*i.e.* finally imported from abroad) or subject to temporary importation in Italy. Therefore, a supply of goods in view of their exportation is subject to VAT, even if this is a case of exemption with credit, see para. 8–012, "Exemptions".

There is no special rule concerning chain transactions. In fact, every transaction is treated as a single supply according to general rules.

### Supply of services

#### General rule

Services are deemed to be rendered in Italy if the supplier has his domicile (registered office) or a permanent establishment (from which the service is supplied) within the territory of the State.

The following are exceptions to the general rule:

— services connected with immovable property are deemed to be rendered where the property is situated; **8–007**

— services connected with movable tangible property; ancillary transport activities; cultural, artistic, sporting, scientific, educational and entertainment activities are deemed to be rendered where those services are physically carried out;

- services derived from the hiring out of movable tangible property other than means of transport are deemed to be rendered where the relevant asset is used;
- the place where transport services are supplied shall be the place where transport takes place. Only the distance covered in Italy is taxable;
- transfer and assignment of copyrights, patents, licences, trademarks and similar rights; advertising services; services of consultants, engineers, consultancy bureaux, lawyers, accountants and other similar services, as well as data processing and the supply of information, banking, financial and insurance transactions; the supply of staff; the services of agents who act, either in their own name or in the name of the principal to procure for their principal the services referred to under this point; obligations to refrain from pursuing or exercising a business activity or a right referred to above are deemed to be supplied where the recipient has his domicile or a fixed establishment to which the services are supplied; however, the place of supply shall not be Italy if the services provided are used or enjoyed by the recipient outside the EC. If the recipient is a non-entrepreneur established in the EC, the place of supply shall be deemed to be in Italy.

  When the following services are rendered to entities established outside the EC, the place of supply is deemed to be Italy when the effective use and enjoyment take place in Italy. This applies to the transfer and assignments of copyrights, advertising services, banking, financial and insurance transactions, supply of staff, services of agents relating to those services, obligations to refrain from pursuing a business activity or exercising a right. This last rule, referring to the place of effective use or enjoyment, is specific to Italy.
- hiring of forms of transport are deemed to be supplied in Italy:
  - if the recipient is outside the EC and the services are used or enjoyed in Italy;
  - if the supplier is outside the EC and the relevant services are used in Italy.

## Reverse charge mechanism

**8–008** A very important aspect to be considered is how to charge VAT on supplies made by foreign entities who have no permanent establishment in Italy and have not appointed a VAT representative in Italy, see para. 8–002, "Who is taxable?". In this situation, the so-called reverse charge mechanism applies. The Italian resident taxable person must account for the supplies received as if he had made the supply himself. In other words, he replaces the foreign entity. At the same time, he may recover the VAT charged as input tax, according to the general rules, see para. 8–014, "Credit/Refund for input tax". This is achieved by the recipient issuing a so-called "auto" invoice to himself.

# 5. BASIS OF TAXATION

## *Supplies within Italy*

The taxable basis is everything which constitutes the consideration received or to be received by the supplier from the customer (or from a third party) in connection with a certain supply. Such a consideration does not include: 8–009

- price reductions by way of discounts provided for in the relevant invoice;
- packing expenses, when packages must be returned to the supplier;
- late payment interest;
- amounts due by the customer as reimbursement for expenses paid by the supplier in the name and for the account of the former.

When the consideration is denominated in a foreign currency, the exchange rate to be used is that of the date on which the chargeable event has occurred, see para. 8–010, "Chargeable event/Time of payment". When no consideration exists or it is in kind, VAT is assessed on the open market value of the supply.

## *Self-supplies*

In case of self-supplies, the tax basis is the open market value of the goods or services at issue. The taxable event occurs at the moment of appropriation.

## *Imports*

VAT due on import of goods is charged on the value assessed for customs purposes, plus freight costs to the first place of destination in the country, plus customs duties paid on the importation itself. As to the goods that were transferred, before customs clearance, from the importer to another taxable person, the taxable basis is the consideration of the last supply.

## *Chargeable event/Time of payment*

As a general rule, a taxable event occurs: 8–010

- for immovable goods: when the transfer deed is signed;
- for movable goods: when supplied or dispatched;
- for services: when the relevant price (or consideration) is paid;
- for importation: when the goods are released from the customs.

There are a number of exceptions which take into account specific situations (*e.g.* goods to be resold on commission, supplies to the State and other public bodies, situations where delivery does not coincide with the actual transfer of ownership).

In principle, an invoice must be issued when a chargeable event occurs. In any case, if an invoice is issued or the price or an advance payment is received prior to the date of the taxable event, VAT becomes nonetheless due.

The rules governing the issue of invoices are explained in para. 8–016, "Administrative Obligations".

VAT charged to customers is offset against input tax on a monthly basis (see para. 8–018, "Small entrepreneurs". The net balance, if any, must be paid by the 22nd of the month after the one of reference. Note that invoices not yet settled must be taken into account as well.

Regular exporters may be entitled to make purchases without paying VAT either on internal supplies or on imports, see para. 8–012, "Exemption with credit".

### *Credit notes/Bad debts*

If the taxable amount is modified after the issue of the relevant invoice or if the supply is cancelled, a credit note may be issued by the supplier to offset such an invoice and reimburse the customer for VAT paid. The original supplier deducts VAT so reimbursed. When the partial or total annulment of the transaction is due to an agreement entered into after the performance of the original transaction, no credit note can be issued if more than a period of one year has elapsed.

No particular procedure governs the case of uncollectable invoices (bad debts). Even when a credit note can be issued this rarely happens because it could jeopardise the collection of the debt for civil law and income tax reasons.

## 6. TAX RATES

The present rates are as follows:

**8–011** 0%— Strictly speaking, such a rate does not apply in Italy. The same results are however achieved through exemption with credit, see para. 8–012, "Exemptions".

4%— Basic consumption goods such as butter, vegetables, fruits, devices for disabled people, sales of buildings qualifying as "non-luxury immovables" and services relating to their sale.

9%— Other important consumption goods such as meat, oil, coffee, chocolate, textile goods, electricity for certain purposes, medicines, hotel and restaurant services, telephone.

19%— (standard rate) It applies when no specific rate is applicable.

38%— Luxury goods such as platinum, furs, artistic carpets, cars and motorcycles exceeding certain cylinder capacity.

Services relating to the construction of goods and financial leasing are subject to the same rate as applicable to the sale of the goods themselves.

## 7. EXEMPTIONS

### *Exemptions with credit for input tax*

This regime applies to the exportation of goods, the sale of aircraft and ships and so called international services, *i.e.* services related to import-export. **8–012**

It works like the 0 per cent. rate regime in other countries and it is intended to permit the taxation of goods in the country of destination. All the formal VAT requirements must be met but no VAT is charged and input tax is recoverable in full.

The most important international services are as follows:

- transport of goods intended for import or export; leasing of means of transport in order to perform such transport services;
- forwarding agent services with respect to the above mentioned transport;
- loading, unloading, maintenance, handling, storage relating to goods intended for export or import.

In case of imported goods, these services are exempt provided that their cost is included in the tax basis of VAT to be paid on import. Since all these exempt transactions do not bear any tax, the entrepreneur performing them on a regular basis (regular exporter) ends up in a permanent credit position due to input tax paid. The refund of this credit tends to be rather slow in Italy. In order partially to avoid this effect, regular exporters are entitled to obtain their purchases free of VAT, to the extent that the amount of such purchases does not exceed the total exports made during the previous calender year or 12 months, according to the exporter's choice. From the supplier's viewpoint, this is another case of exemption with credit.

### *Exemption without credit for input tax*

Exempt transactions do not bear any VAT. Nonetheless, all the formal requirements provided by the VAT law must be met (for some exceptions see para. 8–020, "Retailers & Banking and Financial Institutions"). Input VAT incurred in connection with these kind of transactions is not recoverable (see para. 8–014, "Credit/refund for input tax").

The most important exempt transactions are as follows:

- the granting and negotiation of credit and financing, including the discounting of bills of exchange and cheques and any dealings in credit guarantees;

- — insurance and reinsurance transactions;
- — transactions concerning currency, bank notes and coins used as legal tender in a foreign country (transactions concerning Italian money as well as those concerning deposits, current accounts and other financial items are non-taxable transactions);
- — transactions (except management and safe keeping), concerning shares, interests in companies, debentures and other securities, excluding documents establishing title to goods;
- — the leasing of immovable property; excluding financial leasing (to which the same rate as for actual negotiation applies), leasing of commercial buildings (*i.e.* which cannot be used as houses: standard rate), leasing of houses performed by real estate companies (4 per cent. rate) and leasing taking place in the context of a business lease (standard rate);
- — many activities performed in the public interest (medical assistance, transactions on human blood, milk or organs, educational services provided by qualified bodies, etc.).

## *Non-taxable transactions*

**8–013** They are:

- — the transactions which would be subject to tax as a consequence of the general definition but nonetheless excluded by a specific provision. With respect to these transactions no VAT obligation exists and they do not affect the deductibility of input tax incurred in conjunction with transactions subject to VAT. In Italy, these non-taxable transactions are also referred to as being outside the scope of VAT. Exempt transactions are considered as within the scope of VAT.
- — the transactions which do not comply with the definition of taxable supplies.

The most important non-taxable transactions are:

- — transfers of currency and credits;
- — transfers of a business as a going concern;
- — contribution of goods in exchange for shares or quotas;
- — transfer of goods in the context of company reorganisations or mergers;
- — transfer of land intended for agriculture;
- — the supply of staff, provided the consideration does not exceed the cost incurred;
- — the supplies of goods with respect to which input tax was not recoverable at the time of purchase because of specific regulations *e.g.* cars and luxury goods, see para. 8–014, "Credit/Refund for input credit";
- — exploitation of copyright by the author.

In many cases, these transactions are subject to registration tax.

**Subsidies/Penalty payments/Compensation**

They are not taxable when they do not represent a consideration for a supply. It may, however, be difficult to determine the exact nature of the payments and professional advice should be obtained in each specific situation.

### *Election to be subject to VAT*

No election can be made to be subject to VAT when an exemption applies.

## 8. CREDIT/REFUND FOR INPUT TAX

### *General rule*

Taxable persons have the right to recover input tax incurred for the purposes of their taxable transactions. This means that input VAT paid in relation to exempt transactions (treated in para. 8–012, "Exemption without credit") cannot be deducted. The same applies to supplies obtained for private consumption or intended to be used for non-commercial purposes. VAT is not recoverable on a number of expenses which are deemed to be usually incurred for private consumptions, *i.e.*: **8–014**

— purchase or import of means of transport intended to be used both for goods and persons provided they are not the object of the primary activity of the taxable person or a primary instrument of that activity; services related to such means of transport at the same condition;
— purchase or import of goods subject to the 38 per cent. rate, unless they are the object of the primary activity of the taxable person; services related to such goods at the same condition. Recovery is in any case disallowed for liberal professions;
— purchase or import of cars and motorcycles intended for personal transport and exceeding a given cylinder capacity, which do not constitute the primary activity of the taxable person, up to 1990; services relating to such goods subject to the same conditions;
— purchase or import of fuels and lubricants in relation to means of transport which do not give title to deduct VAT;
— hotel and restaurant services;
— motorway tolls;
— transport services concerning individuals.

### *Adjustment of entitlement to credit*

Deductible input tax on depreciable assets (whose depreciation rate is lower than 25 per cent.) must be adjusted if, in each of the four years subsequent to the one of purchase, the partial exemption ratio has changed by more than 10 percentage points. The effect of this adjustment is an additional credit or a partial repayment for the year of the adjustment.

## *Partial exemption*

**8–015** Entrepreneurs making both taxable and exempt supplies are entitled to recover input VAT which is attributable to both only for that part which relates to taxable supplies. This is achieved by computing the ratio between the amount of taxable supplies and the amount of total supplies, including exempt transactions and excluding non-taxable transactions. No other criteria are available nor can they be allowed by VAT authorities.

For the purpose of the ratio, exempt transactions do not include occasional exempt supplies (*e.g.*. the sale of shares in a subsidiary by a manufacturing company). The supply of capital goods (*i.e.* depreciable assets) is not included in the turnover and therefore has no impact on the determination of this ratio. The entrepreneur can make an election to compute a separate ratio for each sector of his business, provided that each sector is separately accounted for.

## *Time of recovery*

Input VAT can be recovered when the relevant invoice is accounted for in the VAT books, see para. 8–016, "Administrative obligations". Input VAT on invoices recorded in a given month (or quarterly as the case may be) is offset against VAT charged to customers on invoices recorded in the same period. If the former exceeds the latter, the balance (credit) is carried forward to the next period.

## *Refund for foreign entrepreneurs*

Foreign entrepreneurs without a permanent establishment in Italy do not qualify as taxable persons. Nonetheless, they may incur an input VAT on supplies made to them by a taxable person. To recover such VAT they have two possibilities:

- they may appoint a VAT representative in Italy who will file an annual return and claim the refund according to general rules; or
- they may apply directly to the VAT authorities in Rome. This is only possible for EC residents who have performed no transactions in Italy (apart from exempt international services) and excluding VAT on immovables. The application must be made on a specific form and addressed to:

  VAT office<br>
  Via Tolstoi 5<br>
  00144 Rome.

The original invoices giving rise to the claim must be attached to the form, as well as a certificate from the VAT authorities of the applicant's country confirming that he is a taxable person in that country. The refund may be applied for quarterly or annually. In any case, applications must be received before June 30 of the year following the one for which the refund is required. It is also possible to have the relevant refund remitted abroad to a given bank account of the claimant.

## 9. ADMINISTRATIVE OBLIGATIONS

### *Registration*

Each taxable person must register with the local VAT office and get his own VAT number. This applies also to very small undertakings, since no income or revenue limit exists in Italy. The application must be filed on a specific form within 30 days from the start of the activity. When changes in the data communicated to the VAT authorities occur, the taxable person must inform the authorities within 30 days. **8–016**

### *Books and records*

Supply invoices must be accounted for in a specific book within 15 days of the date of issue. Invoices received from suppliers must also be recorded in another book, before the end of the month following the one of receipt. Taxable persons entitled not to issue invoices must record payments collected in a third book.

All VAT books before they are used must be "validated" by a VAT office or a notary public. All the pages are stamped and numbered and the total number of pages is indicated on the last one. In the absence of these formalities, book entries are void.

### *Invoices*

In principle, each VAT transaction must be documented by an invoice containing the following elements:

- date of issue;
- chronological number;
- identification data of the customer, including VAT number (if any);
- description of the transaction;
- consideration, rate of VAT, VAT amount, total amount. In case of exempt transactions, reference must be made to the specific law provision granting the exemption.

Invoices must be issued when chargeable events occur. As a derogation, a unique invoice can be issued for the supplies of goods of a given month, before the end of the following one, provided that the delivery of the related goods is documented by special transport documents (such as delivery notes) regulated by VAT law.

In some cases (*e.g.*. retailers, banks, insurance companies) the issue of invoices is not compulsory, unless expressly asked for by customers.

Taxable persons, who in the conduct of their business or profession make taxable purchases (either of goods or services) in respect of which the issue of the invoice is compulsory, must take good care to receive such an invoice. If, after four months from the date of the supply, no invoice is received, the customer must go to the competent VAT office within 30 days, pay himself the VAT due (if any) and show two copies of a document which is intended to replace the invoice. One copy of it will be returned by the VAT authorities and will be registered in the customer's books. If an invoice received is not in accordance with the law, the customer must go to the VAT office within 15 days from the date on which the invoice was recorded and pay the additional VAT due (if any). Again, two copies of a document which is intended to replace the invoice must be shown to the VAT office, which will return one copy for the records.

Heavy fines are imposed on customers in cases of non-compliance.

## *VAT returns*

**8–017** VAT returns must be filed annually by March 5 of the year following the one of reference. Nonetheless, VAT is paid on a monthly basis, *i.e.* the net VAT due of a given month is payable by the 22nd of the following one. Where the input VAT exceeds the output VAT the excess is carried forward to the subsequent period. Only the additional VAT (if any, usually due to adjustments of exemption ratio) is paid in connection with the annual return. If an excess of input VAT over output VAT arises, it can be either carried forward or reimbursed. Small undertakings (*i.e.* whose annual turnover is lower than 360 million lire) and liberal professions, can pay VAT on a quarterly basis.

## *Powers of the authorities*

VAT authorities are of course entitled to check that VAT provisions are respected. Should the VAT return not be filed, they can make an estimated assessment. The same applies if the return is not signed, compulsory records have not been kept, or the VAT authorities can give evidence that the taxable person's records are not reliable. Returns filed within 30 days from the due date are considered valid, though penalties for late filing apply; they range from 100,000 lire to 500,000 lire. Should the return be filed within 90 days from the due date, the taxable person avoids criminal penalties but he is subject to the penalties for absence of filing: between two and four times the VAT due for the calendar year. No correction of the annual return can be made. It is only possible to file a new return within the above mentioned term of 30 days after the due date. Input VAT not claimed in the annual return of the year in which it should have been recorded is lost forever. In case of late payment of the balance shown by the annual return, the penalties are 50 per cent. of the amount due, plus the annual 9 per cent. interest. In case of late payment of the periodic amounts, either monthly of quarterly, the penalties go from two to four times the amount due, plus interest.

VAT authorities are entitled to check VAT returns up to four years after the end of the one of reference. They have one more year in case of estimated assessments.

### *Objections/Appeals*

Disputes of any kind are settled before tax courts (Commissioni Tributarie). The claim must be raised within 60 days from the date on which the tax assessment is notified. There are four degrees of judgment. Even if the taxable person challenges the assessment, one-third of the tax assessed must be paid at once. Penalties are imposed only at the end of the whole procedure. Disputes concerning VAT on importations are settled according to customs provisions.

## 10. SPECIAL VAT REGIMES

### *Small entrepreneurs*

Small entrepreneurs are those taxable persons whose total supplies do **8–018**
not exceed 360 million lire in the calendar year prior to the one of reference. Total supplies comprises exempt transactions and excludes non-taxable transactions. Small entrepreneurs are entitled to simpler formalities with regard to the issue of invoices and records. They may also pay VAT on a quarterly basis instead of a monthly basis.

Within the category of small entrepreneurs it is necessary to distinguish the category of minimum entrepreneurs, that is, those entrepreneurs whose total supplies do not exceed 18 million lire in the calendar year prior to the one of reference.

Only individuals, partnerships and non-profit making organisations can be minimum entrepreneurs, while limited companies are excluded. Minimum entrepreneurs may elect to pay VAT on the basis of a given rate applied to taxable supplies.

### *Agricultural enterprises*

The supply of certain agricultural products by the producer is subject to a special regime with respect to the determination of input tax, *i.e.* input tax is computed in such a way as to be in any case equal to VAT charged to customers. VAT due on the purchase of depreciable assets can be recovered to the extent that it exceeds deductible input tax according to the mentioned automatic system.

Agricultural products eligible for that regime are expressly listed. Such a list also comprises some fishing products. For this purpose, agricultural producers are those so defined by the civil code, including most breeders, and certain fishing entrepreneurs, *i.e.* those whose activities are comparable with breeding activities.

Where supplies qualifying for this regime are made in conjunction with non-qualifying supplies, input tax relating to the latter is computed according to the ratio between them and total supplies.

Agricultural producers with very low total supplies (less than 10 million lire) are excluded from all VAT formalities except for the obligation to keep received invoices.

In any case, agricultural producers may elect to compute VAT pursuant to ordinary rules. This election is binding for three years.

## *Travel agencies*

**8–019** A special regime applies for travel and tourist agencies which do not act in the name and for the account of their customers, in which case, the supply is considered as taking place directly between the final supplier and the customer and is regulated by general rules. On the contrary, when travel agencies act in their own name and for the account of their customers, a unique supply of services is taxable if carried out within the EC, while considered as exempt (with credit) otherwise.

The tax basis is the difference between the consideration paid by the customer and the expenses, including VAT, incurred by the third parties to the customer. Special provisions exist for supplies made partly inside and partly outside the EC. Travel agencies cannot deduct VAT on supplies made by third parties to their customers.

Travel agencies do not have to issue an invoice for their services, unless it is expressly asked for by the customer no later than the taxable event. The taxable event is the payment of the consideration or the beginning of the journey, if it happens prior to the payment. In any case, customers are not entitled to deduct VAT paid in connection with such services.

There are specific provisions regulating books and records of travel agencies, as well as the determination of the VAT payments during the year and at the end of the year. A special form must be submitted together with the annual return.

## *Second-hand goods*

They are treated in the same way as newly manufactured goods.

### *Retailers*

They are entitled not to issue invoices, unless expressly asked for by their customers. Some of them must, nonetheless, issue a special fiscal receipt where the tax is not given separate evidence. This applies to restaurants and hotels. **8–020**

Retailers can record payments received, including VAT, in a special book; when goods for sale are subject to different rates, it is necessary to distinguish payments relating to the various goods. Nonetheless, the Ministry of Finance has authorised certain categories of retailers (notably pharmacies and food and dress shops) to record sales without reference to the diverse applicable rates. Total supplies are then attributed to the various rates in the same proportion as purchases. Once the various categories have been determined, output VAT is computed by applying specific ratios to the recorded payments.

### *Banking and financial activities*

Most transactions performed by banking and financial institutions are exempt (without credit). They do not have to issue invoices unless their customers explicity ask for them.

With respect to taxable transactions, these entities may elect to give up their right to recover input VAT. In such a case, their administrative obligations are simplified. This election is binding for three years.

Special VAT provisions apply with respect to the issue of invoices, accounting and VAT payments.

### *Entertainment activities*

With respect to these activities, the VAT tax basis is the same as for entertainment tax and is collected according to the rules governing this latter tax. Input tax is equal to two-thirds of output tax and no obligation exists with respect to issue of invoices, accounting for VAT, or the annual returns. Entertainment entrepreneurs may however elect to be subject to VAT according to the general rules. This election is binding for three years.

### *Free Port areas*

The municipalities of Campione d'Italia and Livigno on the Swiss border, though part of the Italian Republic, are outside the customs border so that the goods brought there from abroad are not considered as imported goods. **8–021**

### *Different activities conducted by the same entity*

Entrepreneurs conducting different activities may elect to account separately for each of these activities. Notice to the VAT office must be given in the annual return concerning the previous year and it is binding for three years. The validity of the election is longer if depreciable assets are purchased with respect to which the adjustment of entitlement to credit applies, see para. 8–014, "Credit/refund for input VAT". Separate accounting is usually adopted when exempt transactions take place together with taxable ones (*e.g.*. banking activity and leasing activity), so that input tax attributable to taxable transactions can be recovered fully. Allocation of input tax among the various activities does not take place according to definite criteria but on a case by case approach. There are certain cases in which separate accounting is compulsory (*e.g.*. agricultural and retailing activities). Supplies of goods and services from a taxable activity to an exempt one (or to an activity with a special regime concerning input tax, like agriculture or entertainment) must take place at the open market value.

# 9. Luxembourg

## 1. GENERAL BACKGROUND

In 1969, the Grand-Duchy of Luxembourg adopted value added tax which replaced cumulative turnover tax with effect from January 1, 1970. The law of February 12, 1979 implemented the Sixth Council Directive which lays down a uniform basis for assessment of value added tax. This law came into force on January 1, 1980. **9–001**

VAT in Luxembourg is administered by the "Administration de l'Enregistrement et des Domaines" and it is known as "taxe sur la valeur ajoutée".

## 2. WHO IS TAXABLE?

### *General*

Any person who carries out independently, in any place, any economic activity, is liable to the tax. **9–002**

Economic activities comprise all activities of producers, traders, persons supplying services, including agriculture, mining activities and activities of the liberal professions. The exploitation of tangible or intangible property for the purpose of obtaining income is also considered an economic activity.

Anyone who carries out on an occasional basis a transaction relating to the activities referred to above is also treated as a taxable person.

The use of the word "independently" excludes employed and other persons from the tax insofar as they are bound to an employer by a contract of employment or by any other legal ties creating the relationship of employer and employee.

Small entrepreneurs whose turnover is less than FLux 200,000 are not liable to VAT. They are, however, required to register for VAT purposes.

#### Transactions with branch/subsidiary

Branches and subsidiaries of foreign companies supplying taxable goods or services in Luxembourg are treated in the same way as other entrepreneurs.

Supplies of goods or services between a subsidiary and the parent company are within the scope of VAT. Transactions between a Luxembourg branch and its foreign head office or vice versa are treated as internal supplies and, therefore, outside the scope of VAT.

### Government bodies

Government bodies are not subject to VAT on their activities of an administrative, social or cultural nature.

However, commercial activities or activities which are deemed to be in competition with other commercial companies are subject to VAT.

## *Fiscal unity/Group taxation*

The concept of fiscal unity does not exist in Luxembourg VAT law. Each taxable person (individual or legal body) must account for the tax independently in the same way as any other taxable person. It is not possible for a group of taxable persons to file joint returns.

### Foreign entrepreneurs

**9–003** Foreign entrepreneurs who have no establishment in Luxembourg are subject to VAT in Luxembourg when they deliver goods in Luxembourg or supply services which are taxable in Luxembourg.

Foreign entrepreneurs are considered as having an establishment, for VAT purposes, if they keep a regular place of activity (office, factory, etc.) in Luxembourg. Non-resident entrepreneurs with an establishment in Luxembourg are treated as local entrepreneurs and comply with all the rules applicable to Luxembourg companies.

### Representative office

Representative offices of foreign entrepreneurs who only carry out activities of a preparatory or an auxiliary nature are not treated as taxable persons. VAT incurred in Luxembourg can be recovered by the foreign entrepreneurs, see para. 9–013, "Refund for foreign entrepreneurs".

### VAT representatives

Foreign entrepreneurs who do not maintain a fixed establishment in Luxembourg but making supplies within Luxembourg which are within the scope of VAT are required to appoint a VAT representative who will be responsible for fulfilling the administrative obligations and for payment of the tax due by the foreign entrepreneur.

### Reverse charge mechanism

The liability for payment of VAT of a non-resident entrepreneur who does not maintain a fixed establishment in Luxembourg will normally fall on the VAT representative referred to above. In the absence of a

VAT representative, the liability is shifted to the recipient of the goods or services.

### Importers

Goods imported into Luxembourg by resident entrepreneurs or by foreign entrepreneurs with a fixed establishment in Luxembourg are liable to VAT. The tax is not due until the next VAT return has to be filed and it can be recovered by taxable entrepreneurs.

This rule applies also to foreign entrepreneurs who do not have a fixed establishment in Luxembourg if they can prove that they are registered in Luxembourg and if the customs documents show that they are the recipient of the goods.

Goods imported into Luxembourg by persons who are not registered for VAT purposes are liable to VAT at customs clearance.

## 3. WHAT IS TAXABLE?

VAT is levied on the supply of goods and services in Luxembourg and on importation of goods. **9–004**

### Supply of goods

The term "supply" means the transfer of the right to dispose of tangible property as owner. Generally, the transfer is effected by sale. The remittance of goods is also treated as a supply.

The term "goods" applies to all tangible movable properties. Utilities such as electricity, gas, heat and similar intangibles qualify as goods.

Land and buildings are not subject to VAT, see para. 9–016, "Real estate".

### Supply of services

The term "services" applies to all transactions which are not treated as a supply of goods.

The transfer of intangible properties such as patents, know-how, software, etc., is considered as a supply of services.

Services also include:

- leasing, renting;
- transport of persons and goods;
- commissions;
- research and expertise;
- agreements to refrain from certain activities.

### *Self-supply of goods/services*

A taxable self-supply of goods is deemed to arise if:

- goods acquired in the course of a business and giving rise to an input tax credit are used for non-business purposes;
- goods are extracted, manufactured, built or transformed by the entrepreneur himself for the use of his business. A self-supply also arises if the manufacturing, building or transformation is carried out by a third party at the request of the entrepreneur.

The rule of taxable self-supply intends to avoid distortion of competition caused by the fact that otherwise an entrepreneur making exempt supplies would make a saving by not paying non-deductible VAT if he manufactured certain goods himself instead of acquiring them from third parties.

Self-supply of services is normally not deemed to constitute a taxable supply.

### *Imports of goods*

This is the introduction of goods into Luxembourg. In limited cases, the importation of goods into Luxembourg is exempt from VAT, see para. 9–010, "Exemptions with credit for input tax".

Goods imported into bonded warehouses are not subject to VAT until they are removed for sale, see para. 9–016, "Bonded warehouses".

## 4. PLACE OF SUPPLY

**9–005** VAT is chargeable in Luxembourg only when goods and services are supplied or deemed to be supplied in Luxembourg.

### *Supply of goods*

Where the goods are to be transported:

- the goods to be delivered are in Luxembourg before transportation: the supply is taxable in Luxembourg with the exception of export sales;
- the goods to be delivered are abroad before transportation: the supply is not subject to VAT in Luxembourg. However, VAT is nevertheless due on importation at the point of importation and payable by the importer or by the final customer in Luxembourg.

Where the goods are not transported:

- the supply is taxable in Luxembourg if the goods are in Luxembourg at the time of delivery or transfer of ownership.

Assembly or installation of goods in Luxembourg before they are delivered is also taxable in Luxembourg.

## *Supply of services*

### General rule

Services are normally considered to be supplied at the place where the entrepreneur supplying the services is established or has a fixed basis from which the services are supplied.

### Exceptions

There are a few exceptions to the general rule:

- services connected with real estate (real estate agents, architects, etc.) are supplied where the real estate is situated. **9–006**
- transport of goods and persons is subject to VAT where it effectively takes place; thus, only transport within Luxembourg is subject to VAT.
- the place of supply of the following services is deemed to be where they are physically carried out:
  - cultural, artistic, sporting, scientific, educational and entertainment services;
  - ancillary transport activities, such as loading, unloading, handling and similar activities;
  - valuations of movable tangible property;
  - work on movable tangible property.
- the following services are deemed to be supplied at the recipient's place of business if he is a registered entrepreneur;
  - transfers and assignment of trademarks, licences, copyrights, patents;
  - advertising services;
  - services of consultants, engineers, accountants;
  - data processing and supply of information;
  - financial, banking and insurance services;
  - supply of staff;
  - hire of movable property (except the hire of means of transport);
  - accepting to refrain from carrying out an activity or exercising rights;

### Reverse charge mechanism

The liability for payment of VAT of a non-resident entrepreneur who does not maintain a fixed establishment in Luxembourg will normally fall on the VAT representative. In the absence of a VAT representative, the liability is shifted to the recipient of the goods or services.

## 5. BASIS OF TAXATION

### *Supplies within Luxembourg*

9–007 VAT is calculated on the total price charged for the supply of the goods or services. Ancillary expenses, commissions, wrapping expenses, interest relating to the supply, customs duties are part of the acquisition price. If the total price is not expressed in currency, VAT is charged on the total value of the consideration.

If a larger amount is received than invoiced, VAT is payable on the amount received.

### *Self-supplies*

VAT due on self-supplies is calculated on the basis of the purchase price of the goods or on the cost of the supplies. In the case of goods manufactured by an entrepreneur for his own business, the cost will include the value of the raw materials, the services obtained for the manufacturing and the salary expenses if the work was carried out by the entrepreneur's own staff.

Self-supply of services is not a taxable transaction.

### *Imports*

On the importation of goods, VAT is calculated on the higher of the amount charged to the recipient or its value for import duty purposes. This amount includes freight charges, taxes and other duties, except VAT.

### *Chargeable event/Time of payment*

9–008 VAT becomes due at the time the goods are supplied or the services are rendered or when goods are imported into Luxembourg.

The tax payable falls due on the 15th day of the month after the end of the tax period and must be remitted together with the VAT return, see para. 9–015, "VAT return".

The tax is payable even when the invoice has not yet been paid.

An entrepreneur regularly importing goods into Luxembourg can defer payment until the moment he has to file his periodic VAT return. In the same return he can claim a credit for the tax, see para. 9–003, "Importers".

The liability for VAT is generally linked with the issuance of the invoice. In principle, invoices are to be issued, at the latest, by the 25th day after the end of the month in which the supply was made. Each entrepreneur is obliged to issue an invoice for supplies made to another entrepreneur.

Certain entrepreneurs can account for VAT on a cash basis. In such cases, VAT is payable or recoverable at the time the consideration for the supply is actually received or paid.

### *Credit notes/Bad debts*

If an entrepreneur gives a credit, he is allowed to claim a refund of VAT, provided a credit note is issued to the customer.

When payment is not obtained from a customer, the output VAT paid on the supply can normally be recovered by the supplier.

## 6. TAX RATES

The following rates are applicable under Luxembourg VAT law: **9–009**

0%— see para. 9–010, "Exemptions with credit";

3%— The annual budgetary laws since 1972 provide a rate of 3%, which is not officially contained within the law itself and, therefore, subject to removal each year. This rate applies to certain goods considered as essential (*e.g.*, certain foods, pharmaceutical products, etc.);

6%— This reduced rate applies mainly to food, agricultural and fish products, electricity, gas, books, transport of persons, lodging, hotel accommodation, advertising, advisory and similar services (*e.g.*, lawyers and accountants);

12%— The standard rate is applicable to all supplies of goods and services not subject to another specified rate.

## 7. EXEMPTIONS

### *Exemptions with credit for input tax*

The main exemptions are: **9–010**

- goods transported out of Luxembourg by a resident or non-resident entrepreneur;
- delivery of goods to be placed under customs duty suspensions;
- services connected with goods under customs duty suspensions, such as transport, handling and wrapping;

— work, repairs performed for the account of a foreign client, on goods to be exported;
— services connected with imports of goods, the cost of which is already included in the taxable basis of the goods imported;
— sale and hire of ships and aircraft engaged in international trade or professional fishing;
— repair, transformation, maintenance performed on ships and aircraft engaged in international trade or professional fishing;
— international transport of persons or goods.

Certain exemptions apply for the import of goods, including personal effects of travellers, goods imported by diplomats, household contents of persons moving into Luxembourg and certain goods to be imported temporarily.

## *Exemptions without credit for input tax*

An entrepreneur engaged in exempt activities is not permitted to charge VAT and is not entitled to a credit for VAT incurred on expenditure made in connection with those activities.

The main exemptions are:

— medical care or services provided by hospitals, doctors, dentists, laboratories;
— transactions on human blood, milk or organs;
— social and cultural services;
— educational services provided by schools and universities;
— public postal, telephone and telegraph services;
— insurance and reinsurance transactions (input VAT may be recovered in certain cases);
— financial and banking services (input VAT may be recovered in certain cases);
— supply and leasing of real property (for exceptions see para. 9–017, "Transfer and rental of buildings");
— supply of gold, silver;
— transactions of shares.

## *Non-taxable transactions*

### Transactions within the same legal entity

**9–011** Supplies within the same VAT entity are considered to be outside the scope of VAT, see para. 9–002, "Branch/subsidiary".

### Transfer of business

Transfer of a business or an independent part thereof is not subject to VAT provided the transferee continues to use the assets in carrying on the business.

This exemption does not prevent the recovery of the input VAT paid on other services related to the transfer of the business.

### Subsidies/Penalty payments/Compensation

Subsidies are subject to VAT when the payments:

- constitute in fact the consideration for supplies by the recipient; or
- are directly connected with the price of the supplies made.

Subsidies are not subject to VAT when the payments provided by the government are not directly connected with the price of the supplies made.

Penalty payments arising from taxable transactions are generally subject to VAT.

Payments of compensation normally are not within the scope of VAT since these payments are not made as a consideration for a supply.

## *Election to be subject to VAT*

Entrepreneurs making certain exempt supplies may elect to be subject to VAT. Election will enable them to charge VAT and to recover the input tax relating to these supplies.

Election is possible for:

- agricultural and forestry enterprises;
- supply and leasing of real property.

# 8. CREDIT FOR INPUT TAX

## *General rule*

Generally, all the VAT paid on goods and services by a Luxembourg entrepreneur within the course of business is recoverable. **9–012**

No credit is granted for input tax on:

- goods and services used for non-business purposes;
- goods and services used for exempt transactions, with the exception of input tax related to exempt banking and financial and insurance transactions, provided the recipient of these services is established outside the EEC;
- expenditure for private purposes (*e.g.*, hotel accommodation, travel and restaurant expenses, expenses for food, for goods and services for maintaining a private lifestyle or for other private purposes).

## Adjustment of entitlement to credit

Throughout a period of four book years for movable depreciable goods and nine book years for immovable goods following the year of purchase, the entitlement to a credit for input tax may be adjusted on a *pro rata* basis, depending on whether the use of the goods changes from use for exempt transactions to the use for taxable transactions and vice versa.

## Partial exemption

An entrepreneur making taxable and exempt supplies is allowed to recover only the input tax relating to the taxable supplies.

If goods or services can be attributed to being used for taxable supplies, the credit for input VAT will be fully allowed. If the attribution is made to exempt supplies, it will be totally disallowed.

If the goods or services are used for taxable and exempt supplies, the creditable input tax is calculated in the ratio of the turnover of supplies entitled to credit to the total turnover.

The ratio is established according to the available data at the time the entrepreneur started to use the goods or services. In the final VAT return of the year, an adjustment for creditable input tax must be made according to the information available for the entire year.

On request, the entrepreneur may be allowed to use another ratio, if this gives a fairer split (*e.g.*, actual use of the purchased goods).

The tax authorities may also oblige the entrepreneur to use a ratio other than the turnover ratio.

## Time of recovery

**9–013** A credit for input tax can be claimed in the VAT return for the tax period (calendar year, quarter or month) during which the supplier made the supplies. If the VAT credit is higher than the VAT liability, the tax credit will be repaid and carried forward if the credit amount is less than FLux 50,000.

## Refund for foreign entrepreneurs

Foreign entrepreneurs not established in Luxembourg and who do not supply goods or services in Luxembourg may obtain a refund of VAT paid on goods or services purchased in Luxembourg.

Claims for refund must be requested on a form addressed to:

Administration de l'Enregistrement et des Domaines
Boîte postale 1004
L—1010 LUXEMBOURG

The claims must be filed within 6 months following the end of the calendar year during which VAT was incurred in Luxembourg.

The claim must be accompanied by the original invoices and a certificate confirming the status as a taxable person issued by the tax authorities of the EC Member State where the applicant is established.

Entrepreneurs resident outside the EC must prove that they are considered as an entrepreneur according to Luxembourg VAT law.

## 9. ADMINISTRATIVE OBLIGATIONS

### *Registration*

An entrepreneur engaged in an industrial, commercial or professional activity must register with the VAT authorities as soon as the activities begin. **9–014**

### *Books and records*

An entrepreneur is obliged to keep accounts in sufficient detail to permit application of the VAT and inspection by the tax authority. The records must be kept for a period of 10 years.

### *Invoices*

In principle, invoices are to be issued for each supply to another entrepreneur before the 25th day following the end of the month in which the supply was made.

All invoices must contain the following information:

— name and address of the purchaser;
— price of the goods or services excluding VAT;
— rate of the tax and the corresponding VAT due.

Other information required by commercial law:

— supplier's name or corporate name;
— form of the company;
— address;
— registration number;
— share capital;
— date of the invoice;
— description of the supply.

### *VAT returns*

An entrepreneur is obliged to file a monthly, quarterly or annual tax return before the 15th day of the month after the end of the taxation period depending on the annual turnover. **9–015**

**Annual turnover without tax**

| | |
|---|---|
| FLux 1— 600,000 | tax return (annual)<br>payment (annual) |
| FLux 600,001— 1,800,000 | tax return (annual)<br>payment (quarterly) |
| FLux 1,800,001— 6,000,000 | tax return (quarterly)<br>payment (quarterly) |
| FLux 6,000,001—18,000,000 | tax return (quarterly)<br>payment (monthly) |
| FLux >18,000,000 | tax return (monthly)<br>payment (monthly) |

A final annual tax return must be filed before May 31 following the end of the year.

An entrepreneur who has not filed monthly or quarterly tax returns must file his final tax return before March 31 following the end of the year.

### *Powers of authority*

If a tax return is not filed after expiration of the time limit for submission, the tax authorities may issue an assessment for an estimated amount. Penalties of FLux 1,000–50,000 may be fixed.

Penalties for late payment may not exceed 10 per cent. of the tax due.

The statute of limitations is five years from the end of the calendar year in which the VAT liability arose.

### *Objections/Appeal*

An appeal against an assessment of tax must be lodged within three months of receipt of the notice of assessment.

Further appeals are possible within three months to the District Court and to the Supreme Court (Conseil d'Etat).

## 10. SPECIAL VAT REGIMES

**9–016** Special VAT rules apply to a number of activities as in the following examples.

**Agricultural and forestry enterprises**

Agricultural and forestry enterprises are excluded entirely from VAT. They are not entitled to a credit for input tax. An option to be taxed as a normal entrepreneur can, however, be made.

### Banking and financial institutions

Most of the activities of these institutions are exempt from VAT. In practice some activities which are taxed permit them to obtain a relatively low tax credit.

### Small enterprises

Entrepreneurs whose annual turnover is less than FLux 200,000 are not subject to VAT, see para. 9–002, "General".

Special tax reductions are given to other small entrepreneurs whose annual turnover is less than FLux 1,000,000.

### Bonded warehouses

Goods imported into bonded warehouses are not subject to VAT and customs duty until they are removed for sale in the EC. Imports of goods into a bonded warehouse are subject to the prior approval of the customs authorities.

### Travel agencies

Special rules apply to activities carried out by travel agencies.

### Real estate

*Land*

The acquisition of land is not subject to VAT but to a transfer duty at **9–017** a rate of approximately 10 per cent. of the acquisition price.

### Transfer of buildings

*Before construction*

The acquisition of a building before its construction is subject to VAT. The rate is 12 per cent. of the acquisition price.

*During construction*

The acquisition of a building during its construction is subject to:

- transfer duty at a rate of about 10 per cent. for the finished part;
- VAT at a rate of 12 per cent. for the part that is not yet finished.

*After completion*

The transfer of a building after completion is subject to transfer duty at a rate of approximately 10 per cent. of the total price.

An entrepreneur purchasing a building for business purposes may obtain refund of VAT.

## Rental of buildings

### *Residential buildings*

Rental income of a residential building is not subject to VAT.

### *Buildings used for business purposes*

Rental income of these buildings is normally not subject to VAT. However, the lessor and lessee may opt for a taxable lease by filing a joint request.

If the lessor does not opt for a taxable lease, refund of the input tax is not allowed.

# 10. The Netherlands

## 1. GENERAL BACKGROUND

A general indirect tax on consumption, "Value Added Tax" (VAT), in Dutch "Belasting over Toegevoegde Waarde" (B.T.W.), was imposed as of January 1, 1969. Following EC tax harmonisation, the VAT Act has been amended to comply with the Sixth EC Directive, since January 1, 1979. **10–001**

VAT is levied on entrepreneurs on the supply of goods and services in the Netherlands and generally, on the import of goods. The Netherlands means the Kingdom in Europe, thus not including the overseas territories of the Netherlands Antilles.

VAT is administered by the various Value Added Tax Inspectors throughout the country in as far as the tax is not levied on importation. VAT due on importation is dealt with by the Inspectorate of Customs and Excise.

## 2. WHO IS TAXABLE?

### *General*

An entrepreneur supplying goods and services within the Netherlands is liable to the tax. This is "anyone who conducts a trade or business (or a liberal profession) independently." A profit motive, however, is not necessary. Persons making supplies exclusively free of charge do not qualify as entrepreneurs. Generally, a person who makes an occasional transaction is not deemed an entrepreneur liable to VAT. Also, an employee is not a taxable person for VAT purposes. **10–002**

A "trade or business" includes the exploitation of tangible or intangible goods (*e.g.* copyrights, patents, trademarks, etc.) in order to derive income from them on a regular basis.

The taxable person is determined by economic and social considerations rather than legal concepts. The entrepreneur can be a resident or non-resident, an individual, an association of individuals (*e.g.* a partnership), a legal person, a combination of legal persons or any other economic entity.

Registration is required as soon as the definition of entrepreneur is satisfied. There is no monetary limit below which VAT is not chargeable.

### Transactions with branch/subsidiary

Branches and subsidiaries of foreign companies from which supplies of goods and services are made in the Netherlands are treated in the same way as other entrepreneurs. Crossborder supplies between a subsidiary and the parent company abroad or vice versa are within the scope of VAT.

Crossborder supplies between a branch and its foreign head office or vice versa are, however, outside the scope of VAT and thus not taxable, since these are internal transactions within the same VAT entity.

### Government bodies

Public entities such as the State and municipalities may also be subject to VAT. These entities may, in fact, act in three different capacities, *i.e.* as "government", non-entrepreneur or entrepreneur. When fulfilling a governmental function (*i.e.* which they are required to perform by public law) these entities do not act as entrepreneur. Public entities making supplies can be deemed to qualify as entrepreneurs with respect to certain supplies which may distort competition with commercial enterprises.

## *Fiscal unity/Group taxation*

**10–003** The requirements for a fiscal unity are different for VAT purposes and corporate tax purposes.

Two or more Dutch resident entrepreneurs or fixed establishments constitute a fiscal unity for VAT purposes, if they are so closely integrated by financial, organisational and economical links, that they form one single taxable entity. This is determined on the facts and circumstances. In order to be recognised as such, a formal decision from the tax inspector is, however, required. Entrepreneurs can also request such a decision. The fiscal unity will have consequences from the first day of the month following the tax inspector's decision.

All members of the fiscal unity are normally registered under the name and number of the representative member of the group. One single VAT return is filed by the representative member. Fiscal unities for VAT and corporate tax purposes do not have to have the same members.

Internal transactions between members of a fiscal unity are disregarded for VAT purposes. In particular, when (partly) exempt entities are part of a fiscal unity, this creates an advantage where it prevents incurring irrecoverable VAT on charges for internal transactions, in proportion to the extent the fiscal unity as a whole is engaged in taxable transactions. Special care must also be taken with reorganisations, which may result in breaking up the fiscal unity.

A disadvantage of the fiscal unity is that each member of the fiscal unity is jointly and severally liable for the VAT due by the fiscal unity, irrespective of by whom the liability arose. Should, due to changing facts and circumstances, the requirements for a fiscal unity no longer be met, then the entrepreneur will have to inform the tax inspector. If he is not notified, the several liability for each of the previous members of the fiscal unity will continue.

## *Foreign entrepreneurs*

Non-Dutch entrepreneurs become liable to VAT when supplying goods and services within the Netherlands in the course of their business, even if no fixed establishment is maintained in the Netherlands.

If the foreign entrepreneur has a fixed establishment in the Netherlands from which supplies to third parties are made (*e.g.*, workshop, a plant, sales office, central depot), it is treated as a domestic entrepreneur. Registration requirements apply as for Dutch entrepreneurs.

Note that the concept of fixed establishment for VAT purposes is not the same as that of the permanent establishment known for corporate and income tax purposes. It is normally required that supplies are made from the fixed establishment in order to be recognised as such for VAT purposes.

### Representative offices

Representative and information offices of foreign entrepreneurs, **10–004**
through which only activities of a preparatory or auxiliary nature are performed, do not normally qualify as fixed establishments for VAT purposes. The same generally applies for branches taxed on a cost-plus basis for corporate tax purposes. As a consequence, the Dutch VAT incurred will have to be recovered under the "mutual recovery procedure", see para. 10–015, "Refund for foreign entrepreneurs" instead of the normal procedure of claiming a credit when filing the quarterly or monthly VAT returns.

### VAT representatives

Foreign entrepreneurs making supplies within the Netherlands but who do not maintain a fixed establishment here from where the supplies are made, do not have to employ a tax representative or appoint someone who is severally and jointly liable for the tax.

### Reverse charge mechanism

If no fixed establishment exists, a special provision (see para. 10–008, "Reverse charge mechanism") shifts the VAT liability for its transactions, for both the supply of goods and services, from the foreign entrepreneur to the Dutch resident recipient, provided the latter is an entrepreneur or an entity according to the General Act on Taxation. Registration by the foreign entrepreneur is then not required.

This reverse charge mechanism does not apply if the recipient of the goods and services is a non-resident entrepreneur who does not maintain a fixed establishment in the Netherlands or is a non-entrepreneur not qualifying as an entity under the General Act on Taxation (*e.g.* an individual person). In that case, VAT is still due and payable to the tax authorities by the foreign entrepreneur. Registration with the Inspectorate of Customs and Excise in Rijswijk is then compulsory.

Note that contrary to most other EC countries this reverse charge mechanism in the Netherlands is not restricted to certain specific services.

### *Importers*

When goods are brought into the Netherlands and cleared by customs a VAT liability arises. VAT due must be paid by the importer (entrepreneur or private individual) in the same way as if it were an import duty, before the goods are released by the customs authorities. For resident entrepreneurs and foreign entrepreneurs with a fixed establishment in the Netherlands who regularly import goods, a deferral scheme (postponed accounting system) may defer the VAT becoming due until the next VAT return must be filed, see para. 10–015, "Time of payment".

Note that it is not necessary to actually own the goods in order to declare them for importation. It is not uncommon that the goods are imported by an authorised (forwarding) agent, who will report the VAT due on importation. These amounts are subsequently charged through to his customer, who may credit this VAT as input VAT.

## 3. WHAT IS TAXABLE?

**10–005** VAT is levied on the supply of goods and services in The Netherlands and the importation of goods. The distinction between a supply of goods or services is important, because of the different rules governing the time and place of supply. It may decide whether the supply is taxable or not and the applicable VAT rate.

### *Supply of goods*

Generally, a supply includes any transaction resulting in a transfer of title or possession of goods which then cease to form part of an entrepreneur's business assets. As well as an outright sale of goods (including sale through a commission agent or by auction), this includes, for example:

— the handing over under a hire-purchase, conditional sale or credit-sale agreement;

— the handing over by a manufacturer who produces goods from materials provided by the customer;
— the transfer of goods under an agreement to install or incorporate them into other goods.

All tangible goods qualify as goods. Electricity, gas, heat, cold and similar intangibles are deemed to be tangible goods.

The establishment, transfer, amendment, and cessation of rights *in rem* to real property (with the exception of mortgages, and ground rents) are also considered to be a supply of goods.

## Supply of services

For VAT purposes a service is any transaction for consideration which does not otherwise qualify as a supply of goods. When there is no consideration, the service is not taxable. Services include:

— the outright transfer of rights, such as patent rights, trademarks, licences, securities etc.;
— providing of management, staff hire, the leasing of goods, granting (sub) licences;
— agreements to refrain from certain activities or to tolerate activities of others.

If the service is rendered as a gift, the related input VAT may be disallowed, see para. 10–014, "Credit—General rule".

## Self-supply of goods/services

VAT is normally not charged on self-supplies. However, a taxable **10–006**
supply of goods is deemed to arise if:

— goods are produced or acquired in the course of business and are appropriated permanently for other than business purposes (*e.g.*, personal use);
— goods are manufactured within the enterprise and used for business purposes, but only if the entrepreneur is not or only partially, entitled to a credit for the input tax had he purchased the goods instead of manufacturing them.

The latter provision aims at avoiding distortion of competition caused by the fact that otherwise an entrepreneur making *e.g.* exempt supplies (and thus not entitled to a credit for input tax) would save in not paying non-deductible VAT by manufacturing goods in-house instead of acquiring them from third parties. For example, a builder who himself builds houses which are subsequently rented out free of VAT.

Goods produced by a third person, upon request of the entrepreneur, from goods belonging to that entrepreneur, are deemed to be goods manufactured in the entrepreneur's own enterprise. Land also qualifies as "goods" for this purpose.

Although the VAT Act enables the Ministry of Finance to prescribe similar rules for the self-supply of services, no such order has, as yet, been made. Consequently, the self-supply of services is not taxable.

Donations of goods and services for business purposes (*i.e.* gifts) are not liable to VAT. However, in some cases the credit for related input VAT may be disallowed, see para. 10–014, "Credit—General rule".

## *Imports of goods*

"Importation of goods" is the introduction of goods into free circulation in the Netherlands. Importation is a taxable event unless exempt (see para. 10–012, "Exemptions with credit for input tax"), irrespective of whether the importer is a private individual or an entrepreneur. Payment of VAT may be deferred by provisionally storing the goods in a bonded warehouse, see para. 10–019, "Free port/Bonded warehouse".

The input VAT due at importation can be credited by the person for whom the goods are destined (*i.e.* the addressee). The entitlement to the credit must, however, be evidenced with proper documentation.

# 4. PLACE OF SUPPLY

**10–007** It is essential to determine the place of supply since VAT is imposed only when goods and services are supplied or deemed to be supplied in The Netherlands.

## *Supply of goods*

The place at which a supply is deemed to take place is:

— if the goods are transported in connection with the supply, the place where such transport begins;

— in other cases, the place where the goods are at the time of the supply.

Assembly, installation and incorporation of goods into other goods in the Netherlands is taxable in the Netherlands, irrespective of their transportation from abroad.

### Chain transactions

A special rule applies if several entrepreneurs enter into subsequent transactions involving the same goods (chain transactions). Then each entrepreneur within the chain is deemed to have made a taxable supply, even if the actual ownership is transferred directly from the first entrepreneur to the last recipient in the chain. When these transactions involve transportation of the goods from a place outside the Netherlands to a place within the Netherlands, all transactions are deemed to be in the Netherlands and thus subject to Dutch VAT. A 0 per cent. rate applies to the transactions preceding the supply made by the actual importer.

## *Supply of services*

### General rule

Services are normally considered to be supplied where the entrepreneur supplying the services is established or has a fixed establishment from which the services are supplied. There are, however, various exceptions. **10–008**

### Exceptions

There are a number of exceptions to the general rule:

— services with respect to real estate (real estate agents, architects, etc.) are supplied where the real estate is situated;

— transport of goods and persons takes place where the actual transport occurs. Only the transport within Dutch territory is subject to Dutch VAT (transport of goods for export or to the place of destination after importation qualifies for the 0 per cent. rate);

— services consisting of cultural, artistic, sportive, scientific, educational, entertainment or similar activities are supplied where the activity is physically carried out. This rule also applies to services consisting of loading, unloading or similar activities in connection with transport and to services supplied with respect to tangible movable goods, including examination by experts;

— transfer and assignment of copyrights, patents, licences, etc.; advertising; advisory and similar services (*e.g.*, lawyers, accountants), as well as data processing and supply of information; the leasing of tangible movable goods with the exception of means of transport (to which the general rule applies); banking, financial and insurance services, secondment of personnel, and the obligation to refrain, partly or fully, from pursuing a professional activity or from a transfer or assignment of copyrights, patents, etc., are all supplied where the recipient of the services resides, provided he qualifies as entrepreneur or is resident outside the EC territory.

### Reverse charge mechanism

If a foreign entrepreneur does not maintain a fixed establishment in the Netherlands, the tax liability for both the supply of goods and services shifts from the foreign entrepreneur to the Dutch resident recipient, provided he qualifies as entrepreneur or is an entity according to the General Act on Taxation. Consequently, the tax liability of the foreign entrepreneur is not shifted to the recipient if the latter is a Dutch individual person.

This specific provision avoids problems connected with the Dutch tax authorities having to maintain administrative and financial connections with foreign entrepreneurs who have no fiscal presence in the Netherlands. Under this so-called reverse charge mechanism, the Dutch resident entrepreneur must account for the supplies as if it had made the supply itself. At the same time it may recover the VAT due in full as input tax. As a result, no VAT is actually payable, unless the Dutch resident entrepreneur is (partially) exempt.

## 5. BASIS OF TAXATION

### *Supplies within the Netherlands*

**10–009** VAT is calculated on the total amount charged. If this amount is not expressed in currency, VAT is charged on the total value of the consideration. If a larger amount is received than invoiced, VAT is payable on the amount actually received.

Some amounts are excluded from the tax basis, *e.g.* cash discounts, certain incidental charges, such as itemised insurance costs which the entrepreneur supplying the goods pays to another entrepreneur and certain transitory amounts, import duties and other taxes paid on behalf of the recipient.

When goods are traded in exchange for other goods of the same kind, the tax is calculated only on the difference between the selling price of the "new" goods and the trade-in value of the "old" goods.

### *Self-supplies*

For the self-supply transactions and the permanent appropriation of goods produced or acquired in the course of business for non-business purposes (see para. 10–006, "Self-supplies of goods and services"), the basis of taxation is the present cost of purchasing or producing the goods, *i.e.*, the price, exclusive of VAT, for which the goods can be acquired or the costs of manufacturing, including overhead but excluding fixed general costs, interest and profit mark-up. Note that self-supply of services is not a taxable transaction.

### *Imports*

On the importation of goods, VAT is calculated on the higher of the amount charged to the recipient or the goods' value for import duty purposes. This amount is inclusive of freight costs to the destination, taxes and other levies, but exclusive of VAT due at import.

## Chargeable event/Time of payment

Generally, the VAT becomes due at the time the goods are supplied or the services are rendered or when goods are imported into the Netherlands. **10–010**

The tax payable falls due one month after the end of the taxation period and must be remitted together with the VAT return.

Note that the tax is payable even if the customer has not yet paid the invoice. When VAT is accounted for on a cash basis, the tax is only payable in as far as the consideration was received.

Where VAT arises on goods on import, the tax must normally be paid before the goods are released by the customs authorities. However, a resident entrepreneur regularly importing goods can defer payment until the moment he has to file his periodic VAT return. In the same return he can normally claim a credit for the tax. This deferral scheme ("postponed accounting system") thus avoids any cash flow problems. This so-called "verleggingsregeling" will be granted together with a special VAT code number by the tax inspector upon request.

Non-resident entrepreneurs who maintain no fixed establishment in the Netherlands do not have this possibility of deferral, unless they import specifically designated goods, mainly raw materials and non-consumables. Therefore, they will normally have to pay the VAT on importation and subsequently set off this amount in a domestic return or request a refund at the Inspectorate for foreign entrepreneurs in Rijswijk. Payment of VAT may, however, be deferred by provisionally storing the goods in a customs warehouse.

## Cash/Invoice basis

The liability for VAT is normally linked with the issuance of the invoice. Invoices are to be issued before the 15th day after the month in which the supply was made. An entrepreneur is obliged to issue an invoice for supplies made to other entrepreneurs. No invoice is required for supplies made to non-entrepreneurs.

Certain designated entrepreneurs (generally retailers, etc.) can account for VAT on a cash basis. VAT then becomes due at the time the consideration for the supply is actually received. Note, however, that even when VAT is accounted for on a cash basis, invoices need to be issued for supplies made to entrepreneurs.

## Credit notes/Bad debts

Entrepreneurs accounting for VAT on the invoice basis who do not receive or only partially receive payment, or to whom the consideration was repaid because a discount was given, or the goods were returned, can have their VAT liability adjusted on application. The application must be filed with the tax inspector together with the normal VAT return, over the period in which the entitlement to refund arises. Note that it is generally not allowed to set off this amount against the VAT due. Proof that the amount will not or cannot be paid by the customer must, however, be provided. Entrepreneurs accounting for VAT on a cash basis automatically obtain bad debt relief.

If the entrepreneur gives a credit, he is also allowed to claim a refund of VAT provided a credit note is issued to the customer. The customer, in turn, must repay to the tax authorities the VAT stated on the credit note in his next VAT return.

## 6. TAX RATES

The present rates are as follows:

**10–011** 0%— The zero rate in The Netherlands, specifically mentioned in the VAT Act, is a technical zero rate which works as an exemption with credit (see para. 10–012, "Exemptions with credit for input tax") for the exportation of goods and services related to export and import, *e.g.* the supply of goods from outside the Netherlands which are not (yet) imported; goods exported; sea-going vessels and aircraft used in international transport; services rendered in connection with the supplies referred to above, such as loading, unloading and repair of sea-going vessels; transport of imported goods to their place of destination; international passenger transport by sea-going vessels and aircraft.

6%— In general, supplies subject to the reduced rate are basic primary necessities (*e.g.* all foodstuffs), medical goods (medicines, medical aids), cultural goods (books, paintings), goods and services for use by the agricultural sector and certain other supplies, such as passenger transport, and hotel accommodation.

18.5%— All supplies of goods and services not exempt or subject to the reduced rates of 6 per cent. or 0 per cent.

## 7. EXEMPTIONS

### *Exemptions with credit for input tax*

**10–012** Generally no credit for input VAT is available for exempt supplies. However, an exception applies for Dutch input VAT incurred in connection with exempt banking, financial and insurance transactions, provided the recipient of these services is resident or established outside the EC territory. Also, the zero rate (see para. 10–011, "Tax rates") referred to above works as an exemption with credit.

Exemptions may furthermore apply for the importation of goods, *e.g.*, personal effects of travellers; goods imported by diplomats; packing containers and means of transport which will be re-exported; certain goods for educational institutions; household contents of persons moving into the Netherlands; certain goods to be imported temporarily; goods re-imported after having been repaired abroad.

## *Exemptions without credit for input tax*

An entrepreneur engaged in exempt activities is not permitted to charge VAT. Moreover, he is not entitled to a credit for VAT incurred on expenditure made in connection with these activities. The main exemptions are:

- supply and leasing of real property, with certain exceptions (see paras. 10–020 and 10–021, "Supply and rental of real property");
- certain supplies of goods and services in the medical, social and cultural areas (such as those provided by doctors, hospitals, youth organisations, museums, etc.);
- insurance, financial and banking transactions (with some exceptions, see above);
- non-commercial activities of public radio and television broadcast organisations. Television commercials are, however taxable;
- public postal, telephone, and telegraph services;
- certain educational services;
- supply of goods which have been used exclusively for exempt activities or were otherwise not eligible for input credit.

## *Non-taxable transactions*

### Transactions within the same legal entity

Supplies within the same VAT entity (internal transactions) are **10–013**
disregarded since they are considered to be outside the scope of VAT. For example, supplies of goods and services between members of a fiscal unity or a foreign head office and its Dutch branch or vice versa.

### Transfer of Business

No VAT is due if an enterprise or an independent part thereof is sold or otherwise transferred as a "going concern," provided the transferee continues to use the assets in carrying on the enterprise. The fact that this is a non-taxable transaction does not affect, however, the entitlement to a credit for input tax on, *e.g.*, the expenditure incurred in connection with transferring the business.

### Subsidies/Penalty payments/Compensation

This is a very complex area and expert advice should always be obtained. Subsidies and grants are subject to VAT when these payments:

- constitute in fact the consideration for supplies made by the recipient; or
- are directly connected with the price of the supplies made (price subsidies), *e.g.*, subsidies paid by the government to entrepreneurs in compensation for charging too low prices to their customers (*e.g.*, agricultural products).

Other subsidies, however, are outside the scope of VAT. In particular subsidies provided by the government for *e.g.*, certain or all activities of some institution in the general public interest. Also, "operational" subsidies are considered outside the scope of VAT. These are subsidies granted to cover budget deficits for which the grantor of the subsidy does not request a supply in return and which are purely given with the object of giving the respective entity assistance.

Payment for damage claims (compensation) normally does not fall within the scope of VAT since these payments are not made as a consideration for a supply.

Penalty payments, *e.g.*, to compensate for premature termination of lease agreements are, however, subject to VAT.

### *Election to be subject to VAT*

Entrepreneurs making certain exempt supplies may elect to be subject to VAT, in which case they will be entitled to recover the input tax incurred in connection with these supplies. Election is possible for:

- supply and leasing of real property (see paras. 10–020 and 10–021, "Supply and rental of real property")
- agricultural and forestry enterprises (see para. 10–018, "Agricultural and forestry enterprises").

## 8. CREDIT/REFUND FOR INPUT TAX

### *General rule*

**10–014** An entrepreneur is in principle entitled to recover VAT paid on goods and services and on importation of good within the course of business. However, no credit is granted for input tax on:

- goods and services used for non-business purposes (*e.g.* private use);
- goods and services used for exempt transactions (with the exception of input tax related to exempt banking and financial and insurance transactions, provided the recipient of these services is resident or established outside the EC territory);
- certain categories of expenditure, *i.e.*, for goods and services for maintaining a certain private lifestyle, restaurant expenditure for

meals and drinks, gifts, supplying employees with food, housing, private transport, remuneration in kind or facilities for sport and entertainment or for other private purposes.

Input tax is disallowed on gifts if given to those who, if they are or should be charged with VAT on goods or services, would not at all or not for more than 50% be entitled to a credit for input tax. If the total of the purchase, production or cost price (excluding VAT) incurred for the categories of expenditure referred to above (incurred for one and the same person) does not exceed DFL 500,—in one book year, the disallowance of the input credit can be disregarded.

## *Adjustment of entitlement to credit*

During a certain period (four book years for movable depreciable goods and nine book years for immovable goods following the year of purchase) the entitlement to a credit for input tax at the time of purchase may be adjusted on a *pro rata* time basis, depending on whether the use of the goods changes from use for exempt transactions to use for taxable transactions or vice versa. This may result in, respectively, additional credits or tax payable.

## *Partial exemption*

Entrepreneurs making both taxable and exempt supplies are entitled to recover input tax related only to their taxable supplies. The creditable input tax is calculated based on the ratio between taxable supplies and total supplies. When it gives a fairer split, another ratio may be negotiated with the tax authorities on the basis of, *e.g.*, actual use of the purchased goods and services, for instance, in relation to time spent, employees, floor space, number of transactions, etc.

The ratio is established according to the data available at the time the entrepreneur started to use the goods and services. In the last VAT return of the bookyear, an adjustment for creditable input tax must be made according to the information available for the entire bookyear.

## *Time of recovery*

A credit for input tax can normally be claimed in the VAT return for **10–015**
the declaration period (normally a calendar quarter or month) during which the supplier made his supply, as shown on the invoice. If the VAT liability for a particular declaration period is less than the VAT credit, the difference will be refunded on application.

## *Refund for foreign entrepreneurs*

Non-resident entrepreneurs who are not liable to Dutch VAT need not register. Nevertheless, they may incur Dutch input VAT, *e.g.*, with respect to imports, costs incurred by representative offices in the Netherlands (*e.g.*, office lease, cars, computers, etc.) or by employees for courses and exhibitions in the Netherlands. This Dutch input tax can not be credited in another EC Member State. A refund of Dutch input tax can, however, be obtained under the so-called "mutual recovery procedure," on special application to:

Customs and Excise
P.O. Box 5408
2280 HK
Rijswijk,
The Netherlands.

Entrepreneurs resident outside the EC can also obtain this refund.

The application must be completed in Dutch on a special form (OB.97). In practice English and German may also be accepted. Filing must take place within six months of the end of the preceding calendar year. In practice, however, the Dutch tax authorities may also consider the refund request for which the application period has expired. The application form must be accompanied by the original invoices and a certificate of status confirming the status as a taxable person from the official tax authorities of the EC Member State where the applicant is established. Applicants resident outside the EC must otherwise demonstrate that they are considered as an entrepreneur according to Dutch VAT law.

It is not necessary for a foreign entrepreneur to use an agent or (fiscal) representative in the Netherlands nor to elect domicile, although this may be more practical.

VAT on certain kinds of expenditure, is excluded from credit/refund, see para. 10–014, "General rule".

## 9. ADMINISTRATIVE OBLIGATIONS

### *Registration*

**10–016** If there is a Dutch place of business, registration is required at the VAT office in the district in which the business is located, as soon as the definition of entrepreneur is satisfied and liability to VAT arises, see para. 10–002, "Who is taxable?". There is no monetary limit below which registration is not required.

Foreign entrepreneurs who do not maintain a Dutch place of business and whose liability is not shifted to the recipient of the supply (see para. 10–004, "Reverse charge mechanism") will have to register with Customs & Excise in Rijswijk, (foreign entrepreneurs department). It is not required to appoint a VAT agent, but this may be more practical

Provisional registration as an "intending trader" is possible. After a registration form has been completed, the Tax Inspector will normally grant the entrepreneur a VAT registration number.

## *Books and records*

The entrepreneur is obliged to keep detailed records and accounts of the supplies made by and to him, as well as his imports and exports. Failing to do so may result in a penalty of Dfl. 5,000.—(maximum). The records must be kept for a period of 10 years.

## *Invoices*

Invoices are to be issued before the 15th day after the month in which the supply was made. Normally, an invoice must contain the following information:

- a VAT registration number;
- the date of supply;
- the name and address of the entrepreneur supplying the goods and services;
- the name and address of the entrepreneur to whom the goods and services are supplied;
- a clear description of the goods and services supplied;
- the quantity of goods supplied;
- the consideration (excluding VAT);
- the amount of VAT due.

Please note that where no liability to VAT arises, no VAT should be stated on the invoice. This is of importance, for example, for the non-entrepreneur, but also for the foreign entrepreneur whose liability to VAT is shifted to the recipient of the supplies under the reverse charge mechanism, see para 10–008, "Reverse charge mechanism". The latter might consider stating on the invoice, "VAT liability shifted to recipient under article 12, para. 2, VAT Act."

Incorrectly stated VAT will, nevertheless, be due to the tax authorities. Furthermore, an inadequate invoice will normally jeopardise the right to claim a credit for input tax by the recipient.

## *VAT returns*

The entrepreneur is obliged to file a tax return (including remittance **10–017** of any VAT due) within one month of the end of each calendar quarter.

The tax inspector can require that a tax return be filed monthly or the entrepreneur may elect for monthly filing should this be more favourable for him (*i.e.* when his input tax regularly and significantly exceeds his output tax). Filing annually is only possible with approval from the tax authorities.

### *Powers of authorities*

If no VAT return is received after expiration of the time limit for submission of the return, the tax authorities will issue an assessment for an estimated amount.

Failing to file, the late filing or late payment will result in penalties in the form of additional assessments. In principle, the fines amount to 100 per cent. of the additional tax due. However, normally the penalty is reduced considerably to 10 per cent., 25 per cent. or 50 per cent., depending on the circumstances.

The statute of limitations is five years for additional assessments from the end of the calendar year in which the VAT liability arose. The VAT authorities will audit the period of the five preceding years to check whether the VAT due is also collected.

### *Objection/Appeal*

An additional tax liability assessed on a VAT return or a decision of the tax inspector regarding the reduction of a fine or denial of a request for refund can be appealed with the same inspector within two months from the date of assessment or decision. Further appeals are possible to the District Court and, if necessary, the Supreme Court, also within two months.

## 10. SPECIAL VAT REGIMES

**10–018** A special regime applies to, *e.g.*, the following categories.

### *Agricultural and forestry enterprises*

These enterprises are excluded entirely from VAT with respect to their transactions performed for "agricultural" production in the strict sense. At the same time, they are not entitled to a credit for input tax. An option to be taxed as an ordinary entrepreneur can be made. This may be advantageous where substantial investments are made.

Entrepreneurs purchasing agricultural goods and services from these qualifying "agricultural and forestry enterprises" can, however, credit a fixed 4.9 per cent. of the amounts paid as input tax.

### *Arts and antiques*

No special regime applies to objects of art and antiques. Supplies of objects of art and antiques may, however, be subject to the reduced rate of 6 per cent., provided certain conditions are met.

### Financial institutions

No special regimes (*e.g.* election to become subject to VAT) apply to financial institutions like banks and insurance companies. A credit is, however, allowed for Dutch input tax incurred in relation to exempt banking, financial and insurance transactions, provided the recipient of these services is resident or established outside the EC territory.

### Fishing enterprises

A special zero rate applies for the import and supply of fish to a fish auction.

### Free Port/Bonded warehouse

No free port facilities apply in the Netherlands. However, the **10–019**
Netherlands has a bonded warehousing system where goods can be stored without being subject to import duties and VAT. A bonded warehouse is in effect a free trade zone. The goods may be subject to minor handling, such as sorting and testing while stored in a bonded warehouse. Assembly is also possible under certain conditions.

### Retailers

Certain designated entrepreneurs, such as retailers, can account for VAT on the cash basis instead of an invoice basis.

### Second-hand goods

In case of auctions of second-hand goods offered for sale by private individuals, the auctioneer may request that his activities be treated as a supply of services instead of a sale of goods.

When goods are traded in exchange for other goods of the same kind, the tax is calculated only on the difference between the selling price of the "new" goods and the trade-in value of the "old" goods.

### Small entrepreneurs

A special tax reduction is given to small entrepreneurs who are either individuals or associated groups of individuals (*e.g.*, partnerships) and who owe an amount of VAT of no more than DFL. 4,150 per year after credit for input VAT.

## *Travel agencies*

Special rules exist for the tax treatment of activities of travel agencies regarding trips, organised transport, the supply of food and beverages during the trips, commissions on sales of organised trips and the letting of holiday bungalows and appartments.

## *Transfer and leasing of real property*

**10–020** VAT treatment of property transactions is very complex and great care needs to be taken when acquiring or disposing of any real property interest (freehold or lease hold). Expert advice should, therefore, always be obtained.

### Supply of real property

The transfer of real property constitutes a taxable supply from the moment of construction until two years after it has been taken into use for the first time. Subsequent transfers will be exempt from VAT, unless both buyer and seller make a joint election for a taxable supply.

Election for a taxable transfer may be advantageous, depending on the circumstances. The question of whether or not an option will be favourable is closely connected with a 10–year adjustment period, during which the entitlement to a credit is reviewed, see para 10–014, "Adjustment of entitlement to credit".

The adjustment is made on the legal assumption that the supplying entrepreneur continues to use the property supplied within the course of his business until the end of the adjustment period:

- exclusively for exempt transactions, when the supply of the property is exempt; or
- exlusively for taxable transactions, when the supply of the property is taxable.

For example, for the selling entrepreneur who is not entitled to credit the VAT paid upon acquisition of the property (*e.g.* banks, insurance companies), option for a taxable transfer may result in recovering a proportionate amount of the previously uncreditable VAT. For an entrepreneur entitled to credit VAT, an option for a taxable transfer may avoid the situation where a proportionate amount of previously credited VAT becomes uncreditable.

Election for a taxable transfer must, however, be made jointly and thus requires the co-operation of the buyer, whose VAT position and interests may not coincide with those of the seller. Also, in case of a joint election for a taxable transfer, a special provision shifts the liability for VAT due by the seller to the buyer, who will have to declare this VAT due on his VAT return. To the extent entitlement to a credit exists, he can again credit this VAT.

In addition to VAT, the buyer will also have to consider the fact that the transfer of real property may be subject to a 6 per cent. transfer tax.

Generally the buyer can claim an exemption from transfer tax if the transfer is also subject to VAT. Nevertheless, such a duplication can at times take place.

The exemption from transfer tax does *not* apply if the following two conditions are met simultaneously: **10–021**

— the entrepreneur supplying the real property has used it as a business asset in the course of his business; and
— the acquirer qualifies as an entrepreneur who will use the real property in the course of his business for taxable transactions for VAT purposes and who is therefore entitled to a full (or partial) refund of VAT charged to him on acquisition.

In general, if the buyer is not entitled to a credit for input tax, an election for a taxable transfer is not likely to be favourable for him, as this will result in an uncreditable 18.5 per cent. VAT charge, although the transfer of real property will then be exempt from transfer tax. If, however, the buyer is entitled to a credit, he may be inclined to co-operate in making an election. The 18.5 per cent. VAT can be credited and the only charge will be a 6 per cent. transfer tax, which can then not be avoided.

### Rental of real property

The hiring and letting of real property is normally exempt from VAT except for:

- the renting of machines and business installations;
— the rental of accommodation within the framework of the hotel business to persons who only stay there for a short period;
— the rental of parking space for motor vehicles and boats, etc.;
— the rental of safe deposit boxes;
— the rental of real property, other than buildings or parts thereof used as a dwelling.

The lessor and lessee of real property may opt for a taxable lease by filing a joint request provided it will not be used as a dwelling. The advantage of such option for the lessor may be that it will enable him to claim a refund of input tax. If the lessee is an entrepreneur who is in a position to credit input tax charged to him, an option for a taxable lease will be more advantageous than a tax-exempt lease.

# 11. Norway

## 1. GENERAL BACKGROUND

Norway, which is not a member of the European Community, introduced VAT in 1970 through the Value Added Tax Act of June 19, 1969. The territory of Norway for VAT purposes does not include Svalbard or Jan Mayen. **11–001**

The principal indirect tax in Norway is VAT. The Norwegian VAT system is, in the main, based on the same principles as those applicable to the European Community.

The local VAT authority is the regional County Inspector of Taxes ("Fylkesskatteshefen") or the customs authorities for imported goods. The Directorate of Tax is the superior authority.

A special tax on investment etc. was introduced on January 1, 1970 in conjunction with the VAT system and is called Investment Tax (IT).

The Acts of June 19, 1969 No. 66 and No. 67 relating to VAT and IT, have both been amended by subsequent Acts and are supplemented by a number of regulations issued by the Ministry of Finance and Director of Taxes. The rate of VAT and IT is stipulated annually by the Parliament (Stortinget).

VAT on imports is levied by the Norwegian Customs Office and is paid according to the same procedure as customs duties.

## 2. WHO IS TAXABLE?

### *General*

The basic rule is that liability to pay VAT arises whenever turnover of taxable goods or services occurs in Norway in commercial activity. Any physical or legal person (limited company, partnership, etc.) conducting a taxable activity is liable to pay VAT. Special rules apply for certain partnerships, trading companies, corporate groups, estates of deceased persons and estates in bankruptcy. **11–002**

A business must register for VAT once its taxable sales exceed a certain limit—at present NKR 12,000—in the last 12 months period (not necessarily the calender year). All entrepreneurs selling goods and services subject to VAT must be registered in the VAT register. This is done by notifying the County Inspector of Taxes in the county in which the entrepreneur has his permanent place of business on a specially prescribed form.

### Transactions with branch/subsidiary

Transactions between a head office and a branch are deemed not to be a supply because they are looked upon as the same taxable person.

### Government bodies

Government bodies are liable to VAT if they supply goods or services in competition with private entities.

## *Fiscal unity/Group taxation*

**11–003** Several activities operated by the same owner (corporate or personal) are, as a general rule, regarded as a single taxable entity for VAT purposes, provided they are not established as separate legal entities. If separate accounts are kept for one or more of these activities, they may, upon application, be registered separately in the VAT register.

Affiliated joint-stock companies may, upon application, be treated as a single entity for VAT purposes, when at least 85 per cent. of the capital in each company is held by the same owner or owners. Goods or services may then be transferred between the companies without charging VAT. The companies will, moreover, be entitled to a combined deduction for input VAT on goods and services for operating buildings, machines and other operating assets. Such companies may have the right to deduct input VAT relating to such buildings, machinery, etc. even if it has been transferred to a separate real-estate company, which is not engaged in activities liable to VAT (for example, it operates a purely rental business).

An entity which is merely renting out real estate is, individually, unable to be registered in the VAT register, but as affiliated joint-stock companies they could be registered together and make a full deduction for input VAT.

If part of an entrepreneur's business consists of activities for which no credit is allowed (*e.g.* sales of real-estate), VAT paid on purchases and imports must be split between those related transactions benefiting from the right to a credit and those not so benefiting. The VAT paid on purchases of a mixed character must, however, be apportioned so as to reflect the transactions carrying the right and those not carrying any right to a credit.

## *Foreign entrepreneurs*

Foreign enterprises supplying taxable services or selling goods in Norway are fully liable to VAT as Norwegian enterprises. Such foreign suppliers must be registered in the VAT register and are subject to the tax and accounting rules for VAT purposes. Application for registration is made to the County Inspector of Taxes where his representative has a place of business or registered office or his residence and the foreign trader will be given a registration number.

The foreign enterprise will then be entitled to claim credit for the input tax if this has been paid, for instance, on import.

A foreign entrepreneur who makes no taxable supplies in Norway has no right to deduct input VAT.

If a foreign supplier who is making taxable supplies in Norway, fails to register, the Norwegian customer may be liable for the VAT.

Foreign entrepreneurs may thus incur VAT liability under the Value Added Tax Act even if they are not liable for income/corporation tax in Norway.

#### Representative office

The supplies of a representative office in Norway are treated in the same way as an ordinary entrepreneur with the same rights and obligations. **11–004**

#### VAT representative

Where the foreign supplier does not maintain a place of business or a registered office in Norway, registration and remittance of VAT must be undertaken through a representative.

#### Reverse charge mechanism

The reverse charge mechanism is not used in Norway.

### *Importers*

The main rule is that VAT is payable on all imports of goods.

Regulations for the calculation and collection of VAT on imports were issued in December 1975 with several amendments later.

A customs clearance agent may pay the VAT due on import on behalf of the importer, and pass it on to the importer.

## 3. WHAT IS TAXABLE?

### *Supply of goods*

Sales of all goods are liable to VAT, unless otherwise provided by the Act. "Sales" is defined in the Act as the supply of goods or the performance of services against payment, including the exchange of goods and services. **11–005**

A sale or a service in a chain transaction is looked upon as an individual supply for VAT purposes. If the transaction in the chain is, for instance, exported, it is only the last transaction which is exempt from VAT.

### Supply of services

VAT is payable on the sale of services also, but only of such services as are expressly specified in the Act.

The following are the main taxable services:

- any services relating to goods or real property;
- the renting of goods including machinery, mechanical and electrical equipment connected with real property;
- the transport and storage of goods except transport of goods to foreign countries;
- the assignment of patents, licences, trademarks;
- advertising, including arranging advertising contracts or space for advertisements;
- technical assistance such as projecting, drawing, construction and other technical assistance relating to services supplied in connection with works on goods or real property, for example architects;
- typewriting, copying, office services, mass mailing and computer services;
- telecommunication services, including telephone, telegraph and telex;
- catering in, or from hotels and other catering establishments.

### Self-supply of goods/services

**11–006** VAT is also charged on the withdrawal by the owner of goods and services from his own business when goods and services are for private use or for purposes which fall outside the scope of the Act.

### Imports of goods

VAT must be paid not only on taxable supplies in Norway but also on imports of taxable goods. This applies regardless of the purpose of the import and irrespective of the transaction on which the import is based. Tax on imports is assessed by the Customs Office in accordance with procedures laid down for customs clearance. The Customs Office is also the authority to be consulted regarding VAT on imports.

## 4. PLACE OF SUPPLY

### Supply of goods

**11–007** Goods which are sold to a Norwegian customer before importation are not taxable in Norway. The customer has to pay VAT if he brings the goods into Norway.

Goods which are delivered abroad (export) are not taxable in Norway.

Goods which are supplied to a non-resident entrepreneur's warehouse in Norway are taxable as a main rule.

## *Supply of services*

### General rule

A service is deemed to be rendered at the place where the activities are carried out. Some services which contain a "foreign element" are regarded as export services in Norway.

### Exceptions

VAT exception applies to services supplied by registered Norwegian suppliers for use abroad or for use on foreign ships and aircraft provided that the service is either performed abroad or on the foreign ship or aircraft or is performed in Norway for a customer resident abroad and for use abroad. In the case of work on goods, for example repairs to a machine, exemption is also dependent upon the goods being dispatched through customs by the enterprise supplying the service.

Norwegian VAT law is based on the same principles as the EC Model.

# 5. BASIS OF TAXATION

## *Supplies within Norway*

The main rule is that output VAT must be calculated on the sales **11–008**
value. The ordinary sales value is the amount the business in question demands for its goods or services in the normal course of its operations.

The sales value includes all costs and incidental expenses, such as:

— cost of packing, transport, insurance and the like included in the price, or for which separate payment is demanded;
— customs duties and other excises;
— selling charges, fees, commissions and other expenses incurred in connection with the delivery but excluding VAT.

Discounts and bonuses agreed upon and given are deducted from the sales value.

## *Self-supplies*

When goods or services are exchanged or when they are withdrawn from a business for private use, the sales value on which VAT is charged must not be lower than the sales value of similar goods and services sold by the enterprise.

### *Imports*

The basis for the calculation of VAT on imported goods is the customs value for the goods. This includes customs duties and all other duties except VAT. When goods are re-imported after repair abroad the taxable value is the cost of such repair with the addition of the cost of transport to and from Norway.

VAT on imports is payable when the goods pass through customs. It is calculated and collected by the customs authorities.

### *Chargeable event/Time of payment*

Returns must be submitted for each two calendar month period. The VAT due for each period is payable within 40 days of the end of the VAT period. The date of payment for output and input VAT may not normally be used as a basis for the recording and settlement of VAT for each VAT period. The cash basis of accounting will only be permitted in exceptional cases, *i.e.* where a small entrepreneur has few employees with less than 600 man days worked.

### *Credit notes/Bad debts*

Where a debtor defaults in the payment of an account due as a consequence of a taxable supply, in respect of which the registered supplier has reported and accounted for VAT, a deduction may be made of an amount corresponding to the VAT paid. The deduction is made by reducing the figure for output VAT. To qualify for the deduction, the loss in question must be an actual or formally declared loss on accounts receivable. If payment is received for a previously deducted loss, VAT must be reported for the payment received.

## 6. TAX RATES

**11–009** The rate is at present 20 per cent., charged on net price before VAT. It is charged on the supply of goods and services in Norway. It is also charged on the import of goods and in certain circumstances services into Norway.

The tax is levied at all points in the chain of supply, but the full amount of VAT ultimately falls on the individual consumer and will not, in most circumstances represent a cost of business.

# 7. EXEMPTIONS

A person who sells exempt goods or services does not incur VAT liability and is not entitled to deduction for tax paid on acquisitions for the business. 11–010

## *Exemptions with credit for input tax (zero rate)*

The following exemptions are with credit for input tax:

- goods to foreign countries and to Svalbard and Jan Mayen;
- goods for use in the North Sea, in connection with the exploration and exploitation of submarine resources;
- goods supplied to foreign ships and aircraft;
- goods supplied to Norwegian ships over a certain limit and aircraft used in international trade;
- services to foreign ships and aircraft;
- services to Norwegian ships over a certain limit and aircraft used in international trade;
- supply of services to non-registered suppliers of services to investments in the North Sea.

The entrepreneur is allowed a credit for the VAT imposed on him. Credit for previously paid VAT is available only to an entrepreneur engaged in trade or business. The input VAT is only deductible if it relates to purchases of goods and services for use in the registered enterprise.

It is of no consequence whether the goods are new or used.

## *Exemptions without credit for input tax*

The main transactions which are outside the scope of VAT are: 11–011

- renting out of real property;
- passenger transportation;
- banking and financial transactions;
- education;
- legal, auditing and book-keeping services. Works of visual art (when the artist himself or his estate is the seller);
- products for personal use at importation;
- postage stamps;
- showing of motion picture films;
- medical services.

## *Election to be subject to VAT*

A person supplying the following exempt services may elect for voluntary registration, within regulations issued by the Ministry of Finance. 11–012

— Commercial agents
— Shipbrokers
— Book-keepers
— Public accounting firms
— News agencies
— Shipping and airline companies
— Private planning consultants

Through voluntary registration the suppliers obtain the right to deduct input VAT on purchases made for their activities, but they are then subject to the rules governing Investment Tax (IT), see para. 11–021, "Investment Tax". Furthermore, VAT is then chargeable on the relevant services supplied by the voluntarily registered supplier, even though normally, such services are not chargeable to VAT under the Act.

## 8. CREDIT/REFUND FOR INPUT VAT

### *General rule*

**11–013** An entrepreneur who is liable to report VAT is entitled to claim a deduction in his tax return for VAT paid on acquisitions and imports for the purpose of his taxable business. The right to deduction is essentially general in nature, that is, it covers all types of acquisitions with a few exceptions.

No credit is allowed for VAT suffered on the following:

— meals and other benefits for use by the owner or employers;
— housing and recreational purposes;
— entertainment and gifts for advertising purposes;
— costs of acquisition and running expenses of passenger vehicles, without regard to the use to which the vehicles are put. The only exemption is passenger cars used in rental services.

### *Adjustment of entitlement to credit*

There are no special rules with regard to the review of apportioned input credits in respect of capital goods as provided for in Article 20(2) of the Sixth EC Directive on VAT.

### *Partial exemption*

Where part of the turnover consists of supplies which are not liable to VAT, the input tax attributable to purchases which are used for the purposes of the non-taxable activities may not be claimed.

VAT paid on purchases which are used for the purposes both of taxable and exempt supplies must be apportioned so as to reflect the suppliers who carry the right and those who do not carry any right to a credit.

### *Time of recovery*

A taxable person is entitled to recovery of input tax, subject to the rules to entitlement outlined above when he has a valid VAT invoice or stamped customs entry. It is *not* necessary that he had paid for the goods or that the supplier has paid the output tax to the authorities.

The claim to input tax credit should be made in the VAT return for the period in which the invoice or import documents are issued.

### *Refund for foreign entrepreneurs*

Norwegian VAT suffered by foreign entrepreneurs who do not make taxable supplies in Norway cannot be recovered.

## 9. ADMINISTRATIVE OBLIGATIONS

### *Registration*

All taxable enterprises selling goods or services subject to VAT have **11–014**
to register at the regional tax office if the turnover exceeds 12,000 NKR in a 12 month period.

Entry in the VAT register is made by notifying, on a specially prescribed form, the County Inspector of Taxes in the county in which the enterprise has its permanent place of business.

When an enterprise is entered in the VAT register, it is obliged to collect and remit VAT and is entitled to deduct input VAT.

### *Books and records*

The VAT Act requires registered enterprises to organise their book-keeping in such a manner that the VAT authorities may at any time check sales, withdrawals if any, purchases, output and input VAT and the accuracy of the VAT calculation.

Regulations relating to the keeping of accounts were issued by the Director of Taxes on August 20, 1960 with amendments of December 15, 1977.

### *Invoices*

Regulations relating to the contents of sales documents, etc., which are to serve as evidence for the calculation and collection of VAT, were issued on October 14, 1969 by the Ministry of Finance.

VAT registered entrepreneurs must always issue a written sales document (note, invoice, bill) when selling goods and services to other registered enterprises. A contract note or other voucher issued by the purchaser may also be regarded as evidence of sale. The document shall be numbered and dated, shall state name and address of both seller and buyer, shall clearly describe the product or service, the price and give the other relevant information. It must be issued in duplicate and one copy must be kept by the supplier.

For sales between registered entrepreneurs, the sale document must state the price excluding VAT and the VAT amount separately ("open invoicing"). If the sale document covers both taxable and non-taxable sales, the figures relating to the taxable sales must be shown and summarised separately.

A non-VAT registered entrepreneur may not show a VAT amount on its sales document.

All books of accounts kept by an enterprise liable to VAT together with vouchers, notes, contracts, correspondence, invoices and other account documents, must be retained for at least 10 years.

## *VAT returns*

**11–015** All VAT registered suppliers must submit a sales and turnover return ("omsetningsoppgave") to the County Inspector of Taxes for each VAT period. The return shall be made on a special form. It shall contain details of total sales (and withdrawals, if any) in the VAT period, a calculation of the output VAT, deductible input VAT, and shall state the difference between the output and input VAT amounts. Sales of VAT exempt goods and services shall also be shown.

The figures must normally be based on the invoicing principle, *i.e.* both output and input VAT must be included in the return for the VAT period during which the sale or purchase was invoiced by or to the taxable entity. The accounting records of the enterprise must be arranged accordingly (accounting basis). Advance or part payments shall be included in accordance with special regulations issued by the Ministry of Finance on September 9, 1974.

If deductible input VAT in any one VAT period exceeds payable output VAT, the excess is refunded by the taxation authorities to the taxable entity.

A claim for refund automatically arises when the tax return shows a negative VAT amount. The claim need not, therefore, be submitted separately. If the credit regularly exceeds VAT liability on sales by more than 25 per cent., the administration may shorten the declaration period to one month. If the credit VAT regularly exceeds sales by more then 50 per cent. the tax administration may shorten the declaration period further but never to less then one week.

**11–016** The Act requires that the taxation authorities ensure that refunds are made within three weeks of the receipt of the tax return. The taxable entity is entitled to interest on any overdue refund.

Even if refund has not taken place within the three-week time limit, the enterprise is entitled to deduct the refundable amount in its subsequent returns.

As the final date for submitting the tax return is 40 days from the end of the VAT period, 40 + 21 days may thus pass before refund takes place. Shorter VAT periods may be permitted in situations where the input VAT regularly exceeds the output VAT. In any case, the enterprise may shorten the refund period by submitting its return as early as possible after the end of the VAT period.

## *Powers of the authorities*

VAT is administered in each country by the County Inspector **11–017** of Taxes ("Fylkesskattesjefen"). His office conducts the day-to-day administration and control of the tax system and makes decisions in the first instance where authority has not expressly been vested in others. The County Inspector of Taxes also maintains the VAT register.

The central administration of the tax system lies with the Director of Taxes ("Skattedirekoren"), Oslo.

Any person who wilfully gives wrong or insufficient information in a tax return or in any other form of information given to the tax authorities and by those means withholds tax or obtains an incorrect deduction for input tax, is punishable by fines or imprisonment according to the provisions given in the Act of Punishment, 1969.

Any person who wilfully fails to register or to file returns when required to do so or who violates the regulations concerning book-keeping, accounting and information is liable to fines or imprisonment for a period of up to three months. The same applies to violations of the Regulations issued under the VAT Act. If the intention was to withhold tax or to obtain an incorrect deduction, the punishment may be imprisonment for a period of up to three years, as well as fines; accessories to a wrongdoing are liable to the same punishment.

If violations of the Act occur through negligence, the taxpayer is liable only to fines.

These provisions apply where the offence is not covered by more stringent penal provisions.

Any person who wilfully or negligently contravenes the Act or any regulations issued by pursuant to the VAT Act, with the result that the Treasury has been or could have been deprived of tax, may be ordered to pay an additional tax of up to 100 per cent. over and above the tax assessed according to the procedure for discretionary assessment. Such an order may be made up to 10 years after the expiry of the period in question.

If payment is not made on the due date, interest is due on the delayed tax at 1.75 per cent. per month or part of a month until the tax is paid, if the tax declared on the return is higher than 500 NKR. Very often interest will be as large as the additional tax, especially when the assessment covers a longer period of time. Interest of less than 50 NKR can be ignored.

When sales returns have not been rendered in time or in the prescribed form, the output tax for the period concerned may be increased by at least 100 NKR. The increase may be made up to three years after the expiration of the period concerned.

Even though a return has been rendered in time and in the prescribed form, output tax can be increased in the same manner for the three preceding periods, if the account books, etc., have not been submitted, made available or sent, upon request, to the tax authorities.

### *Objections/Appeals*

**11–018** Appeals over decisions made by the County Inspector of Taxes lie with the Director of Taxes. The time limit for appeals is three weeks from the date the decision is communicated to the person or company in question.

If the Director of Taxes has made the decision in the first instance, the appeal lies with the Ministry for Finance.

The customs and excise authorities collect the VAT on imports of goods and services and functions as tax authority in the first instance. Decisions made by the customs authorities may be appealed to the Customs Directorate ("Tolldirektoratet"), Oslo, within the same three weeks time limit.

A special appeals board (the VAT Board of Appeals) has been established to deal with certain appeals, for example, where VAT has been arbitrarily assessed because returns have not been filed ("omsetningsoppgave"—chapter XIII of the Act). The Board is appointed by the Ministry for Finance. The latter may reverse the Board's decision.

## 10. SPECIAL VAT REGIMES

### *Exports*

**11–019** Exports also include trade inside Norway in the following cases:

1. Delivery of goods in a free port, provided the goods are not intended for use in the free port.
2. Delivery of goods to or for use or trade on board a ship or aeroplane in international service.
3. Delivery of beer, wine, spirits and tobacco products for sale in a tax-free shop.
4. Advertising or other publicity on behalf of a foreign client.
5. Transport of goods directly to or from a foreign country.

### *Non-profit organisations*

There are no special rules applying to social organisations or charities if they deal in business liable to taxation. Charities, however, are often considered to be non-profitable or not to be carrying on business transactions liable to taxation, even if they do take money for their goods or services.

## *Agents and auctioneers*

### Agents

Agents do not sell goods and the services they supply are not mentioned in the Act as being liable to taxation. An agent may, however, apply for voluntary registration. If the agent does not merely bring together a supplier and buyer but also sells goods on his own account, he is liable to taxation for this business activity.

A commission agent—a person who acts in his own name on behalf of a third person in the supply of goods—is liable to registration. Both the commission agent and the principal are considered as independent persons regarding the VAT liability and sale on commissions are considered as sales by both the principal and the commission agent.

### Auctioneers

Auctioneers are liable to be registered under the normal rules. Tax is **11–020** calculated and paid by the auctioneers. Output tax is due on the selling price and no credit is given as there is usually no input tax paid. If, however, the owner of the goods is registered, input tax will be paid by the auctioneer and credit will be given for the tax thus paid. In other words, the owner and the auctioneer are treated for VAT purposes as though the owner sells the goods to the auctioneer. Sales by auction in execution of a legal judgement are not subject to VAT.

## *Small entrepreneurs*

If turnover does not exceed the financial limit of 12,000 NKR, the entrepreneur need not be registered. Voluntary registration is not possible for such small entrepreneurs, no regulations having been issued.

# 11. INVESTMENT TAX (IT)

## *Introduction*

The special tax on investments, etc., was introduced on January 1, **11–021** 1970 in conjunction with the VAT system. It is levied on durable items of business equipment and is payable by entrepreneurs which are registered under the VAT Act. Investment Tax does not carry any right of deduction and is therefore finally borne by the enterprises.

## *The tax rate*

The rate of IT is stipulated annually by the parliament ("Storting") in connection with the annual budget. The normal rate is at present 9 per cent. Enterprises engaged in industrial manufacturing and mining are zero rated. The reduced rate applies to certain kinds of business equipment which the owner uses in industrial manufacturing and mining.

### *Entrepreneurs liable to IT*

Only entrepreneurs which must be registered under the VAT Act and those voluntarily registered, are liable to IT. For example, banks, insurance companies etc. are not liable to IT. Such enterprises must pay VAT on all VAT liable purchases, without being entitled to deduct input VAT.

### *Items subject to IT*

The tax is levied on purchases of, and work on durable business equipment for use in VAT-liable activities. A number of detailed regulations apply to IT as a result of its close connection with the VAT Act.

IT is chargeable on goods purchased by the enterprise for use as business equipment for use in the manufacture of such equipment, provided the enterprise is entitled to deduct the input VAT on such purchases. It is also chargeable on goods which the business itself manufactures for the same purpose.

### *Import*

**11–022** Goods imported as business equipment are subject to IT at the same extent as domestic purchases. IT is calculated on the customs value.

Equipment rented from abroad is IT liable. This ensures equal treatment vis-à-vis domestic suppliers of business equipment for rental.

### *Use of own goods*

IT is also levied if the entrepreneur takes into use, as business equipment, goods which are normally intended for sale or for use as raw materials or semi-manufacturers.

### *Exemptions for non-durable equipment*

The Act provides that non-durable equipment should be exempt from IT. The Ministry for Finance is authorised to draw the distinction between durable and non-durable equipment. Under the regulations on November 18, 1969 (No. 10), the following have been exempted from IT:

fuel, electric power, gas and water;
motor fuel (but not petrol), lubricating oil and lubrication grease;
soap, detergents and cleaning agent;
advertising material for use abroad;
Goods intended for sale which in accordance with trade custom are taken into use as samples or for demonstration purposes and which thereafter are returned to store to be sold in the normal course of business.

For enterprises engaged in the manufacturing industry or in work on goods and real property, including buildings and plants, the IT exemption is more extensive. Such enterprises are not liable to IT in respect of goods used as non-durable business equipment in the production of goods for sale or for use in the enterprise itself or in respect of work on goods, real property, buildings or plants for others.

The regulations define "non-durable" equipments as goods normally consumed or considerably depreciated by being used once or a few times in the course of normal manufacturing operations or during work on goods, etc. This means that business equipment that is consumed in the course of manufacturing, the processing of goods or construction activities, is IT-free.

Repairs, maintenance and cleaning of an entrepreneur's business performed by its own employees, is not liable to IT. However, materials, etc., consumed during the work are IT liable.

## *Basis for calculations of IT*

The main rule is that IT is levied on the purchase price, excluding VAT. The taxable value is therefore the same as for VAT purposes. Freight, customs duties, taxes other than VAT and other delivery costs must be included. **11–023**

## *Refund of IT on re-export*

On July 27, 1970, the Ministry for Finance issued regulations regarding the refund of IT on the re-export of equipment imported for hire or loan. The enterprise may claim refund on re-export of this kind of the IT charged upon import, less 5 per cent. for each month or part thereof. Thus, no refund may be claimed after 20 months. The claim for refund is included in the return for the tax period during which the equipment is re-exported.

No refund of IT may be claimed on the re-export of taxable objects other than those which have been hired or borrowed from abroad.

# 12. Portugal

## 1. GENERAL BACKGROUND

VAT was introduced in Portugal to overcome certain deficiencies in the tax system on consumption and also to comply with the requirements of the EC following the accession of Portugal from January 1, 1986. **12–001**

Harmonisation with the Sixth EC Directive was achieved on January 1, 1989.

Portugal comprises the continental territory plus Madeira and Azores Islands.

Administration of VAT has been given to a central service in Lisbon which handles VAT on imported goods as well as VAT on internal transactions.

## 2. WHO IS TAXABLE?

### *General*

The following persons are subject to VAT: **12–002**

- a person or group of persons who independently and regularly engages in production, commerce or in the supply of services;
- persons who engage in occasional transactions which qualify as commercial transactions according to the law (*e.g.* purchase of a building for resale);
- any importer;
- persons who inadvertently mention VAT on invoices or on documents equivalent to invoices.

An exemption applies when transactions are below PTE 800,000 annual turnover. This limit goes to PTE 1,700,000 if the taxpayer is deemed to be a small entrepreneur, see para. 12–015, "Special VAT regimes".

### Transactions with branch/subsidiary

No special regulation applies to transactions between a branch and its foreign head office. They are considered to be two independent taxpayers and therefore supplies between them are subject to VAT.

### Government bodies

The State and other public entities are taxable persons in respect of onerous transactions which do not constitute mere acts resulting from their powers of authority.

## *Fiscal unity/Group taxation*

The fiscal unity concept is not applicable to Portugal.

## *Foreign entrepreneurs*

**12–003** Foreign entrepreneurs with no establishment in Portugal are subject to VAT in Portugal when they make taxable supplies in Portugal. This is the case when foreign entrepreneurs import goods into Portugal. This is also the case when they perform services which are deemed to be supplied in Portugal.

### Representative office

Representative offices of foreign entrepreneurs are not regarded as liable to VAT when they carry out only activities of a preparatory or auxiliary nature. The foreign entrepreneur will be able to claim from the Portuguese VAT authorities a refund of the input VAT incurred in Portugal through its representative office, see para. 12–012, "Refund for foreign entrepreneurs".

### VAT representative

Foreign entrepreneurs making taxable supplies within Portugal must appoint a VAT representative who will fulfil all the administrative obligations and pay the tax in their names.

### Reverse charge mechanism

Foreign entrepreneurs supplying services such as royalties, advertising, consultancy, etc., do not have to account for VAT in Portugal. The tax is due by the recipient entrepreneur, see para. 12–006, "Reverse charge mechanism".

### Importers

Goods brought into Portugal are subject to VAT at customs clearance. The tax is due by the importer.

## 3. WHAT IS TAXABLE?

VAT is due in Portugal on the supply of goods and services effected for consideration within Portugal by a taxable person acting as such, as well as on the import of goods. **12–004**

### Supply of goods

The supply of goods means the transfer of tangible goods. Electricity, gas, heat and refrigeration are considered tangible goods. Assembly and installation of goods in Portugal triggers a liability to VAT. The tax is due when the work is completed.

The transfer of establishments for key money is not considered a supply of goods.

### Supply of services

Supply of services means transactions carried out which do not constitute the supply or import of goods. As such, for example, transfers of intangible assets are considered supplies of services.

### Self-supplies of goods/services

In certain cases specified by law, self-supplies are subject to VAT (*e.g.* use of goods or services for private consumption or for purposes not related to the taxable activity of the entrepreneur).

### Imports

The importation of goods means the entry of goods into the VAT territory of Portugal. The VAT is due at the time of customs clearance.

## 4. PLACE OF SUPPLY

### *Supply of goods*

12–005 The transfer of goods is taxable if the goods are situated in Portugal at the time of transfer. Transfers of goods still in transit are also taxable when the transfer of ownership occurs before the actual import into Portugal.

### *Supply of services*

#### General rule

The supply of services in Portugal is taxable when the supplier has his head office or a fixed place of business from which the service is supplied or, in the absence of these, a permanent address in Portugal.

#### Exceptions

For a number of specified services, the general rule is not applicable. These exceptions are:

- services connected with real estate, such as the services of estate agents, architects, etc., are deemed to be supplied where real properties are located;
- transport of goods and persons and closely related services (such as loading and unloading) are deemed to be supplied where the transport takes place. Only the transport taking place in Portugal is taxable. Exemptions apply to international transport and to exported goods, see para. 12–009, " Exemptions";
- renting of means of transport is deemed to be supplied in Portugal:
  - if the lessor is established in Portugal and the services are used in Portugal;
  - if the lessor is established outside Portugal and the services are used in Portugal by the lessee;
- cultural, artistic, sporting, scientific, educational and entertainment services are supplied where they are physically performed.

12–006 The following services are deemed to be supplied where the recipient of the service usually resides or has a fixed establishment:

- transfers and assignments of trade marks, licences, copyright, patents;
- advertising services;
- services of consultants, engineers, chartered accountants, consultancy offices;
- data processing and supply of information;
- financial, banking and insurance services;
- supply of staff;

— acceptance to refrain from carrying out an activity or exercising any rights;
— renting of movable properties (apart from the renting of means of transport).

According to this rule, no VAT will be due in Portugal when the recipient of these services is established outside Portugal. However, VAT will be due in Portugal if the services are provided to a non-VAT tax payer located in another EC country.

**Reverse charge mechanism**

When a foreign entrepreneur supplies the following services to an entrepreneur in Portugal, VAT is not due by the foreign company but by the recipient entrepreneur in Portugal: royalties, advertising services, services of consultants, engineers, economists and accountants, consultancy bureaux, supply of staff and the hiring of movable tangible goods apart from means of transport.

## 5. BASIS OF TAXATION

### *Supplies within Portugal*

The taxable amount of supplies of goods and services subject to VAT **12–007** is the value of the consideration received, or to be received, by the purchaser, net of any discount, deduction or bonus granted.

If the discount, deduction or bonus is given in a separate credit note, application of VAT is not obligatory.

The taxable value shall include, however, taxes and duties, excluding VAT itself, as well as any other chargeable expenses, such as commission, packing, transport, insurance and advertising costs carried out on the customer's account.

### *Self-supplies*

The taxable value for self-supplies is either the cost of production or the cost of acquisition.

### *Importation of goods*

The taxable amount of imported goods shall be the price paid, or to be paid, by the importer, where this price is the sole consideration and shall include the following elements when they are not already included in it:

— import duties and any other taxes due on importation, excluding the value added tax to be levied;

— chargeable expenses, such as commission, packing, transport and insurance costs, incurred up to the first place of destination within Portuguese territory, excluding transport expenses between the islands making up the Autonomous Regions of Madeira and the Azores, and between these and Continental Portugal and vice versa.

### *Chargeable event/Time of payment*

VAT on goods becomes due as soon as the goods have been delivered. VAT on services becomes due when the services have been rendered. In case of payments in advance VAT is due immediately on the amount paid.

### *Credit notes/Bad debts*

When a credit note is issued cancelling all or part of an invoice, the entrepreneur may deduct the VAT shown on the credit note from output VAT when filing his VAT return.

VAT paid on uncollected debts can be refunded as long as the debts qualify as bad debts as defined by law.

## 6. TAX RATES

The present rates are as follows:

**12–008**

0% The zero rate applies to basic foodstuffs, pharmaceuticals, books and papers, agricultural products, etc.

8% (Maderia & Azores 6%)
This reduced rate applies to other foodstuffs, scholastic materials, petrol and other fuel, unspun textiles, public works contracts, telecommunications, travel agencies, lawyers and other jurists, hotels, restaurants, agricultural equipment, etc.

17% (Madeira & Azores 12%)
The standard rate applies when no other specific rate is applicable.

30% (Madeira & Azores 21%)
The higher rate is due on alcoholic beverages (spirits and liquors), perfumes, furs, jewellery, games, fire-arms, private aircraft, etc.

## 7. EXEMPTIONS

### *Exemptions with credit for input tax*

**12–009** Exemptions with credit, also known as "zero-rated" exemptions, allow the taxable person to reclaim from the State the full VAT incurred on his purchases of goods or services.

These exemptions apply to the following:

- exports and similar transactions;
- the supply of goods such as basic food products, films, newspapers, books, pharmaceutical and similar products, orthopedic equipment, agricultural products;
- general financial transactions and services supplied by insurance brokers and insurance agents when the recipient is established outside the EC;
- international transport of persons or goods;
- exempt imports.

However, certain restrictions defined in law prevent the recovery of input tax paid on a number of items, see para. 12–011, "Credit/Refund for Input VAT".

The most important exempt imports are:

- imports of goods which are exempt from VAT when sold on the internal market;
- imports of goods under International Agreements;
- certain personal and household belongings;

Relief is also available, under certain conditions, for goods which are temporarily imported or which are re-imported after repair abroad.

## *Exemptions without credit for input tax*

These exemptions do not give the taxable person the right to deduct, or reclaim from the State, the VAT incurred on his purchases. The purchaser is deemed to be the ultimate consumer.

Examples of these exemptions are:

- the medical and paramedical professions;
- hospitals, centres for medical treatment, etc.;
- educational establishments within the National Education System;
- public postal services;
- general financial transactions and services supplied by insurance brokers and insurance agents, when the recipient is established in an EC country;
- the renting, purchase and sale of immovable property.

## *Non-taxable transactions*

### Transactions within the same legal entity

Supplies within the same legal entity are not taxable when the branch and its head office are both established in Portugal. However, supplies made between a foreign head office and its branch in Portugal are taxable. **12–010**

### Transfer of business

The transfer of a business or of a complete and independent branch of an activity is not subject to VAT.

### Subsidies/Penalty payments/Compensation

Subsidies are generally subject to VAT when they are directly linked to the cost of a taxable supply. Indemnities either for premature termination of contracts or for repairing a damage are not subject to VAT.

## *Election to be subject to VAT*

Besides real estate—see para. 12–015, "Special regimes"— exempt taxpayers carrying on the following activities can opt to be subject to VAT under normal terms:

— veterinary surgeons;
— interpreters, translators, etc.;
— certain centres for medical treatment;
— agricultural, husbandry and forestry activities.

# 8. CREDIT/REFUND FOR INPUT VAT

## *General rule*

**12–011** Resident taxpayers may recover VAT as follows:

— VAT incurred on the acquisition of goods or services from other VAT taxpayers;
— VAT paid at customs on imports;
— VAT incurred on an operation subject to VAT when effected by VAT taxpayers established abroad who do not have a representative with legal powers in Portugal;
— VAT paid on services such as royalties, advertising services, consultancy, etc. supplied to recipient entrepreneurs in Portugal.

VAT paid on the following expenses is not recoverable:

— expenses concerning acquisition, manufacture, or importation, rental, use, transformation or repairing of passenger cars, yachts, helicopters, planes, motor-bicycles and motorcycles;
— expenses relating to fuel usually used by vehicles, except the acquisition of diesel oil in respect of which 50 per cent. of the VAT is deductible;

— expenses of transport and business travel of the taxpayer;
— expenses relating to accommodation, meals, drinks and tobacco;
— expenses relating to entertainment and luxury goods and services.

## *Adjustment of entitlement to credit*

The credit for input VAT obtained on capital assets may have to be adjusted if one of the following events occurs before the beginning of the fourth year (for movable goods) or the ninth year (for immovable goods):

— transfer of the capital assets (for consideration or free of charge), if the transaction is not subject to VAT;
— transfer of the capital assets from a taxable to an exempt sector of activity;
— termination of business;
— termination of all taxable activities.

Part of the input tax will have to be repaid on a *pro rata* time basis.

## *Partial exemption*

Entrepreneurs making both taxable and exempt (without credit) supplies are allowed to recover only the input VAT relating to taxable supplies, calculated on a *pro rata* basis. **12–012**

## *Time of recovery*

When an entrepreneur has a VAT credit in excess of his VAT liability, a refund can be claimed in the periodical VAT returns.

Reimbursements must be made within 90 days of the claim. This period is reduced to 30 days for taxpayers in a permanent credit situation.

Reimbursements to non-resident taxpayers must be made within six months of the filing of the claim.

## *Refund for foreign entrepreneurs*

Single or collective persons, non-resident or not established in Portugal, who prove that they are subject to VAT in another EC member state are entitled to a refund of VAT incurred in Portugal on the transfer of goods or rendering of services in Portugal, provided that:

— they do not have a residence or a permanent establishment in Portugal;

- they have not effected any sale of goods or rendered any services which are deemed to be supplied in the Portuguese territory, except:
  - transport and related services such as charges connected with imports and exports or entry into duty free zones;
  - rendering of services such as royalties, advertising services, consultancy, etc., for which the tax is due in Portugal by the recipient entrepreneur;
  - rendering of services relating to movable or immovable goods located in Portugal and for which VAT is paid by the foreign entrepreneur when no VAT representative has been appointed in Portugal to act on behalf of the foreign company.

The VAT to be refunded will be that incurred by the taxpayer either on the acquisition of goods and services effected in Portugal or which has been assessed on the import of goods, provided these goods or services are used for the sale of goods or rendering of services subject to VAT and are not exempt without credit.

## 9. ADMINISTRATIVE OBLIGATIONS

### *Registration*

**12–013** Taxpayers must submit a declaration and register as soon as they begin their activity.

### *Books and records*

Accounting should be clear and unequivocal so as to permit control over the calculation of tax and contain all the elements necessary for filing of the VAT periodical returns. Taxable persons who neither have, nor are obliged to have, proper books of account, should keep appropriate records.

### *Invoicing*

Invoices must be issued within a 5 day period or, by option, on a weekly or monthly basis and should show the following elements:

- number, in sequence;
- date;
- name and head office address or place of residence of the supplier and of the recipient or purchaser;
- tax number of the taxable person;
- the quantities and description of the goods or services supplied;

— the net value and any other elements included in the taxable amount;
— the VAT rates and amount of tax chargeable;
— the motive justifying an exemption from tax, where applicable.

All goods in transit must be accompanied by two copies of the delivery note, invoice or similar document, except:

— goods obviously for personal or domestic use by the owner;
— goods from retailers acquired by the final consumer;
— goods from agricultural producers;
— goods from fishermen;
— goods subject to the 0 per cent. rate;
— tobacco, matches and fuel.

## *VAT returns*

VAT returns have to be filed on a quarterly or monthy basis depending on the turnover of the entrepreneur. **12–014**

Taxpayers are required to submit a quarterly declaration when their turnover of the preceding year was below PTE 30,000,000.

The VAT returns and the corresponding payments should be received by the VAT Administration Service before the 15th day of the month following the end of each calendar quarter.

Above the limit of PTE 30,000,000, entrepreneurs are obliged to submit a monthly return. The payment must be made by cheque or postal order at the time the return is sent by post to the VAT Administration Service. It should be received before the end of the second month following the month in which the transactions took place.

Payment is deemed to be received in time if it was posted three weekdays before the due date.

## *Powers of the authorities*

If VAT is not paid in due time a fine between half and twice the VAT overdue is applicable as well as interest of 24 per cent. per annum.

VAT returns or transactions can be corrected by the tax authorities over five years. VAT paid unduly can be corrected by the taxpayer during the year following the date of the transaction.

Refunds of VAT cannot be claimed if there is any VAT overdue relating to previous periods and if no guarantee is provided.

## *Objections/Appeals*

Taxpayers who are individually or jointly responsible for payment of the tax may contest the liability to VAT assessed either by the tax authorities or in the Courts according to the terms of the Tax Procedural Code.

### Annulment of VAT by the tax authorities

This may occur whenever VAT is assessed in excess of that due and if the amount to be cancelled exceeds PTE 500. The right to refund expires after five years.

### Compensatory interest

If the above situation occurs and if it can be proved that the error is the responsibility of the tax authorities, taxpayers are entitled to receive compensatory interest at the rate of 18 per cent. per annum.

## 10. SPECIAL VAT REGIMES

### *Small entrepreneurs*

**12–015** This category includes those taxpayers whose total amount of purchases does not exceed PTE 7,500,000. VAT is assessed on 25 per cent. of the total VAT paid on purchases. Input VAT included in small entrepreneurs' invoices is not recoverable.

### *Travel agencies*

This regime follows the rules of the Sixth EC Directive whereby the taxable amount is the difference between the price paid by the customers and the cost of the expenses paid by the agent to third parties (airlines, hotels, etc.). Input VAT included in these expenses is not recoverable.

The special regime for travel agencies is not applicable to services rendered, by travel agencies and operators, acting in the name and on behalf of their clients.

### *Bonded warehouses*

Goods imported into bonded warehouses are not liable to VAT and customs duty until they are removed for sale in the community. Importing of goods into a bonded warehouse is subject to the prior approval of the customs authorities. The agreement applies for a limited period of time and specifies the conditions in which the goods are to be kept.

### *Free zones*

There are two free Zones in Portugal: the Island of Madeira and the Island of Santa Maria in the Azores. Goods imported to these zones are exempt from VAT.

### *Second-hand goods*

VAT is due on second-hand goods sold by a VAT taxpayer. The VAT is assessed on the difference between the purchase and sale prices. Input VAT related to these sales cannot be recovered.

### *Real estate*

Transactions on real estate are exempt, see para. 12–009, "Exemptions without credit for input tax". However, entrepreneurs may elect to become liable. As a consequence they have to assess VAT on their transactions but they can claim input VAT incurred on their acquisitions.

# 13. Spain

## 1. GENERAL BACKGROUND

As a consequence of Spain's entry into the EC, VAT came into force in Spain on January 1, 1986. VAT replaced 23 indirect taxes, the most important of which were Turnover Tax and Luxury Tax, as well as compensatory tax on imports. **13–001**

From a territorial point of view, VAT is applicable on the Spanish mainland and the Balearic Islands (including Spanish territorial sea to a limit of 12 miles), but not in the Canary Islands, Ceuta and Melilla (North African areas under Spanish sovereignty). The VAT Act of August 2, 1985 and Regulations approved by Royal Decree of October 30, 1985 are the main legislation governing VAT.

For a period of six months, from January 1, 1986, certain entities such as Trade Unions, Professional Associations and Chambers of Commerce were allowed to make submission to the tax administration from whom they received binding replies. These replies are important, since they set out the tax authorities' interpretation of various different VAT aspects. Based on the experience acquired and the answers given, a new VAT law is expected to be enacted in the near future.

VAT is administered in Spain by the tax authorities except for the VAT levied on imports which is collected by Customs.

## 2. WHO IS TAXABLE?

### *General*

An entrepreneur ("empresario o profesional") acting either as an individual or an entity, who supplies taxable goods or services, in the course of business, whatever the purpose or results of that business, is a taxable person. **13–002**

Trading companies are considered to be entrepreneurs in any case. Generally, a person who makes an occasional transaction is not deemed to be an entrepreneur liable to VAT. Employees are outside the scope of VAT.

There is no monetary limit below which VAT is not chargeable.

### Transactions with branch/subsidiary

Supplies between a head office and its branch which are both located in the Spanish VAT territory are outside the scope of VAT because they are the same legal entity. However, if the head office is outside the Spanish VAT territory and the branch is located in it, supplies made between them are subject to VAT since, for tax purposes, the foreign head office and its Spanish branch are different taxable persons. Only in the case of a branch's activity which is only preparatory or auxiliary (*i.e.* a representative office) to that of its head office, are services of such a nature supplied to the head office outside the scope of VAT.

### Government bodies

State, regional and local government bodies are not subject to VAT in respect of the activities which they carry out without consideration or which are remunerated by the payment of a tax. However, these bodies are always considered taxable persons in relation to the following activities:

— telecommunications;
— supply of water, gas, electricity and steam;
— transport of goods and passengers;
— port and airport services;
— supply of new goods manufactured for sale;
— transactions of agricultural intervention agencies in respect of agricultural products regulated by the common EC agricultural policy;
— running of trade fairs and exhibitions;
— warehousing;
— activities of commercial publicity bodies and travel agencies;
— running of staff shops, cooperatives and industrial canteens and similar institutions;
— commercial activities of radio and television.

## *Fiscal unity/Group taxation*

**13–003** The concept of fiscal unity does not exist in Spanish VAT law.

## *Foreign entrepreneurs*

A foreign entrepreneur or an entrepreneur from the Canary Islands, Ceuta or Melilla who supplies goods or services in Spain without a fixed establishment is deemed to be a taxable person, except when the taxable person is deemed to be the recipient. However, there is no specific provision regarding the procedure for payment of the tax due by the foreign entrepreneur and no obligation to appoint a VAT representative.

If the foreign entrepreneur has a fixed establishment within Spain from which supplies to third parties are made, it is treated as a local entrepreneur and should comply with all the rules applicable to an established entrepreneur. Generally, a non-resident entrepreneur is considered as having a fixed establishment for VAT purposes if he keeps a regular place of business in the Spanish VAT territory such as a branch, office, shop, factory, warehouse, installations, workshop, etc., where an entrepreneurial activity is performed.

#### Representative office

A representative office of a foreign entrepreneur which only performs activities of a preparatory or auxiliary nature is not considered to be a fixed establishment. The services supplied to its head office are not subject to VAT. Input VAT of the representative office can be claimed by the head office according to the procedure established for foreign entrepreneurs, see para. 13–014, "Refund for foreign entrepreneurs".

#### Reverse charge mechanism

Foreign entrepreneurs with no establishment in Spain supplying to other entrepreneurs (Spanish or not) goods or services which are deemed to be supplied in Spain are not liable to VAT in Spain since the tax in these cases is due by the recipient, see para. 13–006, "Place of supply".

### *Importers*

With regard to importation of goods, the importer is always the taxable person and the tax is due at customs clearance.

## 3. WHAT IS TAXABLE?

VAT is levied on the supply of goods and services in the Spanish VAT **13–004**
territory and on the import of goods.

### *Supply of goods*

Supply of goods means the transfer of the right to dispose of tangible property as owner.

Gas, heating, refrigeration, electric current and the like are considered tangible property. Real estate is also considered as tangible property.

The following are also treated as supply of goods:

— the establishment, extension and transfer of rights *in rem* over real property, except mortgages;

- the transfer of the ownership of property by order of a public authority or in pursuance of the law;
- the handing over of goods under a hire purchase contract;
- sales with retention of ownership until full payment;
- contribution in kind to a corporate body;
- the delivery by a contractor of movable property made or assembled from materials supplied in whole or in part by a customer (in the case of building construction, when the cost of the materials supplied by the contractor exceeds 20 per cent. of the taxable amount, the delivery is a supply of goods);
- the self-supply of goods.

## *Supply of services*

Supply of services means any supply which does not constitute a supply of goods.
It also applies to:

- transfer of intangible property such as rights on trademarks, patents, knowhow, software, etc.;
- leasing, renting;
- agreements to refrain from certain activities;
- building constructions when it is not a supply of goods;
- commissions;
- transport;
- transfer of a lease contract on a business premise;
- self-supply of services:

## *Self-supply of goods/services*

**13–005** The supply of goods is deemed to be a self-supply of goods when:

- goods are transferred by an entrepreneur from his business to his personal patrimony or for consumption;
- goods are supplied to third parties without charge;
- goods are acquired or produced by an entrepreneur and used in his business as capital assets or transferred from an area of his business to another in which the entitlement to input VAT credit differs by 50 per cent. points.

The supply of services is deemed to be a self-supply of services when:

- goods or rights are transferred from the business for personal consumption and are not any of those goods listed under the title "Self-supply of goods", at para. 13–004.
- business goods are used for private purposes;
- services are rendered without charge.

### *Imports*

Importation of goods means the entry of goods into the Spanish VAT territory, irrespective of their destination or the status of the importer.

Imports of goods are in general taxable. However, in certain cases, a number of exemptions are applicable, see para. 13–011, "Exempt imports".

Services rendered in connection with the import of goods are exempt, provided that the value of services is included in the taxable amount of the import.

## 4. PLACE OF SUPPLY

VAT is chargeable in Spain only if the supply of goods or services takes place in the Spanish VAT territory. **13–006**

### *Supply of goods*

The general rule is that the place of supply is where the goods are physically located at the time of supply.

Special rules apply:

- when goods are transported: the place of supply is where the transport begins. If transport of goods begins outside Spanish VAT territory, the place of supply by the importer and the place of any subsequent supplies is deemed to be Spain;
- when goods are installed or assembled, the place of supply is where they are installed or assembled;
- when immovable property is supplied, the place is where it is situated.

### *Supply of services*

#### General rule

The place of supply is where the supplier has established his business or has a fixed establishment from which the service is supplied or, in the absence of such a place of business or fixed establishment, where he has his registered office or permanent address.

#### Exceptions

The place of supply of:

- services connected with immovable property, is where the property is located;

- transport services is where the transport takes place, considering distances covered. Only transport supplied within the Spanish territory is taxable;
- services relating to:
  - cultural, artistic, sporting, scientific, educational, entertainment or similar activities;
  - ancilliary transport activities such as loading, unloading, handling, storing and similar activities;
  - work on movable tangible property and its evaluation;
  - hotel and restaurant services

  is where these services are physically carried out.
- renting of means of transport is where the transport is used, only when the lessor is established outside the EC and the means are used in the Spanish territory or vice versa. In all other cases, the place of supply is determined according to the general rule. The supply is deemed to be in Spain:
  - if the lessor is established outside the EC and the means of transport are used in the Spanish territory;
  - if the lessor is established in the Spanish territory and the means of transport are used in an EC country or in Spain.

**13–007** The place of supply of the following services:

- transfers and assignments of copyrights, patents, licences, trademarks and similar rights;
- advertising services;
- services of consultants, engineers, auditors, tax experts, lawyers, accountants and other similar services;
- data processing services and the supplying of information;
- banking, financial and insurance transactions including reinsurance;
- management data processing;
- the supply of staff;
- the hiring out of movable tangible property, with the exception of all forms of transport;
- obligation to refrain from pursuing or exercising, in whole or in part, a business activity or a right referred to above;
- the services of agents who act in the name and for the account of another, when they procure for their principal the services referred to above

is where the recipient of the services has established his business or has a fixed establishment to which the services are supplied or, in the absence of such a place, where he has his registered office or permanent address.

This rule does not apply when the recipient is a non-entrepreneur resident in an EC country. In such a case, VAT is due by the Spanish supplier.

**Reverse charge mechanism**

When, according to the above rules, supplies of goods and services are deemed to be made within the Spanish VAT territory by a foreign entrepreneur to another entrepreneur, the reverse charge mechanism applies. The taxable person is not the supplier but the recipient entrepreneur, who has to pay the VAT due on these supplies. This VAT can be deducted as input VAT on the next VAT return if the entrepreneur is established in the Spanish VAT territory or through the special procedure explained below—see para. 13–013, "Credit/Refund for input tax"—in the case of foreign entrepreneurs with no establishment in the Spanish territory. The reverse charge does not apply when the supplier is established in the Canary Islands, Ceuta or Melilla. In such a case the taxable person is the supplier and not the recipient.

## 5. BASIS OF TAXATION

### *Supplies within the Spanish territory*

With regard to supplies of goods and services the taxable amount is the total consideration which has been or is to be obtained by the supplier, including: **13–008**

- commissions, containers, packing, transport, insurance, interest and any other amount charged to the customer;
- interest for late payments;
- subsidies directly linked to the price;
- taxes, duties, levies and charges on the same supply, excluding VAT.

Not included are:

- indemnities;
- discounts and rebates;
- expenses incurred in the name and on behalf of the customer.

When the consideration is not payable in cash, or is not wholly for cash, the open market value is applied.

In case of transactions between related parties at a price lower than the market price, the taxable basis cannot be lower than the full cost to the supplier.

### *Self-supplies*

For self-supply of goods the basis of taxation is the historical cost (excluding VAT) of the goods or services purchased or used to produce the goods. In respect of self-supply of services the taxable basis is the full cost incurred by the taxable person in providing these services.

### Imports

With regard to importation of goods, the taxable basis is the customs value, plus the following items, insofar as they are not already included in the customs value:

— taxes, duties, levies and other charges due by reason of importation, excluding VAT;
— incidental expenses, such as commissions, packing, transport and insurance incurred up to the first place of destination within the Spanish VAT territory.

### Chargeable event/Time of payment

13–009 VAT becomes chargeable when the goods are delivered or the services are performed. With regard to supplies of electricity, gas, and the like and supplies of services which give rise to successive payments, VAT is chargeable at the time each payment becomes due for the period.

However, where a payment is to be made on account before the goods are delivered or the services are performed, the tax becomes chargeable on receipt of the payment and on the amount received.

VAT is due on imports when the importers apply for the clearance of the goods from the customs.

### Credit notes/Bad debts

Taxable amounts can be adjusted in the case of:

— re-usable containers and packing returned to the supplier;
— discounts and rebates subsequent to supplies;
— total or partial cancellation.

In these cases, a new invoice should be issued indicating the changes or modifications to the original transaction and identifying the invoices modified. In case of discounts after the invoice is issued, credit notes can be issued only if the customer is not an entrepreneur or in the case of an entrepreneur, if input VAT cannot be deducted.

VAT charged on invoices which remain unsettled, *i.e.* bad debts, cannot be recovered.

## 6. TAX RATES

The present rates are as follows:

0% Services rendered by lawyers and solicitors before the law courts (applicable in 1987 and 1988 only) and certain services connected with sports (applicable in 1987). The zero-rated supply is similar to an exempt supply with credit, see para. 13–011. **13–010**

6% Applicable to supplies and imports of:

- food (excluding alcoholic and refreshment beverages) for humans and animals;
- books, magazines and newspapers;
- housing;
- materials for schools (except electronic equipment);
- films.

And to the following services:

- overland transport of passengers and their baggage;
- hotels and restaurants (except top-ranking hotels/restaurants);
- services connected with films, plays and musical comedies;
- urban cleaning and rubbish collection;
- services rendered by fairs and commercial exhibitions;
- services rendered by lawyers and solicitors before the law courts;
- housing construction.

12% Applicable to all supplies not liable to a specified rate.

33% Applicable to the deliveries, lease, leasing and import of:

- cars and motorbikes. The rate for car hire under certain conditions is reduced to 12 per cent.;
- boats more than nine metres in length for leisure and waters-ports;
- aeroplanes, aircraft, etc., except those required by the State, public entities, or air companies;
- jewels;
- clothing made with luxury furs.

## 7. EXEMPTIONS

### *Exemptions with credit for input tax*

The following exemptions are with credit for input tax:

- exports; **13–011**

- services rendered in connection with exports (transport, storage, custody, etc.);
- services rendered by agents connected with export operations;
- transport of passengers and their baggage by air or sea from Spain to foreign countries or the Canary Islands, Ceuta and Melilla and vice versa.

## *Exemptions without credit for input tax*

The following exemptions are without credit for input tax:

- public postal services;
- services connected with health care (hospitals, medical assistance, dentistry, etc.);
- services rendered by Social Security;
- services connected with education at all levels;
- insurance and reinsurance;
- banking and other financial transactions;
- conveyances of rural land and second or successive transfers of buildings;
- real estate rentals (except ground rent for parking, storage of goods, lease of business premises which are taxable);
- gambling, games and lotteries;
- deliveries of goods in which input VAT could not be deducted when they were acquired;
- deliveries of pictures, sculptures, etc. made by the artist.

### Exempt imports

Imports of goods are usually taxable. However, in certain cases, exemptions are applicable. It is the case, for example, of:

- imports of goods which would be exempt if supplied within the Spanish territory;
- imports of goods under a declaration for transit arrangements or by recognised international organisations;
- imports of goods to be placed in temporary storage or under free-zone arrangements.

Services rendered in connection with the importation of goods are exempt, provided that the value of services is included in the taxable amount of the import.

## *Non-taxable transactions*

### Transactions within the same legal entity

**13–012** Transactions between a head office and its branch both located within the Spanish territory are not taxable because they are taking place within the same legal entity. However cross border transactions are treated according to general VAT rules and are taxable.

### Transfer of business

When an entrepreneur transfers his entire business (assets and liabilities), it is considered that no supply of goods has taken place provided that the recipient continues with the same business.

### Subsidies/Penalty payments/Compensation

Subsidies are liable to VAT when they are directly linked to the price of taxable supplies. Their amount should be included by the beneficiary in the taxable amount of the supplies to which they are linked.

Penalty payments for breach of contracts are liable to VAT when they relate to taxable transactions.

Sums of money repairing a damage are not subject to VAT.

## *Election to be subject to VAT*

It is not possible to elect to be subject to VAT when an exemption applies.

# 8. CREDIT/REFUND FOR INPUT TAX

## *General rule*

A taxable person may claim input VAT relief in respect of VAT borne on supplies of goods and services received and in respect of VAT paid on the import of any goods, insofar as these goods or services are used or are to be used for the purpose of a taxable business carried out or to be carried out by him. **13–013**

If deductible input VAT exceeds, in a tax period, the amount of output VAT due, the excess can be carried forward to the following period except in case of exporters who can claim VAT refund monthly within certain limits.

Input VAT cannot be claimed on the following items:

- cars;
- leisure aircrafts or boats;
- travel;
- hotels;
- restaurant or entertainment;
- goods or services subject to the top VAT rate;
- gifts to clients, employees or third parties.

## *Adjustment of entitlement to credit*

VAT paid on capital goods can be deducted as any other input VAT. However, during a period of four years for movable property and nine years for immovable property, starting from the time when the goods are first used, the entitlement to a credit for input tax at the time of purchase must be adjusted when the deductible proportion (in respect of partially exempt persons) of any of these years, differs by more than 10 percentage points from that of the year in which the goods were acquired. This may result in an additional credit or a VAT repayment.

## *Partial exemption*

When a taxpayer makes both exempt (exempt with no tax credit) and taxable supplies, only a percentage of the non-attributable input VAT may be deducted.

The general rule to calculate the deductible proportion of non-attributable input VAT is as follows:

$$\text{Ratio} = \frac{\text{Total value of operations entitled to VAT refund} \times 100}{\text{Total value of operations}}$$

**13–014** The following items are not included in that formula:

- VAT;
- sales of capital goods used in the business;
- financial and real estate operations, except if they are the activity of the taxpayer;
- imports;
- acquisitions of goods and services;
- subsidies;
- compensations paid by the administration or an insurance company in the case of accident, fire, disaster, etc.

A special rule applies when a company carries out activities which are clearly different and to which special VAT rules apply. This special rule allows the deduction of the input VAT incurred in the acquisition of goods and services for taxable activities but disallows the deduction of the input VAT for the exempt activities. The input VAT borne for the acquisition of goods and services used in both activities may be deducted applying the above mentioned general ratio.

## *Time of recovery*

Input VAT is deductible when the invoice has been received by the taxable person or when VAT due on imports has been paid. The claim to input tax credit should be made in the VAT return for the period during which the invoice or import document is received.

If at the end of the year input VAT exceeds output VAT, the taxpayer may request a refund for the balance at the time the last return is filed.

Exporters included in the Special Register (exports must be above 20 million pesetas) may request refunds on their monthly returns. This refund is limited to 12 per cent. of exports made in the same period.

## *Refund for foreign entrepreneurs*

There is a special procedure for refund to entrepreneurs established in the Canary Islands, Ceuta and Melilla or in other EC countries as well as in non-EC countries, as from January 1, 1988.

### EC entrepreneurs

The activity of the foreign entrepreneur must be subject to VAT or other similar tax in his country.

He should not have made any supplies of goods or services within the Spanish VAT territory other than the following:

— services connected with exports;
— services connected with imports;
— services for which the resident recipient is the taxable person.

Refund of VAT cannot be claimed if the input VAT refers to goods or services for which an input credit is not allowed, see para. 13–013, "General rule". **13–015**

Refund of VAT over pesetas 25,000 may be claimed for a quarter or a year and must be claimed within a period of six months from the last day of the period to which it refers.

Refunds of over pesetas 3,000 and below pesetas 25,000 may be claimed when they refer to the whole year.

The documents to be filed are the following:

— official form for claiming: the form may be that of any EC country but it should be completed in Spanish;
— certificate issued by the tax authorities of the country of residence of the applicant indicating that the applicant is a VAT taxpayer;
— original invoices and import documents proving Spanish VAT paid.

### Non-EC entrepreneurs

The procedure and requirements are the same as for EC entrepreneurs except for the following points:

— it is necessary to prove reciprocity for Spanish entrepreneurs in the country of the applicant;
— a VAT representative must be appointed.

# 9. ADMINISTRATIVE OBLIGATIONS

## *Registration*

All entrepreneurs who commence activities which are subject to VAT within the Spanish VAT territory must register, using the official form, **13–016** in their tax office before the date of commencement. The right to claim input VAT credit is conditional upon this registration.

## Books and records

The following books must be kept by a taxable person:

- book of invoices issued;
- book of invoices received;
- book of assets (only if the *pro rata* is applicable).

## Invoices

Every taxable person must issue an invoice for each supply, even in case of exemption or self-supply. It is also possible to issue a sole invoice for all the supplies made to the same person during a month.

The invoice should be issued within 30 days from the date of the chargeable event. It should be sent to the recipient within another 30 days.

Invoices must incorporate the following information:

- an identifying number;
- the name, address and fiscal identification number of the supplier;
- the name, address and fiscal identification number of the recipient;
- description of the supply;
- the total amount payable excluding VAT;
- tax rate and tax due;
- place and date of issuing;
- if the invoice corresponds to a payment in advance, it should be clearly indicated.

Failure to comply with these requirements may prevent the recovery of input VAT.

Every taxable person is obliged to keep all invoices received for a period of five years.

## VAT returns

VAT returns have to be submitted every three months, although in the following cases the return must be filed monthly:

- when sales in the previous year exceeded pesetas 1,000 million;
- when the taxpayer is included in the Exporter Register (exports have to exceed pesetas 20 million).

VAT returns must be submitted no later than twenty days after the end of the period to which it relates, except the return for the last period of the year which can be submitted within the following 30 days.

## *Basque Country and Navarra*

Basically, the VAT rules concerning the Basque Country and Navarra are:

— entrepreneurs who carry out activities only within one of these territories are taxed by the Administration of that territory;

— entrepreneurs who carry out activities in the Basque Country and/or Navarra and the rest of the Spanish VAT territory are taxed by the Administration of their registered office or permanent address if their previous year sales were lower than pesetas 200 million;

— if the activities are carried out in both territories and the previous year sales were higher than pesetas 200 million, VAT must be paid to the Administration of all the territories involved according to the percentage of operations made in each territory. There are specific rules to determine in which territory a supply is made.

## *Powers of the authorities*

### Estimate of tax paid

The tax authorities may estimate the tax to be paid if an entrepreneur **13–017** has failed to file VAT returns within the period prescribed and a formal request to do so is not complied with.

### Statutes of limitation

The statute of limitation is five years from the filing date.

### Correction of returns

An input credit which has been omitted on a VAT return can still be claimed for a period of one year from the date on which the VAT became chargeable or import VAT was paid.

If a return needs to be amended, a supplementary return should be filed and any additional tax paid with interest from the original due date. If the supplementary return involves a refund of tax unduly paid it is necessary to file a request to the tax authorities within a period of six to twelve months from the date of filing. However a court decision has declared that VAT unduly paid can be claimed back within the five years of the statute of limitations.

Failure to submit returns in time entails the payment of interest with a minimum of 10 per cent. of the VAT due. If the filing is requested by the tax authorities and output VAT was charged to the customers, a minimum penalty of 150 per cent. of the VAT due is applicable.

Late payment of tax when an application for deferment or partial payment has not been made is punished by a penalty of 20 per cent of the tax due plus late payment interest.

### *Objections/Appeals*

Appeals to the tax authorities or to the Provincial Administrative Court (Tribunal Economico-Administrativo-Provincial) must be made within 15 days from the date of notification of an assessment or a disputed decision. In certain cases, the decision of the trial court may be appealed to the Central Adminstrative Court (Tribunal Economico-Administrativo-Central). Further appeals are also possible to the Territorial Justice Court (Audiencia Territorial) and the Supreme Court (Tribunal Supremo).

A special procedure applies when a dispute arises between the supplier and the recipient concerning the VAT to be charged.

## 10. SPECIAL VAT REGIMES

### *Real property transactions*

**13–018** Specific rules apply to real property transactions. Real property transactions are considered to be supplies of goods. The supply is deemed to be rendered at the place where the real property is located.

The place of the supply of services connected with immovable property, such as lease, services of estate agents and experts, services for preparing and coordinating construction works, services of architects and engineers, mediation in real property transactions, etc., is the place where the property is situated.

The following transactions are exempt from VAT:

— second and subsequent supplies (after that made by the promoter) of buildings or parts thereof, and of the land on which they stand. In this case, transfer tax is due at a rate of 6 per cent., by the purchaser;
— supplies of country land;
— letting of building or parts thereof for housing, including garages and other accessory sections if they are let together (building and garage);

The reduced VAT rate of 6 per cent. is applicable to:

— supplies of buildings or parts thereof to be used for housing, including garages and other accessory sections (if they are sold together);
— building constructions for housing, including premises and garages.

## Small entrepreneurs

Individual entrepreneurs who carry out certain specified activities and whose previous years sales were lower than pesetas 50 million may opt for a simplified procedure for charging and collecting the VAT. The VAT due is determined by applying certain indices or modules approved by the tax authorities. 13–019

## Agricultural, livestock and fisheries activities

There is a special scheme for agricultural, forestry, livestock and fishing enterprises. Entrepreneurs are compensated for the VAT they are charged on their purchases by means of a 4 per cent. flat rate addition to the price at which they will sell their products to VAT taxable persons. Taxable persons to whom the goods or services are supplied are obliged to pay that compensation and may claim input credit in respect of it.

## Travel agencies

A special scheme applies to travel agents and tour operators who deal with customers in their own name and use the supplies and services of other taxable persons in the provision of travel facilities. All transactions performed by the travel agent in respect of a journey are treated as a single service supplied to the traveller. The supply is deemed to take place where the travel agent has established his business or has a fixed establishment from which the service has been provided. The taxable base is the travel agent's margin, that is to say, the difference between the total amount to be paid by the traveller, exclusive of VAT and the actual cost to the travel agent of supplies and services (included VAT) provided by other taxable persons when these supplies are for the direct benefit of the traveller.

Travel agent services are exempt when transactions entrusted to other taxable persons, for the benefit of the traveller and used for travelling purposes, are performed by such persons outside the EC. Where these transactions are performed both inside and outside the EC, only the part of the travel agent's service relating to transactions outside the EC is exempt. This exemption entitles the entrepreneur to input credit.

## Second-hand goods, antiques and art goods

There are special optional schemes for second-hand traders and antique dealers. In these special schemes the taxable persons may choose how to determine the taxable base. It can either be 30 per cent. of the total consideration or the difference between sales price and purchase price. In the latter case the taxable base can never be lower than 20 per cent. of the total consideration. An option for one of these alternatives applies to all the supplies of this nature. 13–020

## *Retailers*

There are two special schemes with regard to retailers:

1. Optional scheme for retailers supplying goods chargeable to VAT at more than one rate. This is the usual scheme for big department stores. The taxable base is determined according to the level of purchases at each rate.
2. Equivalent increase scheme: this scheme is obligatory for individual retailers, with certain exceptions. Entrepreneurs who supply goods to retailers must charge an additional 3 per cent. or 1 per cent. rate (depending whether the general or reduced rate is applicable) on all supplies. The entrepreneur must pay this additional percentage to the Administration. The additional 3 per cent. or 1 per cent. also applies to imports made by retailers. The retailer does not have to pay VAT to the Administration nor can he claim repayment of any input VAT suffered. The retailer must charge his customers VAT at the appropriate rate corresponding to the goods supplied without adding the additional VAT charged to him under this scheme.

# 14. Sweden

## 1. GENERAL BACKGROUND

Sweden, which is not a member of the European Community, introduced VAT in 1969 through the Value Added Tax Act. Although EC Directives have no impact on Swedish VAT legislation, the VAT laws are largely based on the same principles. **14–001**

In Sweden the free ports are treated as Swedish territory if goods are delivered there to be used in the port. Otherwise, such a delivery is regarded as export.

VAT inside the country is levied by the regional tax authority (länsskattemyndigheten), one in every county. VAT on imports is levied by the Swedish Customs Office and is paid according to the same procedure as customs duties.

## 2. WHO IS TAXABLE?

### *General*

According to the basic rule, the liability to pay tax arises whenever turnover of a taxable commodity or service occurs in Sweden in commercial activity. Any physical or legal person (limited company, incorporated association, etc.) conducting a taxable activity in an independent manner is liable to pay tax. Therefore, if a person has two or more distinct enterprises, those enterprises are normally subject to VAT separately. **14–002**

There is a certain limit of SEK 30,000 (ECU 4,500.—) turnover a year, including VAT, over which there is a requirement to be registered for VAT. If the turnover is below that limit, there is still an obligation to charge VAT; however, this will be accounted for in the income tax return. It is possible to be registered for VAT even if the turnover is below the limit. That applies to export business, business in a "starting-up" period and business with zero-rated supplies.

Special rules apply to general partnerships (handelsbolag). They are subject to VAT, as such, although each owner is taxed individually for income tax purposes. A single partnership (enkeltbolag) in business is normally regarded as a trading company and is subject to VAT as such. A single partnership in the building business, however, is not taxable of its own accord. Each of these partners is taxable individually, both for income tax and VAT purposes. For VAT purposes, however, the partners can decide to let one of them do the accounting for the tax authorities.

Estates of deceased persons, estates in bankruptcy and commission companies also qualify as taxable persons.

#### Transactions with branch/subsidiary

A subsidiary will always have its own registration. Supplies between parent and subsidiary are always taxable, although cross-border supplies may be viewed as export or import. A branch will have its own registration only if the activity in the branch is seen as a different line of business income for the company.

Transactions between a head office and a branch are not taxable in Sweden.

#### Government bodies

Government entities are taxable if they deliver goods or provide services to anyone other than government entities.

### *Fiscal unity/Group taxation*

There are no special rules for taxation of companies as a group or fiscal unity. There are possibilities to credit VAT incurred in one company in the group by charging the VAT to another company of the group. The ownership must, however, amount to more than 90 per cent. of the shares and the "charged company" must not supply the refunding company with taxable services.

### *Foreign entrepreneurs*

**14–003** Non-resident entrepreneurs are deemed to carry on a commercial activity if it is conducted in a commercial manner and:

- if the goods traded are stocked in Sweden;
- if the goods are acquired in or imported into Sweden for delivery after assembly, installation or other service; or
- if an entrepreneur provides construction, contracting services or other services in Sweden.

Foreign entrepreneurs may thus incur tax liability under the Value Added Tax Act even if they are not liable for income tax in Sweden.

#### Representative offices

Representative offices (for example, dependent agents who provide services of a supporting and/or auxiliary nature, such as marketing services, etc.) generally do not qualify as a permanent establishment for either corporate tax purposes or VAT purposes.

#### VAT representative

A foreign person is only liable to VAT when taxable supplies are made in Sweden. If this foreign person has no permanent establishment in Sweden, he must register through a representative who is responsible for fulfilling the administrative obligations, but not for paying the tax. The representative must be approved by the regional tax office.

#### Reverse charge mechanism

The concept of reverse charge, as applicable in the EC countries, by which the resident customer becomes liable to VAT rather than the non-resident supplier, is not known in Sweden. All foreign entrepreneurs will be registered and liable to VAT, if supplying taxable goods (under certain circumstances, see above) and services in Sweden.

### *Importers*

Tax liability is incurred by the person submitting the commodity for customs clearance (*i.e.*, the person incurring customs liability).

A forwarding or a customs clearance agent may pay the VAT due on importation on behalf of the importer, or he may elect to account for VAT himself, in which case he will pay the tax on his own behalf and pass it on to the importer.

## 3. WHAT IS TAXABLE?

VAT is levied whenever a turnover of taxable goods or services occurs within Sweden. **14–004**

### *Supply of goods*

"Supply" means a delivery of goods and services.

The term "goods" refers primarily to tangible objects which do not constitute real property. Goods are taxable unless specifically exempt from the tax. Both raw materials and semi-finished goods, etc., as well as finished consumer and capital goods, are subject to tax. It is of no consequence whether the commodity is new or used. The right to lease farmland, patents and the right to computer software are also considered to be a supply of goods.

## *Supply of services*

Services are only taxable when they are specifically mentioned in the law. The following are the main taxable services:

- services with respect to movable goods, the supply of which would normally be taxable, including, *e.g.*, "made-to-order" services, leasing, designing, acting as an agent, repairing, controlling, analysis, maintenance and cleaning, and catering services in restaurants;
- services with respect to land, including, *e.g.*, exploration, levelling, working at the land, blasting, drilling, filling or covering;
- services with respect to growing crops, including, *e.g.*, digging, sowing, planting, valuing, marking, cutting and protecting;
- services with respect to buildings, including, *e.g.*, constructing, demolishing, repairing, altering, maintaining and cleaning;
- project engineering, drawing, designing, control and similar services with respect to land, buildings and other installations considered immovable property by the VAT law;
- transport of goods;
- renting of hotel rooms and similar services;
- electronic data processing and designing computer systems or software;
- publicity and advertising services and marketing for a businessman;
- services concerning the assignment of rights which are taxable;
- book-keeping and some economic services in connection with it.

Please note that when services are not specifically mentioned in the law, they are not taxable (for example, accounting/audit services, consultancy services, lawyers, etc.).

## *Self-supply of goods/services*

Self-supply of goods and services from a taxable business is regarded as turnover and shall be taxed. A self-supply occurs if it involves a taxable person who is entitled to a credit or refund for input tax and takes out goods for private use or for use in a non-taxable part of the business. Services, however, will only be taxed if the self-supplier at the same time takes out goods of a value exceeding SEK 500.

## *Imports of goods*

VAT must be paid not only on taxable turnover in Sweden, but also on imports of taxable goods. This applies regardless of the purpose of the import and irrespective of the transaction on which the import is based. Tax on imports is levied by the Customs Office in accordance with procedures laid down for customs clearance. The Customs Office is also the authority to be consulted regarding VAT on imports.

## 4. PLACE OF SUPPLY

### *Supply of goods*

The place of supply in Sweden includes commodities delivered within the country. **14–005**

Goods which are sold to a Swedish customer before importation are not taxable in Sweden.

Goods which are delivered abroad (export) are taxable in Sweden. They are, however, zero-rated.

Goods which are sold to a non-resident entrepreneur's warehouse in Sweden are taxable.

### *Supply of services*

#### General rule

A service is deemed to be rendered at the place where the activities are carried out.

#### Exceptions

The following services in Sweden which contain a "foreign element" are regarded as export-services. As a consequence, the entrepreneur need not charge VAT, but will nevertheless be allowed a refund for input VAT.

1. Delivery within Sweden if the goods are to be taken directly out of Sweden by a forwarder or carrier.
2. Delivery to a foreign entrepreneur who himself collects the goods to take them directly out of Sweden, if the goods are intended for activity conducted by the entrepreneur outside Sweden.
3. Delivery of goods in a free port, provided the goods are not intended for use in the free port.
4. Delivery of goods to or for use or trade on board a ship or aeroplane in international service.
5. Delivery of beer, wine, spirits and tobacco products for sale in a tax-free shop.
6. Delivery of a passenger car or motorcycle which is included in an exported vehicle list.
7. Delivery of goods to a foreign entrepreneur who is not liable to pay tax in Sweden, provided the delivery takes place under the terms of a warranty commitment made by the foreign entrepreneur.

8. Service performed on a commodity which has been brought into Sweden exclusively for this service and which is subsequently taken out of Sweden.*
9. Procurement of goods on behalf of a foreign client.*
10. Transport or other taxable service in Sweden which relates to an imported or exported commodity and which a forwarder or carrier provides for a foreign client in connection with import or export.*

**14–006**

11. Testing or analysis of a commodity for a foreign client.*
12. Storage of a commodity for a foreign client.*
13. Advertising or other publicity on behalf of a foreign client.*
14. Service on behalf of a foreign client which results only in a report, minutes or the like.*
15. Service on board a ship or aircraft in international service or a service relating to equipment or other goods for use on such ships or aircraft.
16. Transport of goods directly to or from a foreign country.
17. Architects' services or the like relating to real estate outside Sweden.
18. Repairs performed for a foreign entrepreneur who is not liable to pay tax inside Sweden, provided the repairs are performed under the terms of a warranty commitment made by the foreign entrepreneur.
19. Towing or repair of a truck or trailer registered or domiciled in another country, provided the service in question is performed in connection with the use of the vehicle for transport of commercial goods in Sweden. Delivery of equipment to such a vehicle is also classified as export;
20. Services relating to goods are considered as exports if the service is performed for a foreign client and relates to product development, project planning, design, construction or the like.
21. The transfer to a foreign user of patent rights, the permission to use a design or invention relating to a taxable commodity, the right to use systems or programs for automatic data processing and automatic data processing work for a foreign client are all considered as exports.

## Reverse charge mechanism

The concept of a reverse charge mechanism, as applicable in EC countries, does not exist in Sweden.

* In order for export to be deemed to have taken place, the client must conduct business outside Sweden which would entail tax liability under the Swedish Value Added Tax Act if the business were conducted in Sweden. The client should be able to prove that he conducts business activity outside Sweden by, *e.g.*, presenting registration documents or equivalent proof.

# 5. BASIS OF TAXATION

## *Supplies within Sweden*

According to the basic rule, the taxable base consists of the entire payment (see below) including VAT. 14–007

In cash sales, "payment" refers to payment received, *i.e.*, the cash price less applicable cash discounts. The value of a commodity given in exchange is regarded as the equivalent of cash payment. Bills of exchange and other instruments of debt (promissory) do not constitute cash payment.

In the case of credit sales, payment is the price on which the buyer and seller have agreed when entering into their agreement, as evidenced by an invoice or other document made out on the occasion. Such payments shall also include instalment payment charges, financing charges and all other price increments, with the exception of interest which is payable by the customer under the agreement.

If a bill of exchange or other instrument of debt is made out for payment in connection with the agreement, the agreed price consists of the amount payable according to such a document plus any cash payment made over and above this amount. This applies even if a lower price is stated in an invoice or similar document.

For taxable goods and services the taxable base includes;

— the received consideration, including VAT;
— other taxes imposed;
— any additional charges, except interest.

## *Self-supplies*

The tax base for self-supplies and private use is the "market price," *i.e.*, the same price as for external supplies. Tax liability commences when a commodity or service is withdrawn from the business.

## *Imports*

The taxable base is the value of the goods as calculated plus customs duty and other state taxes or charges, including VAT.

## *Chargeable event/Time of payment*

The basic rule is that tax liability arises in connection with turnover, at the time of delivery of a commodity or provision of a service. Liability arises already prior to delivery or provision when advance payment or payment on account is received for a commodity or service ordered. 14–008

For importation the liability arises when importation has taken place.

According to the Accounting Act 1972 the recording of payables and receivables may be made either on a current basis periodically, by notation in lists, or by recording them at the end of the fiscal year. As a result of these alternatives, a book-keeping based form of VAT reporting is to be carried out according to one of two methods, the "invoicing method" or the "final accounts methods."

The final accounts method shall be used primarily by taxpayers who during the current year only record entries for cash receipts and disbursements.

The invoicing method shall be applied in first instance by taxpayers whose book-keeping system provides for chronological recording of items in original books of entry (daybook) or who have a book-keeping system with lists kept on a current or periodical basis.

### *Credit notes/Bad debts*

If a loss should arise on a claim for which the taxpayer has previously reported tax received, a deduction may be made in an amount corresponding to the VAT. The deduction is made by reducing the figure for VAT received. To qualify for the deduction, the loss in question must be an actual or formally declared loss on accounts receivable. If payment is received for a previously deducted loss, VAT shall once again be reported for the payment received.

If a bonus discount (with the exception of so called conditional discounts) has been paid in arrears and VAT has been previously reported, an adjustment may be made for the tax accruing on such a discount, etc. The deduction is made by a reduction of the tax received. No reduction of the taxable base is permitted for a so-called conditional discount, *i.e.*, a discount awarded if payment is made within a certain period of time.

A credit note is a requirement for the seller to be entitled to reduce his tax received.

## 6. TAX RATES

The present rates are as follows:

**14–009** 3.8% (increment 3.95% on the pre-tax price)

This rate is applied for services, like digging and building with respect to:

- outdoor conduits for water, gas, electricity, etc.;
- roads, bridges and parking;
- rail construction, airfields, harbours, canals, etc.;
- grounds for sportfields, school yards, etc.;
- project engineering, drawing, designing in relation to immovable property control and inspection of such property and leading to construction work.

11.4% (increment 12.87% on the pre-tax price):

- some catering services in restaurants;

— renting of rooms in a hotel business;
— construction services;
— prefabricated houses;
— renting of business premises in cases where owner has applied to be liable to pay tax on rental, see para. 14–017.

19% including VAT, which gives an effective rate of 23.46% on the price excluding VAT:

— all goods and services not subject to a lower rate.

## 7. EXEMPTIONS

### *Exemption with credit for input tax*

This category includes: **14–010**

— Ships and aircraft;
— War materials;
— Medicines;
— Fuels;
— Newspapers.

Also:

— services in connection with zero-rated exempt goods, except for transport;
— transport in connection with cleaning;
— salvage operations if carried out on ships and aircraft which are exempt;
— taking care of goods for destruction;
— service related to printed matter, when the publication is exempt;
— exported taxable goods and services are also zero-rated.

Exemptions for importation of goods are the same as for supplies within Sweden. Furthermore, exemptions are allowed, for example, for personal effects up to SEK 1,000.—and for temporary importation of goods.

### *Exemption without credit for input tax*

This category includes:

— certain periodical publications of a non-commercial nature, staff magazines, etc.;
— works of visual art (when the artist himself or his estate is the selling part);
— water from public waterworks;
— stock in trade, furnishings and other assets belonging to a business, when transferred in connection with the transfer of the business or a part thereof, or in connection with a merger or similar procedure;

- films and duty-free printed matter when imported without payment;
- products for personal use at importation;
- postage stamps;
- products of mechanical density;
- advertising in exempt publications;
- showing of motion picture films;
- compulsory control of motor vehicles;
- veterinary services;
- medical services according to inspection and analysis of tests.

## *Non-taxable transactions*

**14–011** For various reasons, certain areas mainly concerned with services of a personal nature have been excluded from VAT, for example:

- rental of residential housing (for rents on business premises, see para. 14–017, "Special VAT regimes");
- banking services;
- insurance services;
- legal services;
- auditing;
- medical and health care;
- education;
- passenger transport and other travel services;
- hygiene and physical care (hairdressers, bathhouses, etc.);
- entertainment (cinemas, evening entertainers, etc.);
- sporting events;
- theatrical performances, etc.

### Transactions within the same legal entity

Transactions within the same legal entity are not taxable as they are not regarded as turnover. Thus, transactions between a foreign head office and a branch in Sweden or vice versa are not regarded as turnover.

### Transfer of business

Assets and other goods are exempted from VAT when they are included in a transfer of a business. In order to be exempt, the transfer must concern the whole business or a certain independent part of it.

### Subsidies/Penalty payments/Compensation

Subsidies, penalty payments and compensation are outside the scope of VAT, provided they are not to be qualified as payments for taxable supplies.

### *Election for taxable supplies*

The government may, upon request, rule that tax liability applies, until further notice, for a person rendering a service, other than those specifically listed in the law, *e.g.*, for forwarding agents according to VAT for import.

## 8. CREDIT/REFUND FOR INPUT VAT

### *General rule*

A person who is liable to report VAT is entitled to claim a deduction **14–012** in his tax return for tax paid on acquisitions and imports for business entailing tax liability. The right to deductions is essentially general in nature, that is, it covers all types of acquisitions with a few exceptions.

No credit is allowed for VAT incurred on the following transactions:

— dwelling houses;
— personal cars and motorcycles for other purposes than dealing in such vehicles or renting them. The right to a deduction for tax paid on the cost of rental (leasing) of a passenger car is limited to 50 per cent.;
— VAT on deductible expenditure on entertainment and representation for income tax purposes.

Some special rules are in force:

— It is possible to credit VAT charged from one company to another in a group where one Swedish company owns more than 90 per cent. of the shares of one or more Swedish companies in the group. This can be seen as the concept of fiscal unity in the Sixth EC Directive.
— An entrepreneur liable to VAT is entitled to a credit for fictitious VAT when he buys taxable goods from a non-taxable person or company. The credit is the amount of VAT which would have been charged by the seller if he had been liable to VAT in the transaction.

Example: If a foreign entrepreneur liable for VAT in Sweden buys equipment from a Swedish bank (not taxable), he can deduct 19 per cent. of the price as VAT, even though VAT was not charged.

### *Adjustment of entitlement to credit*

A partially exempt enterprise deducts input tax based on the previous year's turnover for the different parts of the business. An adjustment must be made when the annual accounts become final.

### *Partial exemption*

14–013 If part of the turnover concerns activities which do not lead to liability for VAT, the input tax must be split between purchases relating to taxable and exempt (no credit) transactions. The input tax may be divided on the basis of the ratio of taxable and non-taxable transactions of total turnover. Other allocation methods are also permitted, *e.g.*, on the basis of how the floor space of the business premises is used or on the ratio between the employees in the different parts of the business.

### *Time of recovery*

When the invoicing method is applied, the right to claim deductions for VAT paid, commences at the time the business transaction on which the right to the deduction is based is entered into the books or when it is recorded in a list. This means that a person filing a return for a certain reporting period is entitled to a deduction—in addition to deductions for VAT on cash purchases—for VAT on unpaid invoices which have been entered into the books or recorded during the period and which relates to deliveries of goods or provision of services made.

The right to claim deductions when applying the final accounts method commences during the current fiscal year when cash payment is made. Debt instruments (bills of exchange and promissory notes) are not considered the equivalent of cash payment. Therefore, deductions may not be made until the debt instrument is traded or redeemed. VAT which has been charged on unpaid payables may not be deducted until the return for the final reporting period of the tax year.

### *Refund for foreign entrepreneurs*

No special rules apply. For obtaining a refund for input tax incurred, the same general rules mentioned above apply to foreign entrepreneurs. Please note that foreign entrepreneurs who have no permanent establishment in Sweden need a VAT representative in order to obtain a refund for input VAT incurred.

## 9. ADMINISTRATIVE OBLIGATIONS

### *Registration*

14–014 All taxable entrepreneurs have to register at the regional tax office if the turnover exceeds SEK 30,000 (ECU 4,500.—) per tax year. There are also possibilities to register voluntarily. This is in some cases particularly appealing to owners of buildings.

## *Books and records*

The basic principle is that liability to report VAT commences when a person becomes liable to enter a business transaction entailing tax liability into his books of account. Similarly, the right to deductions commences when an acquisition is entered into the books. Certain exceptions have been made from this accrual basis principle.

For book-keeping and tax purposes the books and records must be kept 10 years. If no books and records are kept, a penalty is likely to be imposed and the VAT liability will be based on an estimate.

## *Invoices*

All persons incurring tax liability under the Value Added Tax Act are also liable to issue an invoice, settlement or corresponding document for each taxable transaction. There are certain exceptions to this rule.

The invoice, settlement statement or corresponding document must indicate the amounts of payment and tax, as well as other information of relevance for determing tax liability and the right to deductions.

The amount of VAT (not for supplies in retail business if the total amount is less than SEK 200), the name of the purchaser and the seller, the registration number for VAT and a specification of what has been supplied. Under Swedish book-keeping rules, which are also applicable for VAT accounting, the invoice must be issued as soon as possible after the supply has been made.

Retail trade has been exempted from compulsory invoicing. The same applies to persons performing services which are principally directed to the general public, *e.g.*, in the restaurant sector.

## *VAT returns*

Returns shall be filed for a certain reporting period, generally two **14–015**
months, but it is possible to be registered for periods of one month (export companies, *e.g.*) or six months or one year (small companies).

## *Powers of the authorities*

If the tax cannot be reliably computed on the basis of the return or if no return has been filed, the county administration will determine the tax on reasonable grounds by an assessment; (additional) assessments can be imposed during six years following the calendar year during which the tax year expired.

Once the tax return has been submitted, it constitutes a final statement of the tax for the period and shall constitute the basis for the tax assessment. It is, of course, possible to correct errors that may have been made in a return which has already been submitted. The most convenient procedure in such a case is simply to replace the incorrect return by a corrected return for the same reporting period. A return form for this purpose may be ordered from the county administration VAT section. If a corrected return is received by the county administration, an assessment will be made.

Penalty for late payment is 6 per cent. of the tax that has not been paid.

Additional 20 per cent. of the tax amount will be charged if incorrect information is provided in a tax return or other document.

### *Objections/Appeals*

VAT is assessed for each reporting period. Once a return has been filed on time, the tax declared is deemed to have been assessed automatically. No formal notice is given to the taxpayer. If the taxpayer does not think that he can resolve a tax issue in mutual agreement with the county administration, he may appeal the county administration's decision to the County Fiscal Court of Appeal. In order to do so, he must request a final assessment from the county tax administration. The final assessment can then be appealed. The request for the final assessment must be made within six years following the end of the calendar year during which the tax year expired.

The ruling of the County Fiscal Court of Appeal may be appealed to the Fiscal Court of Appeal and subsequently—after special permission—to the Supreme Administrative Court. The appeal must be made within two months after the decision from the County Fiscal Court of Appeal has been received.

## 10. SPECIAL VAT REGIMES

### *Agricultural and forestry enterprises*

**14–016** Growing woodland, crops and other vegetation where sales take place independently of the conveyance of the land are regarded as taxable goods. So are also the rights of:

- agricultural lease;
- timber rights or other comparable rights;
- the right to extract earth, stone or some other natural product;

### *Financial institutions*

Financial activities are normally outside the scope of VAT. Generally, financial companies are liable for VAT for selling of items which have been repossessed by the company under the terms of a purchase.

## *Fishing enterprises*

For fishing companies there are no special rules for the liability of the VAT. Such companies can buy fishing boats without VAT as such boats are exempted.

## *Free Port/Bonded warehouse*

There are free ports in two places in Sweden: Stockholm and Gothenburg. Provided the goods are not intended for use in the free port, delivery of goods in a free port is regarded as export.

It is possible to have bonded warehouses in Sweden. They do not have to be situated in the free port area. Customs duty will be paid when goods are taken out from the warehouse.

## *Retailers*

There are special rules.

## *Second-hand goods/Arts and antiques*

Second-hand goods are treated as normal goods. Works of art are **14–017**
exempted from VAT when the artist or his estate is the seller. For antiques and arts (not from the artist) there is one important special rule. A businessman exporting antique goods or arts is not entitled to a credit for input tax.

## *Small entrepreneurs*

Small entrepreneurs are taxable, but they do not have to be registered if the annual turnover is below SEK 30,000.

## *Travel agencies*

A travel agency business is not liable for VAT.

## *Real property transactions*

Real property is not subject to tax. The term "real property" is highly important in the application of the VAT rules, since there are, in the real property area, special rules governing such questions as to which goods and services are subject to tax, when the liability to report VAT commences, and how the taxable base is determined. For the purpose of VAT real property includes, first of all, everything which is defined to be real property under the Code of Land laws. In addition, real property also includes buildings, conduits, fences or similar facilities which have been installed in or above the ground for permanent use and which are owned by a person other than the owner of the land. Items added to a building are generally regarded as building fixtures if they are designed for permanent use and relate to the general function of the building

### Building fixtures are not subject to VAT

Industrial fixtures which have been procured for direct use in a particular specified business are deemed to be goods, even if they have been permanently installed in the building.

Business fixtures procured for direct use in a particular business are defined as goods.

Equipment for plumbing, sanitation, heating, electricity and the like which is defined by the Land Laws as part of the building shall, however, always be regarded as real property if the equipment is of the type normally used to equip a building for residential housing purposes.

Upon application, the county administration may rule that the owner of real estate shall be liable to pay tax on rental of business premises used in activity which is itself subject to VAT. A lease with rights to a tenant-owner's flat (bostadsrätt) is considered the equivalent of rental in this case. This possibility does not extend to second-hand rentals. The aim here is to allow the property owner to deduct for the tax he has paid on construction costs, etc. He is then to charge the tenant, who is liable to pay tax, for the openly reported tax paid by the owner, which then becomes deductible tax paid for the tenant. Once tax liability has been granted, there are certain possiblities for retroactive deductions. There are also regulations on restoring deductions for tax paid if circumstances are altered, *e.g.*, if the property is sold.

# 15. The United Kingdom

## 1. GENERAL BACKGROUND

Value Added Tax was introduced into the United Kingdom with effect from April 1, 1973, in conjunction with admission to the European Community on January 1, 1973. An indirect tax, it superseded two other taxes, namely Selective Employment Tax and Purchase Tax. **15–001**

For VAT purposes, the "United Kingdom" comprises England, Wales, Scotland, Northern Ireland and (effectively) the Isle of Man, but it does not include the Channel Islands, which are not only outside the United Kingdom, but also outside the EC.

United Kingdom VAT legislation is for the most part contained in the Value Added Tax Act 1983 ("VATA 1983"), as amended, but much detailed legislation is contained in Regulations. Substantial amendments were made to the original legislation with effect from January 1, 1978, in order to make the United Kingdom position correspond more closely with the Sixth EC Directive, but there still remain a small number of areas of divergence (*e.g.* in the rates governing the place of supply of services).

VAT is administered by H.M. Customs & Excise ("Customs"), whilst the direct taxes such as Corporation Tax, Income Tax, etc, are administered by the Inland Revenue. There is currently little interchange of information between the two government departments, and their procedures are in many respects markedly different. This contrasts with the position in many other EC Member States.

## 2. WHO IS TAXABLE?

### *General*

A "taxable person" is any person (individual, company, partnership, etc.) who makes or intends to make taxable supplies while he is or is required to be registered under the provisions of VATA 1983. A taxable supply is a supply of goods or services (other than an exempt supply) made in the United Kingdom in the course or furtherance of any business. **15–002**

The concept of "business" is fundamental in considering whether or not a liability to VAT arises. Certain supplies are deemed always to be business, *e.g.* subscriptions to clubs and the admission of the public to premises, but the definition of business in the VAT legislation is not intended to be exhaustive. There is case law on the subject, and in general "business" is more all-embracing than the equivalent "trading" test for direct taxation. Occasional transactions will thus in general be subject to VAT, providing there is a measure of continuity and substance to them, and they involve making supplies for consideration (though not necessarily for profit). Hobby activities and certain voluntary and charitable activities are treated as non-business. The term "entrepreneur" is not used in the United Kingdom VAT legislation but broadly speaking, a person carrying on a business is very similar to an "entrepreneur" in other EC countries.

Notification of a liability to be registered for VAT is required when taxable supplies are in excess of £23,600 per annum, or £8,000 per calendar quarter (1989/90 figures). In recent years, these figures have tended to be increased each year in March broadly in line with inflation. Stiff penalties exist for late notification of a liability to be registered, and this matter is dealt with further below.

Businesses are able to register for VAT voluntarily when taxable supplies are beneath the registration limits, and such registrations are in fact commonplace. Where a business makes taxable supplies exclusively or predominantly to other businesses that are registered for VAT, no loss of competitiveness arises; registration enables the business to reclaim as input tax VAT arising on expenditure which is attributable to its own taxable supplies of goods and services (but not when there are exempt or not by way of business) and the fact that a business is registered for VAT (demonstrated by a VAT number on invoices) can add credibility to the business.

### Transactions with branch/subsidiary

**15–003** If a branch of an overseas business (as opposed to a subsidiary company of an overseas business) is registered for VAT, any supplies of services to or from abroad with the United Kingdom branch are outside the scope of the tax; this is important where the United Kingdom branch is partly exempt, and is importing certain services from abroad.

### Government bodies

Special provisions enable local authorities and certain other bodies, including certain government bodies, to recover VAT on supplies made to them. They are also obliged to charge VAT on certain supplies made, particularly when in competition with the private sector.

## *Fiscal unity/Group transactions*

The facility of "group registration" allows all bodies corporate resident in the United Kingdom (but not individuals, partnerships, etc) under common control to be treated as one for VAT accounting purposes with just one VAT return submitted to Customs by the "representative member." There are several tests for "common control" but to put it simply, if there is common ownership to the extent of more than 50 per cent. of the ordinary shares being owned by one person, then any combination of such companies may be group registered.

The facility is entirely optional; any combination of United Kingdom resident companies may be group registered. Customs have a power to refuse group registration for the protection of the Inland Revenue and exercise this power where an avoidance motive is suspected. There are many advantages and disadvantages to group registration but it should be emphasised that there are considerable planning opportunities associated with the facility. In particular, there are significant numbers of businesses which are partly exempt (see below) in the United Kingdom, and group registration prevents the unnecessary generation of irrecoverable VAT on cross-charges between companies under common control.

Where companies are group registered, a joint and several liability to United Kingdom VAT arises for each of them. Where the potential liability is material in any instance, the existence of the VAT group registration is normally recorded by way of note to the accounts. **15–004**

The test of "residence" is unusual, and differs from that applied for corporation tax purposes. For VAT group registration purposes, a company is resident in the United Kingdom if at least one director with full voting rights is personally resident in the United Kingdom and regularly attends board meetings. This is a more generous test of residence than applies in most other EC Member States.

## *Foreign businesses*

Foreign businesses which supply goods or services in excess of the registration limits in the United Kingdom must, in general, notify Customs of their liability to be registered in the United Kingdom, in the same way as national suppliers. However, a foreign business supplying services in the United Kingdom, but having no establishment of any kind here, may not have to register—but the services may be subject to the "reverse charge" on importation (*i.e.* taxed in the hands of the customer)—see para. 15–005.

It is possible to be registered through a "VAT agent," although commercially there is much reluctance for businesses to act as such because Customs contend that the "VAT agent" is liable for the VAT debts of his overseas principal. Whilst in theory this problem could be obviated through the use of bank guarantees, the practical problems are such that overseas businesses normally register direct with a special unit of Customs in Aberdeen, if necessary lodging an appropriate bank guarantee there.

### Representative office

A representative office of an overseas business is eligible for United

Kingdom VAT registration, even when it makes no taxable supplies in the United Kingdom. However, registration is limited to those circumstances where the supplies of the business overseas would be taxable supplies if made in the United Kingdom.

### VAT representative

15–005 If a person who belongs outside the United Kingdom is making taxable supplies in the United Kingdom which require United Kingdom VAT registration, the overseas person can appoint a United Kingdom VAT agent who then becomes responsible for the overseas person's United Kingdom VAT liabilities. Alternatively, the taxable person can be registered from his overseas place of business and in such circumstances Customs require a security to be lodged which must be a guarantee from a United Kingdom bank or United Kingdom insurance company.

### Reverse charge mechanism

Where certain services are imported into the United Kingdom by way of business, the importer must account for United Kingdom VAT as if he had made the supply in question himself, to himself. The services in question are as follows:

- transfers and assignments of copyright, patents, licences, trademarks and similar rights;
- advertising services;
- services of consultants, engineers, consultancy bureaux, lawyers, accountants and other similar services; data processing and provision of information (but excluding from this head any services relating to land);
- acceptance of any obligation to refrain from pursuing or exercising, in whole or part, any business activity or any such rights as are referred to in paragraph 15–001 above;
- banking, financial and insurance services (including reinsurance, but not including the provision of safe deposit facilities);
- the supply of staff;
- the letting or hire of goods other than means of transport;
- the services rendered by one person to another in procuring for the other any of the services mentioned in the preceding paragraphs.

15–006 The importation of such services constitutes "taxable turnover" for registration purposes, and might mean, for example, that a business otherwise making only exempt supplies would have to register for United Kingdom VAT if the imports exceeded the registration limits. These provisions, which accurately reflect Article 9(2)(e) of the Sixth EC Directive, are an exception to the normal rule for establishing the place of supply of services (when the supplier is established), the tax charge arising instead in the hands of the customer importing these mainly "intellectual" services from overseas. The charge only "sticks" when the importer is unable to reclaim all his input tax (*i.e.* he is exempt or partly exempt).

## *Importers*

A foreign business is not obliged to register for VAT if title to the goods imported passes outside the United Kingdom, and the customer himself imports the goods. Further, if a foreign business maintains a stock of goods in the United Kingdom, those goods can be imported under the VAT registration number of an import agent, who will then charge VAT as appropriate to the United Kingdom customer. The only complication here is that the import agent will have to charge the foreign business VAT on his commission, which will be irrecoverable; this problem can be avoided if the foreign business is separately registered either through a "VAT agent" (who could be the import agent), or through the special procedure for registration of foreign business with Aberdeen VAT office mentioned above.

# 3. WHAT IS TAXABLE?

Taxable supplies are all supplies made in the course or furtherance of a business which are of a type which would be taxable (at standard or zero rate) when made by a person who is registered or registrable. The standard rate is currently 15% and has been so since 1979—there are no higher or lower rates. The zero rate is, in effect, "exemption with refund" (the term used in EC Directives), and, where it applies, a nil rate of VAT is charged on outputs, but full recovery can be made of VAT on attributable inputs. **15–007**

## *Supply of goods*

The transfer of the whole property in goods is a supply of goods for VAT purposes. The distinction between a supply of goods on the one hand and a supply of services on the other, is sometimes difficult to grasp, but the legislation specifies that the following (*inter alia*) are supplies of goods:

- the application by one person of a treatment or process to another person's goods;
- the supply of any form of power, heat, refrigeration or ventilation;
- the granting, assignment or surrender of a "major interest" in land.

### Assembly/Installation

A supply of goods takes place in the United Kingdom if the specific goods to be supplied are located in the United Kingdom. This applies **15–008** even if an overseas entrepreneur has no place of business in the United Kingdom. However, the supply of assembled or installed goods may be seen as being made outside the United Kingdom provided certain conditions are met.

## *Supply of services*

Anything which is not a supply of goods but is done for a consideration (including, if so done, the granting, assignment or surrender of any right) is a supply of services.

## *Self-supply of goods/services*

**15–009** There are a number of circumstances when a business has to account for VAT on supplies made to it, rather than by it in addition to the case of certain imported services, see para. 15–005 "Reverse charge mechanism".

Where a partly exempt business or unregistered business produces stationery or cars (this applies to car dealers and manufacturers) for its own use, or provides its own construction services or building land, special rules apply to the "value added" element. This is to prevent unfair competition with manufacturers of these goods.

Where the self-supply is of construction services relating to the construction of new buildings or a major extension or enlargement, VAT must be accounted for on the open market value of the construction services when this exceeds £100,000 or more. This provision was introduced from April 1, 1989, and applies to "in house" construction services, including those provided with VAT Groups.

Where a building or civil engineering work is developed by a partly exempt person for his own occupation but not using "in house" labour or when there is to be an exempt disposal of the building or work, a self-supply charge, rather than using outside "in house" labour, arises when the building or work is completed. The value of the self-supply is the aggregate of the historical value of the land on which it stands and the value of all standard rate supplies made or to be made in connection with it. This self-supply was introduced from August 1, 1989. It does not apply where the value is less than £100,000.

## *Imports of goods*

VAT is either payable upon importation of goods, or, more usually, a debit is made to the importer's bank account on the 15th day of the month following removal from the port (deferred duty system). Input relief is then available to the importer in the same way as with normal supplies. A bank guarantee is required from the importer to cover all VAT deferred at importation under this scheme. It is not possible to place goods only liable to VAT on import in a Customs or Bonded warehouse.

Very exceptionally, postal imports of goods worth less than £1,300 are dealt with by "postponed accounting," whereby payment of tax upon importation is postponed until completion of the importer's next VAT return.

In all instances, it is important that the importer has the correct documentation before claiming input relief.

## 4. PLACE OF SUPPLY

### *Supply of goods*

The place of supply of any goods which does not involve their removal from or to the United Kingdom is treated as supplied in the United Kingdom if they are in the United Kingdom. Otherwise they are treated as supplied outside the United Kingdom. Further, if the supply of any goods involves their removal from the United Kingdom, they are treated as supplied in the United Kingdom and if it involves their removal to the United Kingdom they are treated as supplied outside the United Kingdom. **15–010**

### *Supply of services*

#### General rule

Under the normal rule, supplies of services are treated as being made where the supplier belongs. Where a supplier has establishments in more than one country, the supply is treated as being made by the establishment which is most directly concerned with the supply in question. (It should be noted that in certain instances the United Kingdom VAT legislation achieves the effect of the place of supply rules in the Sixth EC Directive by means of zero-rating rather than by treating the supply as outside the jurisdiction or scope of the tax; while the effect is the same for exported services (even though the place of supply is technically in the United Kingdom), it is not necessarily so for the same services when they are imported, *e.g.* entertainment services performed by an overseas person in the United Kingdom—see below).

### *Exceptions*

#### Property

Whilst many supplies of property are currently supplies of goods rather than of services, when they are supplies of services, as a matter of practice they will be treated as being made where the property is situated. **15–011**

#### Transport services

The supply of transport services is treated as taking place in the United Kingdom to the extent that the journey is within the United

Kingdom, although there are exceptions. The transport of passengers or freight outside the United Kingdom or to or from a place outside the United Kingdom is zero-rated. Difficulties occasionally arise as a matter of practice, including conflicts with the jurisdiction of other Member States.

#### Cultural, artistic, sporting, entertainment services, etc.

Generally, the place of supply is effectively treated as being where the performance or service takes place; this is achieved by zero-rating overseas performances etc. by persons established in the United Kingdom. However, in the case of performances in the United Kingdom by an overseas person, VAT will be due under the normal place of supply rules—*i.e.* it will depend on the supplier having a United Kingdom establishment. (In these circumstances Customs will see a hotel room as constituting an establishment, so great care is needed.)

#### Work on movable goods

As noted above, this may constitute a supply of goods rather than a supply of services, in which event the supply is made where the treatment or process is applied.

#### Reverse charge mechanism

In the case of supplies of the mainly intellectual services mentioned above, the supply is effectively treated as being made where the recipient of the supplies belongs. Thus the importation into the United Kingdom of such services is subject to the reverse charge (self-supply to and by the customer), with the export of such services to a person in his business capacity elsewhere in the EC or to any person in a third country being zero-rated. Note that this does not apply to services relating to land or property in the United Kingdom.

## 5. BASIS OF TAXATION

### *Supplies within the United Kingdom*

**15–012** In the simplest of cases, the consideration for a supply is the cash passing. However, where barter trading is involved, there are deemed to be taxable supplies in both directions, each valued at open market value. Where the consideration for a taxable supply does not consist or does not wholly consist of money, the value of the supply shall be taken to be its open market value. Free supplies of services (where there is genuinely no consideration in return) do not give rise to a VAT liability, but it should be noted that where goods or a succession of goods are given away in the course of business and their cost to the donor is more than £10 (exclusive of VAT), then that is deemed to be a supply of the goods.

Special anti-avoidance provisions apply to supplies between connected persons; these apply particularly to circumstances where the recipient of the supply is partly exempt, or not registered for VAT.

## *Self-supplies*

Where the self-supply is of a car, VAT must be accounted for on the VAT-exclusive cost of the vehicle. The tax point is created when the car is transferred from the new car sales floor.

Where the self-supply is of stationery, VAT must be accounted for on the full cost of production of the stationery including overheads. The tax point is created when there is a clear intention to use the stationery in the business. It should be noted that some stationery supplies may be zero-rated.

## *Imports*

The value for calculating VAT on imports follows normal GATT principles. Where Customs duty is payable, the VAT is calculated by reference to the declared price, plus duty.

## *Chargeable event/Time of payment*

The time of supply depends on whether a supply of goods or a supply **15–013** of services is involved. In the case of a supply of goods, the time of supply is the earliest of the following: the date the goods are removed to give effect to the contract; the date the supplier raises a VAT invoice; or the date when the supplier receives consideration.

In the case of the supply of services, the time of supply is the earliest of: the date of completion of the services; the date a VAT invoice is issued; or the date when the supplier receives consideration.

A large number of special rules covers particular circumstances including supplies of goods "on approval," or on "sale or return" terms, goods for private use; imported services; supplies of any form of power, heat, refrigeration or ventilation; continuous supplies of services; supplies in the construction industry, etc.

### Cash/invoice basis ("Cash accounting")

A special relief was made available to businesses making supplies of less than £250,000 per annum in 1987, whereby those opting to use the relief could account for tax by reference to the date of cash payment, rather than by reference to date of issue of invoices. The Cash Accounting Scheme is particularly useful to those small businesses whose customers take extended credit for settling their debts; further, the effect of using the scheme is to give automatic VAT bad debt relief. More generally, suppliers within the retail industry have always been able to elect to account for tax by reference to date of receipt of cash.

### *Credit notes/Bad debts*

A credit note may only be used to correct a genuine mistake; it may not be issued in circumstances where a customer has failed to pay for a supply, for whatever reason. Relief for VAT on bad debts is limited, and generally only applies where the customer is insolvent.

## 6. TAX RATES

The present rates are as follows:

**15–014** 15% All supplies of goods and services are deemed to be liable to VAT at the standard rate of 15%, unless covered by the exemption and zero-rating Schedules in VATA 1983.

0% (Zero-rating) food, sewerage services and water (other than to industry from July 1, 1990), books, etc., talking books for the blind and handicapped and radios and cassette players for the blind, fuel and power (only to domestic and other limited categories of consumers after July 1, 1990) construction and disposal of certain buildings, etc. (but see para. 15–023, "Real property"), protected buildings, international services, transport, caravans and house-boats, gold, bank notes, drugs, medicine on prescription and aids for the handicapped, etc., imports, exports, certain supplies by and to charities, clothing and footwear.

## 7. EXEMPTIONS

### *Exemptions with credit for input tax (zero rate)*

**15–015** The United Kingdom has more zero-rate supplies than almost all the other EC states. In effect, zero-rated is "exemption with credit," but that phrase is unknown in the United Kingdom.

### *Exemptions without credit for input tax*

Land (with certain exceptions *e.g.* holiday accommodation, parking and sporting rights); insurance; postal services; betting, gaming and lotteries; finance; education; health and social welfare; burial and cremation; trade unions and professional bodies; sports competitions; and transfers of works of art, etc., to museums in satisfaction of tax.

Certain imports are not subject to VAT, such as personal effects of travellers, personal goods imported on permanent transfer of private residence, temporary imports, goods re-imported after being repaired abroad and goods in transit. Certain restrictions and qualifications apply to some of these items.

## *Non-taxable transactions*

For a variety of reasons, certain transactions do not give rise to a liability to VAT but the justification for this situation varies according to the circumstances, and it is difficult to categorise the situations under any neat headings. Nonetheless, the following specific items are worthy of note:

- supplies between members of the same VAT group;
- supply of an employee's services under a contract of employment;
- supplies of services for no consideration;
- supplies made outside of the United Kingdom;
- supplies not made in the course of business;
- supplies not made by a taxable person.

### Transactions within the same legal entity

These are outside the scope of VAT, including transactions between branches, divisions of the same corporate body, irrespective of geographical location worldwide. Transactions between different corporate bodies which are members of the same UK VAT Group are also outside the scope of VAT.

### Transfer of business

Provided certain detailed requirements are met, then a transfer of a business, or a part of a business which is viable in its own right, as a going concern, is neither a supply of goods nor a supply of services. Both parties to the transaction must be (or become) VAT registered and there must be an intention to carry on the business in the same way as before the transfer. It should be noted that there is an anti-avoidance provision whereby if the transfer is into a partly exempt VAT Group, then the transferee has to account for VAT under a special "self-supply" rule on the value of all assets less than three years old (but not goodwill).

### Subsidies/Penalty payments/Compensation

Each particular payment must be treated on its own merits, but by **15–016** and large, a subsidy or grant does not represent the consideration for any supply. The question to be asked is whether the payment is, in reality, for anything which is done (or not done, including giving up a right) by the recipient. If it is, then VAT will be chargeable.

The question of the VAT treatment of compensation payments has recently been subject to review by Customs and it should not be assumed that any payment which is described as compensation will not be subject to VAT. In general out-of-court settlements and liquidated damages *e.g.* for breach of contract are outside the scope of VAT; but this is an area where care is needed.

**Dividends**

Dividends represent the distribution of profits, and are not the consideration for any supply.

**Disposals of motor cars (for a consideration less than the purchase price)**

This is not a supply liable to VAT, primarily because input tax would have been blocked on the original acquisition of the car, and its subsequent disposal does not give rise to any "added value".

### *Election to be registered for VAT*

A person who makes taxable supplies where the value of these supplies is less than the registration limits may nevertheless register for VAT in order to reclaim input tax on expenditure. The person must, however, be making taxable supplies in the course or furtherance of a business.

## 8. CREDIT/REFUND FOR INPUT TAX

### *General rule*

**15–017** A registered business is entitled to claim credit in its quarterly VAT Return for input tax suffered on the expenditure by way of offset against output tax. Where input tax regularly exceeds output tax, it is entitled to submit returns monthly. Customs normally make repayments of the tax in question within 14 days of the submission of a return to Southend-on-Sea. Customs are liable to pay a repayment supplement of 5 per cent. (or if greater, £30) if repayment is not made within 30 days of the last day on which the return was due or received (whichever is the later), but the 30 days does not run, if they are carrying out reasonable enquiries, until those enquiries have been completed.

There are a few exceptions to the general principle that a fully taxable business can claim input relief for all VAT suffered on its expenditure. The most notable exceptions are the outright purchase of motor-cars (VAT is reclaimable on leasing of cars) and on entertainment expenditure; input relief is also blocked in the case of private and non-business expenditure.

### *Adjustment of entitlement to credit*

It is proposed that the provisions of Article 20(2) of the Sixth EC Directive (*i.e.* the provision relating to adjustments for capital items) will be introduced from April 1990. This will create a serious administrative complication for the partly exempt sectors of British industry and commerce (most notably the financial and insurance sectors), which are the largest in Europe. In order to minimise administrative complications, adjustment will be required only for computers and computer equipment valued at £50,000 or more and land and buildings (or parts of buildings) value at £250,000 or more. The input tax recovery will be adjusted over a five-year period in the case of computers ad computer equipment and 10 years in the case of land and buildings to take account of changes in the partial exemption recovery position of the business concerned.

## *Partial exemption*

A partly exempt business may have its entitlement to input recovery **15–018**
restricted to the extent that its expenditure relates to making exempt supplies. Before April 1, 1987, different rules applied but since that date the legislation follows the principles of the Sixth Directive, particularly Articles 17 and 19. The basic principle is that input tax must be directly attributable as far as possible to taxable activities on the one hand and exempt and non-business activities on the other. The former input tax can be recovered in full, but the latter cannot be recovered. Any residual input tax which cannot be attributed directly in this way can be recovered according to any "fair and reasonable" apportionment agreed with Customs which relates the input tax to use.

Since the United Kingdom legislation was recently revised, certain difficulties were being experienced, particularly with regard to the position of holding companies and the costs of acquisition of new businesses. Customs have recently reviewed their policy in this regard to achieve a more permissive stance which is more consistent with other EC Member States. Provided that the input tax attributable to exempt activities is very small, certain *de minimis* limits will apply and the business can treat itself as fully taxable. In addition, input tax attributable to certain incidental exempt activities can be treated as input tax attributable to taxable activities in any event; examples are deposit interest and certain commissions, but not when the business is professionally engaged, *e.g.* a bank or insurance company. A partly exempt business will almost certainly need professional guidance in negotiating an appropriate partial exemption method with Customs and securing an agreement in writing. Many such agreements include a provision whereby input relief is provisionally claimed on a quarterly basis, depending on the circumstances prevailing at that time. Subsequently, an "Annual Adjustment" will be called for, whereby the input tax provisionally reclaimed will be adjusted, having regard to the facts of the year as a whole. This "Annual Adjustment" is to be distinguished from adjustments to entitlement to credit, see para. 15–017.

## *Time of recovery*

Businesses may claim input recovery by reference to the supplier's tax-point although in practice, in the absence of a purchase day book, input relief will be claimed by reference to the date of payment. Claims for input relief should normally be made in the quarter in which the expenditure incurred, but this is not essential.

### *Refunds for foreign businesses*

Foreign businesses are entitled to claim relief for VAT suffered on United Kingdom expenditure pursuant to the Eighth and Thirteenth Directives. In other words, businesses registered for VAT in another Member State but not registered or required to be registered in the United Kingdom have been able to claim refunds of VAT incurred in the United Kingdom since January 1, 1981 and businesses established outside the EC since January 1, 1988. Certain expenditure, *e.g.* business entertainment, is not recoverable. The reclaim procedure is known as "mutual recovery," and the detailed provisions are to be found in Customs Notice 723. It is important to note that claims must be submitted to Customs within six months of the end of the relevant accounting year; thus claims by EC businesses must be submitted by June 30 for VAT suffered in the previous year to December 31; whilst non-EC businesses must submit their claims by December 31 in respect of the previous 12 months ended on June 30.

## 9. ADMINISTRATIVE OBLIGATIONS

### *Registration*

**15–019** Any person who makes or intends to make taxable supplies in excess of the turnover limits is required to notify Customs of that fact.

The turnover limits of £23,600 per annum, or £8,000 per calendar quarter, have already been referred to above, as have the concepts of voluntary registration and group registration.

Further different aspects of registration are as follows:

— exemption from registration: it is possible for businesses with taxable supplies over the registration limits to be exempted (*i.e.* exonerated) from registration.

This is the case where a business can demonstrate that if it were registered for VAT, its input tax would always exceed its output tax. The provision is therefore only of interest to businesses with an overwhelming preponderance of zero-rated supplies.

— divisional registration: a company organised into a number of self-accounting units is able to opt to have each of these divisions separately registered for VAT. This facility is very seldom encountered in practice but may be of use where there are practical difficulties in completing one return for the entire company. This facility is not available to persons who are partly exempt.

## *Books and records*

Books and records of a business must be retained for a minimum of six years in order to facilitate the conduct of control visits by Customs Officers.

## *Invoices*

All businesses making supplies of goods or services at the standard rate are obliged to issue a tax invoice within 30 days of the time of supply where the customer is a taxable person. A "tax invoice" must contain certain specified information, although the requirements are less onerous in the case of certain supplies costing less than £50.

## *VAT returns*

VAT Returns must reach Customs Headquarters at Southend-on-Sea, together with a cheque in settlement of the liability where appropriate, by the end of the month following the quarterly period of account. (Monthly returns are normally used for repayment claims, but exceptionally, where a monthly return shows a liability due to Customs, the same deadlines apply as for quarterly returns). An extension of seven days is permissible where the business agrees to make settlement through the Bank Giro system, rather than through the post, although this needs Customs' prior written consent. **15–020**

## *Powers of the authorities*

Given that VAT is administered by the same government department (namely HM Customs and Excise) which seeks to control drug and other smuggling, it is perhaps unsurprising that it should have very extensive powers for collecting VAT. Whilst these powers were re-defined in 1985, they remain very extensive indeed, and prison sentences are applicable in the most serious circumstances.

### Estimated assessments

Where VAT returns are not submitted to Southend-on-Sea within the prescribed time limits, the Customs' computer will automatically issue an estimated assessment. The submission of the return in question will serve to cancel the assessment but in the absence of the return, the estimated tax assessed must be paid.

There is provision in the legislation for registered businesses to estimate net tax due to the customer but this requires Customs' prior consent, which is not easily obtained.

### Periods of limitation

15–021 Except in case of fraud, wilful neglect, etc. there are strict time limits within which Customs must raise assessments covering mistakes discovered during the course of their control visits.

The time limits for making an assessment depend on the provision under which it is made, the conduct giving rise to the assessment and whether the assessment is made before or after the person's death. Basically an assessment must be made within two years of the end of the accounting period concerned or within one year of it coming to the attention of Customs, facts which in their opinion justify an assessment. In either case the assessment may go back only six years.

### Correction of returns

In view of the fact that Value Added Tax has been in operation in the United Kingdom since 1973, it is perhaps surprising that the legal position surrounding the manner in which errors in earlier returns should be corrected has only recently been settled. Following court decisions unfavourable to Customs' argument that repayments of tax overpaid were entirely at their discretion, legislation was passed in 1989 which established a statutory scheme for recovery of overpaid tax except where the claimant would be unjustly enriched (*e.g.* when he had collected VAT from his customers but would not be refunding it to them on receiving the overpayment due to himself).

## *Penalties*

### Late submission of returns and late payment

Until 1985, the criminal penalties for non-compliance with the VAT legislation were seldom imposed, although in serious cases they were imposed with considerable vigour, as a deterrent to others.

This policy has been substantially amended since then and a number of automatic penalties has been introduced.

In the case of late submission of returns and/or payments, after a written warning for earlier transgressions, a surcharge of five per cent. for the first subsequent offence is imposed, rising on a sliding scale to 30 per cent.. These surcharges are not allowable for direct taxation purposes.

### Default interest

15–022 From January 1, 1990, interest will be imposed on assessments made by Customs to correct earlier mistakes. Again, such interest will not be deductible for direct taxation purposes. Interest will also apply to mistakes voluntarily disclosed by registered businesses.

### Serious misdeclarations etc.

In the case of large errors detected by Customs (rather than by the registered business) a "Serious Misdeclaration Penalty" of 30 per cent.

of the tax which would have been lost if the inaccuracy had not been discovered, will be imposed in specified circumstances, again from January 1, 1990. A similar "Persistent Misdeclaration Penalty" of 15 per cent. of the net tax wrongly declared has been imposed from 1988, in prescribed circumstances.

Late notification of registration penalties have been imposed since July 25, 1985 for failure to register for VAT on time. These penalties are not imposed when there is judged to be a "reasonable excuse" but the criteria for such an excuse are tightly circumscribed by law.

### Late notification of registration

Penalties for late notification of a liability to be registered have been in existence since 1985, with a sliding scale of penalty up to 30 per cent. for non-compliance.

## *Appeals*

A wide variety of matters can be taken before a VAT Tribunal on appeal, including assessments for tax due. Whilst it is possible to appeal direct to a VAT Tribunal, in practice most registered businesses ask for the point of dispute to be "locally reviewed" by senior Customs personnel. Such a review may lead to the settling of the dispute without the cost and inconvenience of proceeding to formal litigation. The time for making an appeal to a VAT Tribunal is limited to 28 days. This can sometimes be extended but the time should not run whilst a local review is underway. However this should be confirmed with Customs in writing.

Throughout the United Kingdom, the VAT Tribunal deals with all appeals in the first instance; in England and Wales, subsequent appeals are to the High Court, the Court of Appeal, and the House of Lords, in turn. In Scotland, however, an appeal from the VAT Tribunal is direct to the Court of Session, and then to the House of Lords. Any court can refer a matter of difficulty to the European Court of Justice. VAT appeals all the way to the House of Lords are rare, amounting to perhaps one a year; appeals to the VAT Tribunal are, however, much more commonplace.

# 10. SPECIAL VAT REGIMES

## *Real property*

As a result of the judgment of the European Court of Justice in the infraction proceedings against certain United Kingdom zero rates, substantial changes have been made to the legislation that governs the VAT liability of construction services and property transactions. **15–023**

Some zero rating remains but its scope has been greatly reduced; buildings whose construction and sale qualifies for zero-rating are confined to dwellings and qualifying residential and charitable buildings.

Generally speaking, freehold sales of commercial buildings are automatically standard-rated for three years after completion. The freehold sale of qualifying buildings remains zero rated if the freehold is sold by the person who constructed the building; the freehold sale of qualifying building by other persons is exempt. All other freehold and leasehold disposals of land or buildings are exempt with the option to tax. The option to tax applies to the sale or lease of any land or any non-residential building (*i.e.* qualifying for zero-rating) and is at the vendor or landlord's discretion and on a building-by-building basis.

Leases granted in connection with qualifying buildings fall into two categories; those exceeding 21 years duration, granted by a person constructing, are zero-rated in respect of the premium, if any, or the first payment of rent, and exempt thereafter; all other leases are exempt from the outset (with the option to tax). Leases granted in connection with commercial buildings are exempt, irrespective of duration (with the option to tax).

### *Retail industry*

A variety of different accounting schemes applies, according to the individual circumstances of the retailer.

### *Second-hand goods*

**15–024** Special second-hand schemes apply to sales of the following second-hand goods:

Works of art, antiques and collectors' pieces; caravans; motor-cycles; boats and outboard motors; electronic organs; aircraft; firearms. Where the conditions are met under these schemes, VAT is only charged on the margin between buying and selling prices.

### *Annual accounting*

Introduced in 1988, this scheme enables a business with turnover of less than £250,000 per annum as defined above, to submit just one VAT return a year, with provisional payments on account being made during the interim by way of direct debit to the bank account of the business, calculated by reference to estimates of liabilities.

### *Tour operators*

New provisions were introduced on April 1, 1988, whereby VAT is imposed only by reference to the margin on trading of anyone acting as a principal in putting together and selling tours and holidays, *e.g.* package holidays. The VAT incurred in buying in the ingredients of such tours etc. (whether in the United Kingdom or elsewhere in the EC) is not recoverable.

### *Retail export schemes*

Overseas visitors to the United Kingdom are entitled to export certain retail products free of VAT, under special rules.

### *Oil industry*

Special treatment is accorded to oil companies involved in exploration activities.

### *Financial and insurance institutions*

A wide variety of special rules applies to supplies made by banks, insurance companies, insurance brokers, Lloyd's managing agents and syndicates, and unit trust management companies.

### *Freeports*

A freeport is a designated and enclosed area in which goods may remain without payment of VAT or customs duty arising at importation. Each freeport is run by an independent commercial operator. Customs do not control freeport goods until they leave the freeport. The United Kingdom Government has designated a number of freeport areas of which only Liverpool, Southampton and Belfast and Birmingham International Airports are operational.

# Appendix A—Comparative Charts

**A–001**

## VAT

### INTRODUCTION AND ADMINISTRATION

| *Country* | *Date VAT Introduced* | *Taxes Replaced* | *VAT based on Sixth EC Directive* | *When Brought into Sixth EC Directive Form* | *Full Name of VAT* | *Abbreviation* | *Administered by* |
|---|---|---|---|---|---|---|---|
| Belgium | 1971 | Turnover tax | Yes | 1978 | Belasting over de Toegevoegde Waarde/Taxe sur la Valeur Ajoutée | BTW/TVA | Taxes (1) |
| Denmark | 1967 | Turnover tax | Yes | 1978 | Mervaediafgift | MOMS | Customs |
| France (2) | 1968 | Turnover taxes Value Added Tax (note) | Yes | 1979 | Taxe sur la Valeur Ajoutée | TVA | Taxes (1) |
| Germany | 1968 | Turnover taxes | Yes | 1980 | Mehrwertsteuer | MwSt | Taxes (1) |
| Greece | 1987 | Turnover and stamp taxes | Yes | 1987 | Foros Prostithemenis Axias | FPA | Taxes (1) |
| Ireland | 1972 | Turnover tax | Yes | 1978 | Value added tax | VAT | Taxes (1) |

| *Country* | *Date VAT Introduced* | *Taxes Replaced* | *VAT in Sixth EC Directive* | *When Brought into Sixth EC Directive Form* | *Full Name of VAT* | *Abbreviation* | *Administered by* |
|---|---|---|---|---|---|---|---|
| Italy | 1973 | Turnover tax<br>Complementary tax on importations | Yes | 1979 | Imposta sul Valore Aggiunto | IVA | Taxes (1) |
| Luxembourg | 1970 | Turnover tax | Yes | 1980 | Taxe sur la Valeur Ajoutée | TVA | Taxes (1) |
| Netherlands | 1969 | Turnover tax | Yes | 1979 | Belasting over de Toegevoegde Waarde | BTW | Taxes (1) |
| Norway | 1970 | Turnover tax | No | n/a | Merverdiavgift | MVA | Taxes (1) |
| Portugal | 1986 | Turnover tax and stamp taxes | Yes | 1989 | Imposto sobre o Valor Acrescentado | IVA | Taxes (1) |
| Spain | 1986 | Turnover, luxury and 21 other indirect taxes | Yes | 1986 | Impuesto sobre el Valor anadido | IVA | Taxes (1) |
| Sweden | 1969 | Turnover tax | No | n/a | Mervardeskatt | MOMS | Taxes (1) |
| U.K. | 1973 | Purchase tax<br>Selective employment tax | Yes | 1978 | Value added tax | VAT | Customs |

1. In these countries VAT at the point of importation is administered by the Customs.
2. NOTE: France introduced a partial VAT in 1954 and 1955 covering limited sectors of the economy.

A–002

## TABLE OF VAT RATES IN THE EUROPEAN COUNTRIES (MARCH 31, 1989)

| | *Lower Rates* | *Standard Rate* | *Higher Rates* |
|---|---|---|---|
| Belgium | 1% – 6% – 17% | 19% | 25% – 33% |
| Denmark | | 22% | |
| France | 2.1% – 5.5% – 13% | 18.6% | 28% |
| Germany | 7% | 14% | |
| Greece | 3% – 6% | 16% | 36% |
| Ireland | 0% – 2% – 5% | 10% | 25% |
| Italy | 4% – 9% | 19% | 38% |
| Luxembourg | 3% – 6% | 12% | |
| Netherlands | 0% | 6% | 18.5% |
| Norway | | 20% | |
| Portugal (1) | 8% | 17% | 30% |
| Spain | 6% | 12% | 33% |
| Sweden | 3.8% – 11.4% | 19% | |
| United Kingdom | 0% | 15% | |

Note—(1) There are reduced rates for Madeira and the Azores.

A–003

## VAT RATES APPLICABLE ON BASIC ITEMS

| | *Basic Foodstuffs* | *Clothing* | *Passenger Transport* | *Education Services* (1) | *Health Services* (2) |
|---|---|---|---|---|---|
| Belgium | 6% | 6% | 6% or exempt | Exempt | Exempt |
| Denmark | 22% | 22% | Exempt | Exempt | Exempt |
| France | 5.5% | 18.6% | 5.5% or exempt | Exempt | Exempt |
| Germany | 7% | 14% | 7% or 14% | Exempt | Exempt |
| Greece | 6% | 6% | Exempt | Exempt | Exempt |
| Ireland | 0% | 0% or 10% (3) | Exempt (4) | Exempt | Exempt |
| Italy | 4% | 9% or 19% | Exempt | Exempt | Exempt |
| Luxembourg | 3% | 12% | 6% | Exempt | Exempt |
| Netherlands | 6% | 18.5% | 0% or 6% (4) | Exempt | Exempt |
| Norway | 20% | 20% | Exempt | Exempt | Exempt |
| Portugal | 0% | 17% | 0% or 8% (4) | Exempt | Exempt |
| Spain | 6% | 12% | 0%,6% or 12% (4) | Exempt | Exempt |
| Sweden | 19% | 19% | Exempt | Exempt | Exempt |
| UK | 0% | 0% or 15% (3) | 0% (4) | Exempt | Exempt |

Notes:

(1) Education Services. Most countries treat education services provided by government bodies or other recognised bodies as exempt and "education" services provided by others as taxable.

(2) Health Services. In most countries such services must be provided by members of recognised bodies to qualify.

(3) Ireland and UK. Children's clothing is zero rated.

(4) Passenger Transport. Domestic passenger transport is liable at 5.5% in France, 6% in the Netherlands, 8% in Portugal and 6% (overland) or 12% (sea or air) in Spain. In the UK the zero rate is applied to passenger transportation in vehicles designed or adapted to carry 12 or more passengers. In Ireland all passenger transport is exempt but suppliers of international passenger transport services can recover input VAT.

## REGISTRATION LIMITS

A–004

| | *Annual Turnover Limits (1)* Goods | *Services* | *VAT Reporting Periods* | *Annual Reporting Available (2)* |
|---|---|---|---|---|
| Belgium | No Limit | No Limit | Monthly or quarterly | Yes |
| Denmark | DKK 10,000 | DKK 10,000 | Quarterly | No (3) |
| France | No Limit | No Limit | Monthly or quarterly | No |
| Germany | No Limit | No Limit | Monthly, quarterly | Yes |
| Greece | No Limit | No Limit | Monthly, bimonthly or quarterly and annually | Yes |
| Ireland | IR£32,000 | IR£15,000 | Bi-monthly (Jan-Feb) | Yes |
| Italy | No Limit | No Limit | Monthly or quarterly (4) | No |
| Luxembourg | No Limit | No Limit | Monthly or quarterly and annually | Yes |
| Netherlands | No Limit | No Limit | Monthly or quarterly | Yes |
| Norway | NOK 12,000 | NOK 12,000 | Bi-monthly | No |
| Portugal | No Limit | No Limit | Monthly or quarterly | No |
| Spain | No Limit | No Limit | Monthly or quarterly | No |
| Sweden | SEK 30,000 | SEK 30,000 | Monthly | Yes |
| U.K. | £23,600 | £23,600 | Monthly or quarterly (5) | Yes |

Notes:
(1) Some countries apply different limits to specific services e.g. small retailers and professionals.
(2) Annual reporting is normally only available for certain types of entrepreneurs (e.g. as small traders) with the consent of the authorities. In Germany every entrepreneur must file preliminary and annual returns.
(3) Biannual returns available for farmers and fishermen.
(4) In Italy VAT is payable monthly or quarterly but it is reported annually.
(5) Bimonthly returns available for farmers and fishermen.

A–005

## GROUP REGISTRATION

A Cross border interbranch and head office/branch trading?
B Group registration/fiscal unity.

| | *A* In the case of services is cross border trading between Head Office/ Branch or interbranch taxable? (1) | *B* Is group registration available for the following categories of entrepreneurs? | | | | |
|---|---|---|---|---|---|---|
| | | *Fully Taxable Entrepreneurs* | *Partially Taxable Entrepreneurs* | *Wholly Exempt Entrepreneurs* | *Cross Border Associated Entrepreneurs* | *Non-Incorporated Entrepreneurs* |
| Belgium | No | No | No | No | No | No |
| Denmark | No | Yes | No | No | No | No |
| France | No | No | No | No | No | No |
| Germany | No | Yes | Yes | Yes | No | No |
| Greece | No | No | No | No | No | No |
| Ireland | No | Yes | Yes | Yes | No | Yes |
| Italy | Yes | Yes | Yes | Yes | No | No |
| Luxembourg | No | No | No | No | No | No |
| Netherlands | No | Yes | Yes | Yes | No | Yes (5) |
| Norway | No | Yes | Yes | No | No (2) | No (2) |
| Portugal (3) | Yes | No | No | No | No | No |
| Spain (3) | Yes | No | No | No | No | No |
| Sweden | No | No | No | No | No | No |
| U.K. | No | Yes | Yes | Yes | No (4) | No (5) |

(1) In all countries cross border services supplied to a representative office from a head office are not taxable.
(2) Yes, if they have a fully taxable joint venture in Norway.
(3) There is no fiscal unity/group registration concept in Portugal or Spain.
(4) Overseas subsidiaries or parents can be members of a UK VAT group in certain circumstances.
(5) Companies controlled by non-incorporated entrepreneurs can be members of a VAT group.

**A–006**

VALUE ADDED TAX IN EUROPE
DEDUCTIBLE INPUT CREDITS
(THIS LIST IS NOT EXHAUSTIVE)

GENERAL RATES APPLICABLE TO TRADERS NOT ENGAGED IN THE INDUSTRIES CONCERNED

| | *Belgium* | *Denmark* | *France* | *Germany* | *Greece* | *Ireland* | *Italy* | *Luxembourg* | *Netherlands* | *Norway* | *Portugal* | *Spain* | *Sweden* | *U.K.* |
|---|---|---|---|---|---|---|---|---|---|---|---|---|---|---|
| Cars | Y (1) | N | N | Y | N | N | N | Y | Y | Y | N | N | N | N |
| Petrol/ Gasoline | Y | N | N | Y | N | N | N | Y | Y | Y | N | N | Y | Y |
| Diesel | Y | Y | Y | Y | (+) | Y | N | Y | Y | Y | (+) | N | Y | Y |
| Tobacco | N | N | N | Y | N | Y | N | Y | N | Y | N | N | Y | (+) |
| Alcoholic Drinks | N | N | N | Y | N | N | N | Y | N | N | N | N | N | (+) |
| Other Drinks | (+) | N | N | Y | N | N | N | Y | N | N | N | N | Y | (+) |
| Meals | (+) | N | N | Y | N | N | N | Y | N | N | N | N | Y | (+) |
| Hotel Accommodation | (+) | N | N | Y | N | N | N | Y | Y | Y | N | N | Y | (+) |
| Gifts | (+) | N | (+) | (+) | Y | (+) | Y | Y | (+) | Y | (+) | N | Y | (+) |
| Entertainment | N | N | N | (+) | N | N | N | Y | (+) | Y | N | N | N | N |
| Secondhand Goods | Y | Y | Y | Y | Y | Y | Y | Y | Y | Y | (+) | Y | Y | (+) |
| Works of Art | Y | Y | Y | Y | Y | Y | Y | Y | Y | N | N | N | Y | (+) |
| Luxury Goods | Y | Y | Y | Y | Y | Y | N | Y | Y | Y | N | N | Y | (+) |

NOTES:
Y: Generally deductible as long as expenditure is attributable to a specific taxable activity.
N: Generally not deductible unless expenditure is attributable to a taxable activity.
(+) Deductibility depends on circumstances.
(1) Only 50% reclaimable.

**A–007** VAT AS % OF GDP (EEC ONLY)

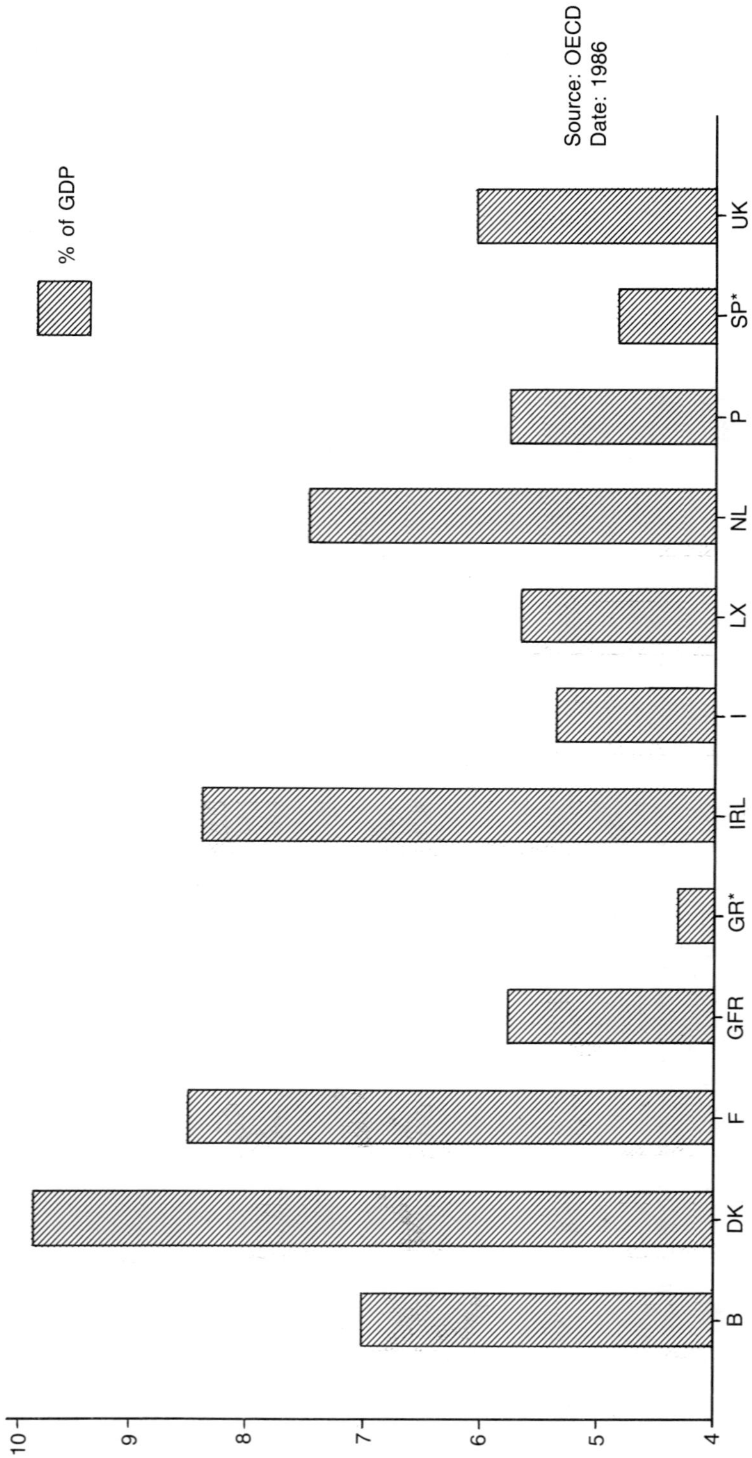

ALL TAXES AS PROPORTION OF TOTAL TAX RECEIPTS **A–008**

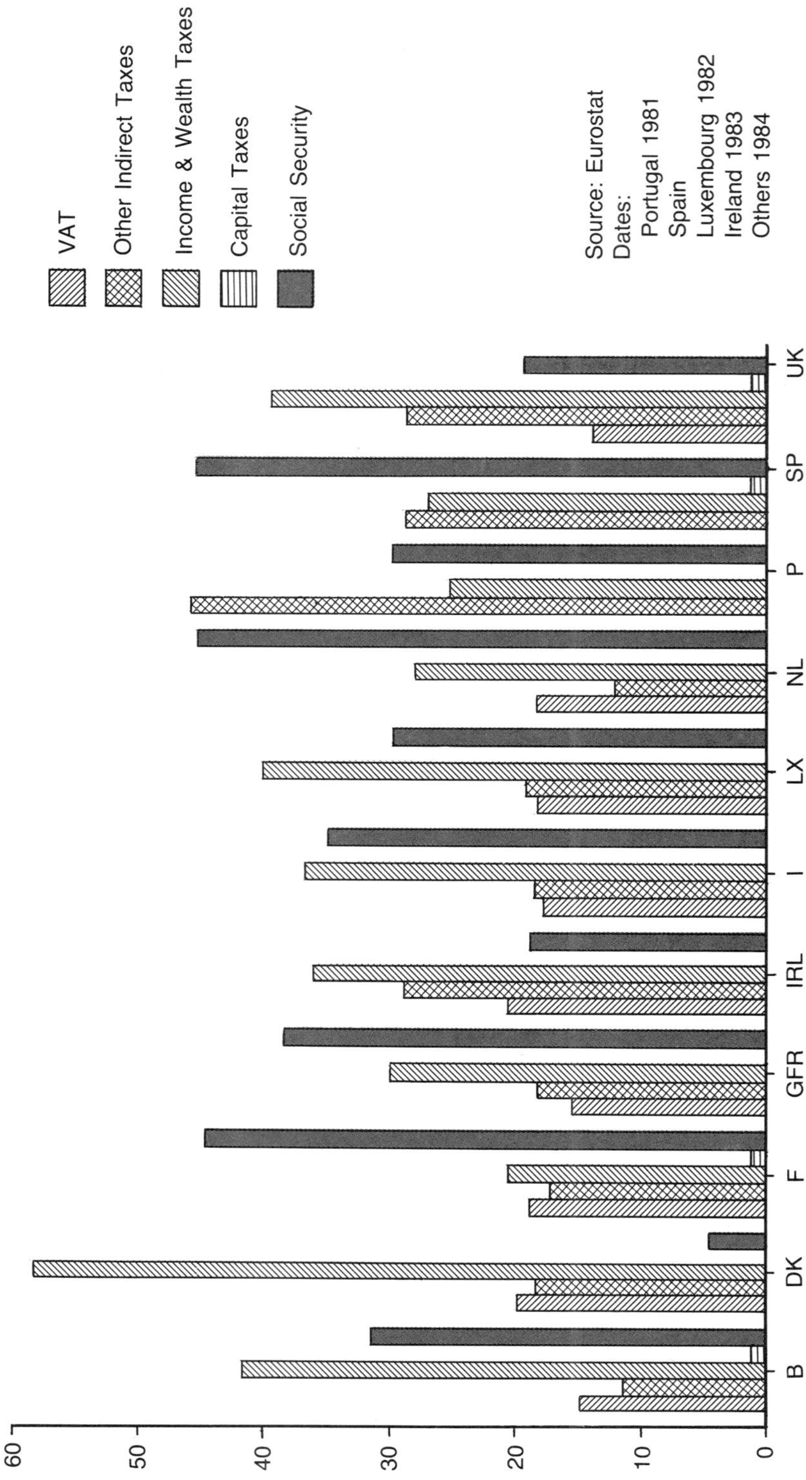

# Appendix B

## EC COUNCIL DIRECTIVES ON THE HARMONISATION OF VAT

The Sixth Council Directive, 77/388 EEC is the cornerstone of the harmonisation of the laws on turnover taxes in the Member States. It introduced a common system of VAT with a uniform basis. Of the subsequent Directives, some have been adopted by the Council of Ministers and thus consolidate community legislation, while others have still not been adopted (see below). **B–001**

| | |
|---|---|
| —First Council Directive (April 11, 1967, no. 67/227, EEC)<br>Harmonisation of legislation of member states concerning turnover taxes. | Adopted |
| —Second Council Directive (April 11, 1967, no. 67/228, EEC)<br>Structures and procedures for application of the common system of value added tax. | Adopted |
| —Third Council Directive (December 3, 1969)<br>Authorised Belgium and Italy to postpone the introduction of a value added tax until January 1, 1972. | Adopted |
| —Fourth Council Directive (December 20, 1971)<br>Authorised Italy to postpone the introduction of a value added tax until July 1, 1972. | Adopted |
| —Fifth Council Directive (July 4, 1972)<br>Authorised Italy to postpone the introduction of a value added tax until January 1, 1973. | Adopted |
| —Sixth Council Directive (May 17, 1977, no. 77/338, EEC)<br>Common system of value added tax: Uniform basis of assessment. | Adopted |
| —Seventh Directive<br>Supplementing the common system of value added tax and amending articles 28 and 32 of Directive 77/388. EEC—special arrangements for second hand goods, works of art, antiques and collectors' items (Submitted by Commission to Council on January 11, 1978, revised version submitted to Council on February 3, 1989). | Amended Proposal |

| | | |
|---|---|---|
| **B–002** | —Eighth Council Directive (December 6, 1979, no. 79/1072, EEC)<br>Arrangements for the refund of value added tax to taxable persons not established in the territory of the country. | Adopted |
| | —Ninth Council Directive (June 26, 1978, No. 78/583, EEC)<br>Harmonisation of the laws of member states relating to turnover taxes. | Adopted |
| | —Tenth Council Directive (July 31, 1984, no. 84/386, EEC)<br>Amending Directive, the Sixth Directive, 77/388 EEC—application of value added tax to the hiring out of movable tangible property. | Adopted |
| | —Eleventh Council Directive (March 26, 1980, no. 80/368, EEC)<br>Exclusion of the French overseas departments from the scope of Directive, the Sixth Directive, 77/388, EEC). | Adopted |
| | —Council Directive of March 28, 1983. (83/181, EEC)<br>Determining the scope of Article 14(1)(d) of Directive 77/388 EEC as regards exemption from value added tax on final importation of certain goods. | Adopted |
| | —Twelfth Directive<br>Common system of value added tax: certain expenditure not eligible for deduction of value added tax (Submitted by Commission to Council on January 25, 1983, amendments submitted on February 20, 1984). | Amended proposal |
| | —Thirteenth Council Directive (November 17, 1986, no. 86/560, EEC)<br>Arrangements for the refund of value added tax to taxable persons not established in the Community territory. | Adopted |
| | —Fourteenth Directive<br>Deferred payment of tax payable on importation by taxable persons (Submitted by Commission to Council on July 19, 1982). | Proposal |
| | —Fifteenth Directive<br>Deferral of introduction of the common system of value added tax in the Hellenic Republic (Submitted by the Commission to the Cuncil on October 26, 1983). | Proposal |
| **B–003** | —Council Directive<br>Amending Directive 83/181 EEC determining the scope of Article 14(1)(d) of Directive 77/388, EEC as regards exemption from value added tax on final importation of certain goods. (Submitted by the Commission to the Council on March 20, 1984). | Proposal |

| | |
|---|---|
| —Sixteenth Directive<br>Common system of value added tax; common scheme for certain goods on which value added tax has been finally paid and which are imported by a final consumer in one Member State from another Member State. | Amended proposal |
| —Seventeenth Council Directive (July 16, 1985, no. 85/362, EEC)<br>Exemption from value added tax on the temporary importation of goods other than means of transport. | Adopted |
| —Eighteenth Directive<br>Abolition of certain derogations provided for in Article 28(3) of Directive 77/388, EEC: on common system of value added tax. | Amended proposal |
| —Nineteenth Directive<br>Amending Directive 77/388, EEC: Common system of value added tax (Submitted by the Commission to the Council on December 5, 1984). | Proposal |
| —Twentieth Council Directive (July 16, 1985, no. 85/361, EEC)<br>Common system of value added tax: derogation in connection with the special aids granted to certain farmers to compensate for dismantling of monetary compensatory amounts applying to certain agricultural products. | Adopted |
| —Council Directive<br>Imposing a standstill on VAT and excise duties. (Submitted by the Commission to the Council on November 21, 1985). | Amended proposal |
| —Twenty-first Council Directive (June 16, 1986).<br>Deferment of the introduction of the common system of value added tax in the Hellenic Republic. | Adopted |
| —Council Directive<br>Concerning VAT rules applicable to the operation of a future cross-channel fixed link. (Submitted by the Commission to the Council). | Proposal |
| —Council Directive<br>Amending Directive 77/388 EEC. In respect of the common value added tax scheme applicable to small and medium-sized businesses. (Submitted by the Commission to the Council on October 9, 1986). | Proposal **B–004** |
| —Council Directive<br>Supplementing the common system of value added tax and amending Directive 77/388 EEC — approximation of VAT rates. (Submitted by the Commission to the Council on August 7, 1987). | Proposal |

| | |
|---|---|
| —Council Directive<br>Instituting a process of convergence of rates of value added tax and excise duties. (Submitted by the Commission to the Council on August 7, 1987). | Proposal |
| —Council Directive<br>On approximation of the rates of excise duties on alcoholic beverages and on alcohol contained in other products. (Submitted by the Commission to the Council on August 7, 1987). | Proposal |
| —Council Directive<br>Supplementing the common system of Value Added Tax and amending Directive 77/388 EEC—elimination of fiscal frontiers. (Submitted by the Commission to the Council on August 7, 1987). | Proposal |

# Appendix C

GLOSSARY

### Appeals

A taxable person may appeal to the Courts to arbitrate in certain disputes between the person and Revenue authorities, *e.g.* additional VAT imposed by the authorities, refusal by the authorities to repay tax which has been overpaid and formal interpretation by the authorities, etc. In Ireland an appeal must first be heard by an independent arbitrator before going to the court. **C–001**

Normally there is a very short time limit within which the aggrieved person must lodge written notice of his appeal.

(see also objections/claims)

### Assujetti

French term referring to any person (individual or corporate body)—carrying out independently transactions of an economic nature.

When a person qualifies as an "assujetti" it means that this activity or the transactions he carries out are within the scope of VAT, although he might not have to pay VAT if part or all of his transactions are specifically exempt.

### Chain transactions

Several entrepreneurs/taxable persons may enter into subsequent transactions, involving the same goods. Then each person within the chain is deemed to have made a supply, even if the actual ownership is transferred directly from the first to the last recipient in the chain.

In some countries special rules apply to determine the place of supply of the goods involved in chain transactions.

### Consideration

This is what is given in exchange for the supply and the charge to tax is based on this. It may take the form of money, barter, the performance of some service, the release from an obligation, etc.

Where goods or services are supplied for a consideration which does consist of money or does not wholly consist of money, the amount on which tax is chargeable is usually the open market value of the goods or services supplied.

When there is no consideration in any form there is no liability to VAT and generally no entitlement to a credit for related input tax.

However, in certain circumstances there may be a liability to tax (*e.g.* self-supplies, gifts).

### Deferred accounting system

C–002 Under the deferred accounting system (as outlined in the narratives of Ireland and the United Kingdom) VAT is due at the time of removal of the goods from the port or is payable by direct debit to the importer's bank account sometime after the removal (*i.e.* on the 15th day of the month following the removal). The importer needs an appropriate guarantee.

### Delivery

Delivery determines the time at which VAT becomes due on the supply of tangible goods. Delivery means the surrendering of possession of goods. It often coincides with the transfer of ownership but in certain cases the delivery is effective before the actual transfer of ownership.

### Domicile

The term "domicile" is used in civil law. It is the place from which a person (individual or corporate entity) conducts his business on a regular basis. It usually has the same meaning as "registered office" where companies are concerned.

### Election to be subject to VAT

In some countries persons supplying certain services and goods which would not otherwise be taxable may elect to become liable persons which will generally entitle them to a credit for input tax (financial services, property, farmers . . .).

### Entrepreneur

Anyone, other than somebody acting as an employee, conducting a trade, a business or a liberal profession independently, will generally qualify as being an entrepreneur, irrespective of whether his activities are taxable or exempt.

One can be an entrepreneur whatever the form of the trade or business. It therefore includes, individuals, companies, trustees, partnerships, public corporations, local authorities, etc.. In Ireland and the United Kingdom, however, the term "entrepreneur" is not used in the legislation. There the term "taxable person" is used, which, in contrast with the term "entrepreneur," does not include persons who make exempt supplies (see "Assujetti" and "Taxable Person").

### Exempt

C–003 This term normally denotes supplies which are not liable to VAT. However, in some countries certain supplies may be exempt with credit or exempt without credit for input tax.

**Exempt—with credit for input tax** This applies to supplies *e.g.* exports, international transport, etc. where output tax is not chargeable but the supplier is entitled to recover input tax subject to local regulations. This is similar to zero rating in other countries.

**Exempt—without credit for input tax** This applies to supplies which are specifically excluded from the charge to tax by local legislation. Persons making such supplies are not entitled to recover any related input tax. They are, in effect, regarded as the end users.

### Imported services

Services received from outside a state are sometimes referred to as imported services. Their liability to VAT depends on the place of supply as defined and they may sometimes give rise to the reverse charge mechanism, which shifts the liability to VAT from the supplier to the recipient of the services.

### Input tax

VAT incurred by a person on the import and acquisition of goods and services is known as input tax. Input tax can be offset against output tax or refunded when it has been incurred in the provision of taxable goods and services. No recovery of input VAT is generally given for VAT incurred in connection with the supply of exempt goods and services or in respect of certain specific items.

### Interest

**Commercial interest** In some countries interest charged by suppliers is regarded as taxable when it relates to the late payment of taxable supplies.

**Financial interest** Interest charged for loans granted by banks, financial institutions or by suppliers independently from the supply of goods or services is exempt.

### Objections/Claims

In order to obtain a reduction or a repayment of VAT wrongly assessed, an entrepreneur must file a formal request to local tax authorities. Objections have to be submitted within certain limits of time which differ from country to country. It is only once the tax authorities have taken their decision that it can be appealed before the Courts. In Italy, the absence of reply within a specified period of time is regarded as a refusal which may be appealed. **C–004**

### Partial exemption

A taxable person who supplies goods and services some of which are taxable and the others exempt (without credit) is regarded as partially exempt. In such circumstances the input tax may only be recovered where it was paid on the purchase or import of goods or services which were used for the purpose of the taxable business. Where tax was suffered on goods or imports which were used for both taxable and non-taxable purposes, only a proportion of the input VAT may be recovered.

### Postponed accounting system

Under the postponed accounting system, entrepreneurs/taxable persons in some countries may import goods without payment of VAT at the point of entry, but defer payment until the next periodic VAT return.

So long as the importer is not exempt, *i.e.*, fully taxable and thus entitled to a credit for input tax, no VAT will actually become payable.

The postponed accounting system is generally applied upon special application with the tax authorities provided certain conditions are met. Normally only resident entrepreneurs qualify for the system.

In some countries (see Ireland) it may be possible to avoid payment of any VAT on the importation of raw materials.

### Real estate/Real property/Immovable property

These terms apply to land and buildings, and fixtures permanently attached thereto.

### Registered person

C–005 A taxable person who has complied with the obligation to register with the Revenue authorities is a registered person. Not every taxable person is obliged to register for VAT because of *de minimus* turnover limits or special regimes (*e.g.* for farmers and fishermen).

Some taxable persons who are not required to register may do so voluntarily in order to entitle them to take credit for input VAT incurred. In some countries persons supplying certain exempt goods or services may elect to be subject to VAT and thus also may register voluntarily.

Normally a taxable person is registered only once in respect of all his business activities but in some countries it is possible to register separate parts or divisions of the same business.

### Reverse charge mechanism

In certain cases liability to tax shifts from the supplier to the recipient.

This mechanism applies differently in the various EC countries *e.g.* in the Netherlands, it concerns goods and services provided in the Netherlands by foreign non-resident entrepreneurs. In many other countries it only concerns the supply of specified services, (*e.g.* United Kingdom, Ireland and France), provided by foreign non-resident entrepreneurs without a place of business in that country.

### Taxable person

Any person who supplies or intends to supply taxable goods or services in the course or furtherance of business is a taxable person.

As in other fields of taxation, the word "person" does not refer simply to individuals but also to trustees, partnerships, companies, public corporations. In some countries it also applies to local authorities in certain circumstances.

In most countries, except Ireland and the United Kingdom, the term "entrepreneur" is used instead of "taxable person." In contrast to the term "taxable person," the term entrepreneur includes persons engaged in exempt commercial activities (see "Entrepreneur" and "Assujetti"). In some other countries both terms are used to convey the same meaning.

### Taxable supply

C–006 The definition of taxable supply is very wide. In respect of goods it covers the transfer of the right to dispose of tangible property (goods) as owner. This includes, but is not restricted to, the voluntary or involuntary transfer of (legal) ownership whether by delivery or otherwise. In respect of services it includes the performance, omission or toleration of any act or any other activity, which is not a supply of goods.

Certain supplies of goods and services are specially excluded from a charge to tax, *i.e.* they are exempt.

The distinction between supplies of goods and services is very important because different rules apply with regard to time and place of supply.

### Trader

A registered person is often referred to as a trader.

### Transfer of business

The sale of the assets and liabilities of a business by one taxable person to another is not regarded as a taxable supply in most countries. Normally input tax suffered in connection with such a transfer is recoverable.

In some countries all of the business or an independent part thereof must be sold as a going concern; in others, sale of part of a business which is not a going concern may also qualify as a non-taxable supply.

### Zero rate

In some countries the rate of tax applicable to some taxable supplies, *i.e.*, exports, foods, etc., is zero. Because the supply is liable to VAT, the supplier is entitled to recovery all input tax subject to local regulations. It is similar to the term "exemption with credit" used in some other countries.

***

# INDEX

*References are to paragraph numbers*

# Ernst & Young Addresses

D–001

BELGIUM

Avenue Louise 523, Bte 30
B–1050 Brussels
Tel: (32) 2/640.29.20
Fax: (32) 2/641.90.95
VAT specialist:
Roger COUTEAU

DENMARK

Finsensvej 15
DK–2000 Frederiksberg
Copenhagen
Tel: (45) 1/87.53.35
Fax: (45) 1/33.10.11
VAT specialist:
Mogens KREWALD

FRANCE

150, Boulevard Haussmann
B.P. 209–08
75364 Paris Cedex 08
Tel: (33) 1/49.53.12.34
Fax: (33) 1/45.61.08.09
VAT specialist:
Anne ERMEL

GREECE

Dorileou 10/12
11521 Athens
Tel: (30) 1/6447.413
Fax: (30) 1/644.8334
VAT specialist:
Themis LIANOPOULOS

IRELAND
Stephen Court
18/21 St. Stephens Green
Dublin 2
Tel: (353) 1/760151
Fax: (353) 1/616971
VAT specialist:
Jim SOMERS

THE NETHERLANDS

Hoogoorddreef 66
NL 1101 BE Amsterdam
Tel: (31) 20/966861
Fax: (31) 20/963961
VAT specialist:
Andele BOOMSMA

NORWAY

Nedre Storgt 46
N–3015 Drammen
Tel: (47) 3/83.88.90
Fax: (47) 3/89.08.18//83.86.25
VAT specialist:
Kjell ANDERSEN

PORTUGAL

Avenida Antonio Augusto
de Aguiar 19
1003 Lisbon Codex
Tel: (351) 1/524849
Fax: (351) 1/524849
VAT specialist:
Albino JACINTO

SPAIN

Alberto Alcocer 24
28036 Madrid
Tel: (34) 1/250.28.00
Fax: (34) 1/457.89.17
VAT specialist:
Eduardo SANFRUTOS

SWEDEN
Kungsgatan 37
11156 Stockholm
Tel: (46) 8/723.3350
Fax: (46) 8/11.15.30
VAT specialist:
Per SNELLMAN

**D–002** ITALY

Via Daniele Manin 6
37121 Verona
Tel: (39) 45/595.255//595.570
Fax: (39) 45/800.3993
VAT specialist:
Nicola FIORINI

LUXEMBOURG

25 B, Boulevard Royal
Forum Royal
L–2449 Luxembourg City
Tel: (352) 27961//22210
Fax: (352) 27964
VAT specialist:
Jos JUNKER

UNITED KINGDOM

Becket House
1, Lambeth House
London SE1 7EU
Tel: (44) 1/928.2000
Fax: (44) 1/928.1345
VAT specialist:
James DIXON

FEDERAL REPUBLIC OF GERMANY

Eschersheimer Landstrasse 14
D–6000 Frankfurt am Main 1
Tel: (49) 69/1520801
Fax: (49) 69/15208.247
VAT specialist:
Brigitte EBELING